GREGORIAN
SEMIOLOGY

Dom Eugène Cardine,
in collaboration with
G. Joppich & R. Fischer

GREGORIAN SEMIOLOGY

Translator:
Robert M. Fowells,
*Professor of Music,
California State University,
Los Angeles*

SOLESMES

It is my pleasure to express gratitude to Dom Godehard Joppich who first conceived this publication and who is entirely responsible for the first edition in Italian.

I would also like to thank those who have helped in this project through both their suggestions and their criticism. Special thanks belong to Dom Rupert Fischer, whose careful work has greatly facilitated the research for the examples, as well as to Rev. Mother Marie-Elizabeth Mosseri, and Brother Gregory Casprini, collaborators for the French and English translations.

ISBN 2-85274-067-2

Extracts from ÉTUDES GRÉGORIENNES
Tome XI, 1970

© Abbaye Saint-Pierre de Solesmes, 1982.
F-72300 SABLÉ-SUR-SARTHE

INTRODUCTION

I. PALEOGRAPHY AND SEMIOLOGY

Paleography is the study of ancient handwriting in order to establish its interpretation, date and place of origin. The term refers mainly to the study of Greek and Latin handwriting.

In an analogous manner, one can speak of musical paleography, defining it as the science of ancient systems of notation employed to express music in the visual domain. In a large sense, its object is the reading of ancient manuscripts in view of a musical interpretation and restoration. In a more precise sense, musical paleography is today limited exclusively to the study of musical symbols, their various forms, their history and their geographic distribution[1].

In the field of Gregorian chant, paleographic work in the above sense seemed to have been completed with the Vatican Edition. By drawing on the most important sources from diverse centuries and regions, it obtained a rather faithful melodic restitution of the authentic Gregorian repertory.

The Vatican Edition however shows only part of what the most ancient neumatic signs express. Although its representation of the melodic design, shown by symbols which have existed for many centuries, is nearly perfect, it almost completely neglects the fact that the ancient notations possessed different symbols for similar melodic designs. One can find, for example, at least five very distinct signs for the torculus alone (ᶌ ᶘ ᶐ ᶍ ᶓ). By transcribing them all in an identical fashion, the Vatican Edition omits their particular signification which can only be of an interpretative nature, since the melody remains the same.

Something therefore was lost in the Vatican notation which is only capable of expressing the most material element of the music − the melodic relation of the notes between themselves. For the thing which gives form to melodic material and causes a succession of notes to become music and, consequently, art, is the combined interplay of the duration and intensity which was intentionally conceived by the composer and which the interpreter must rediscover and bring to life.

Now although the first copyists of Gregorian chant were very imperfect in diastematic matters (the precise notation of melodic intervals), they very carefully notated the expressive part, the " musicality " in the melody. The oldest symbols thus have a double signification − melodic and expressive.

As time went on copyists tried to represent the melodic intervals more exactly. In this they succeeded but the interpretive particularities and the finesse of the notation gradually disappeared as a result and before long they came to write all the notes in an identical way. Because of this simplified uniformity, Gregorian chant appeared to be, and in fact became, a " cantus planus ", that is, a chant free of all expressive values. The term " plainchant ", which so often designates Gregorian chant today, should be discarded because it is based on a false premise.

These considerations indicate the necessity of a return to the MSS. This is the objective that we have set in mind. The method that we follow rests on two principles :

1. *Paleographic* study of the neumatic signs and their melodic signification.

2. *Semiological* study which examines the reasons (logos) for the diversity of the signs (semeion) in order to deduce the fundamental principles for an authentic and objective interpretation. Instead of drawing on modern aesthetic concepts or rhythms foreign to the Gregorian era, this interpretation must be guided by the facts that comparative work or the diverse signs reveals tu us. This is the only realistic basis for sound performance practices.

II. THE ORIGIN OF NEUMATIC SIGNS

The first copyists of Gregorian melodies used signs which had already been employed in literary texts. The original meaning of the signs (acute or grave accents) was retained or adapted in a way more or less analogous to the musical phenomenon which was to be expressed.

By their very nature, the acute accent and the grave accents of the grammarians were suitable for distinguishing higher and lower notes : the virga and the tractulus.

Because of the lightness of their designs, abbreviation signs, ⟩ ∴ , were used for depicting those sounds which were to be lightly repercussed : the stropha and the trigon.

The signs for contraction, ∼ ⟩ , were given to sounds particularly tied to their neighbors : the oriscus.

The question mark, ⌣ ⌒ , was borrowed to represent a vocal phenomenon similar to the ascending modulation of an interrogative phrase : the quilisma.

As can be seen, care was taken to use several graphic methods in order to express variety in the notes. The basic intention of the system is to denote a melody through a gesture and to fix this gesture on the parchment. A neume is actually a " written gesture ".

III. MANUSCRIPTS

1. Saint Gall

The MSS from St. Gall, the celebrated Swiss abbey, seem to be the richest in differentiated neumatic signs. Preserved in large numbers, they have the advantage of presenting an imposing and obviously coherent testimony. Study of the St. Gall notation is essential for anyone wishing to investigate Gregorian chant. The most important documents are :

– St. Gall 359, Cantatorium of St. Gall, from the beginning of the tenth century. It is the oldest, the most perfect and the most precise of the MSS in the St. Gall school. It contains only music for the soloists – graduals, alleluias and tracts.

– Einsiedeln 121, a Gradual from St. Gall, eleventh century. It is the most important of the complete MSS. Along with the pieces for the soloist, it contains the antiphons for the Introit, the Offertory, and the Communion. It is also rich in symbolic letters.

– Bamberg, State Library, lit. 6, the Gradual of St. Emmeran of Ratisbon (Regensburg), written about the year 1000. It features a special use of episemas.

– St. Gall 339, a Gradual from St. Gall, eleventh century.

– St. Gall 390-391, the Antiphonary of B. Hartker, a monk of St. Gall, who wrote about the year 1000. It is probably the best source for the chants of the Office.

2. *Laon*

Laon 239, a Gradual book written in about the year 930 near the city of Laon. Recent studies have established its particular value in the field of rhythm. L is frequently compared here with the St. Gall MSS and it is this which has formed the principal basis of our semiological study. For this reason we have attempted to give, further on, a classification of the signs from L.

3. *Other families of notation*

In order to illustrate the facts studied, we will also rely on certain MSS from other families :

– Chartres 47, tenth century. In Breton notation, it presents numerous rhythmic signs.

– Montpellier, Library of the Faculty of Medicine, H. 159. A Gradual from the eleventh century. Used for musical instruction in Dijon, it contains double notation – neumatic and alphabetic.

INTRODUCTION

– Benevento, Bibl. Cap., VI 34. A Gradual from the eleventh or twelfth century. Written on lines with a stylus, it is especially important for melodic reduction.

– Paris, B.N., lat. 903. A Gradual from St. Yrieix from the eleventh century. It is an important source from the Aquitaine tradition (southern France and Spain)[2].

IV. EXPLANATION
OF THE " TABLE OF NEUMATIC SIGNS
FROM ST. GALL "

The table is arranged in two ways:

1° Vertically: A triple division corresponding to the diacritical signs used:

– symbols based on accents: 1-14;

– signs of elision: 15-17 (sign 19, although formed with acute accents, is placed here because of the unison that it depicts);

– undulating signs for contraction: 20-24 and the quilisma, 25, derived from a question mark. As for the pes stratus, 26, it belongs in the fringe area, as we will see later.

2° Horizontally: opposite the simple or basic symbols in column (a) are aligned other symbols which are differentiated by additions or various modifications designed to signify rhythmic nuance (b, c, d, e) or melodic (f) and phonetic (g, h) indications.

The principal part of the table consists of the four columns (b, c, d, e) arranged in the order of the discovery of the meaning of the signs which are found there. For it is thanks to the "letters" (b) explained by Notker († 912) that we have been able to understand first the meaning of the episemas (c) and next the signification of the angular, twisted and enlarged forms (d). As for the neumatic break (e) its value was the very last to be recognized.

TABLE OF NEUMATIC SIGNS FROM ST. GALL

symbols including a unison							
15 apostropha	[.]			[2]	[z]		[/]
16 distropha	[,,]	[,, x]		[,,]			[,,]
17 tristropha	,,,	[,,, x]		,,,		,'	,,
18 trigon	.˙.				[.˙. .˙. .˙. .˙.]	[.˙.]	
19 bivirga & trivirga	// ///			// ///			//
symbols carrying a qualifying sign							
20 pressus							
21 virga strata							
22 oriscus							
23 salicus							
24 pes quassus			[ ]				
25 quilisma							
26 pes stratus	[ ]						

Brackets enclose neumatic forms used only in combination.

TABLE OF NEUMATIC SIGNS FROM LAON 239

Name of Symbols	Simple Symbols	Symbols differentiated by			Symbols indicating a special meaning		
		the modification		the addition of letters	melodic	phonetic	
		of the mark	of the grouping (neumatic break)			Liquescence	
						augment.	diminut.
	a	b	c	d	e	f	g
1. uncinus	⌒					⸱	
2. punctum	·						
3. virga	[⁄]	[⁄] (.·⁄·:)					
4. tractulus	[—]	(—) (·· —)		[E] (·, ɛ)			
5. clivis	⌐		⁓	⌐ₙ ⌐ᵣ ⌐ₛ		⌐	⌐
6. pes	⌐		⁓	⌐ᵣ ⌐ᵣ ℮		℮	℮
7. porrectus	⋎		⋎	⋎ᵣ	⋎	⋎	
8. torculus	⌒	⌒	⌒	⌒ᴧ ⌒ₐ ⌒		⌒	⌒
9. climacus	⋰	⋰	⋰	⋰ₙ		⋰	⋰

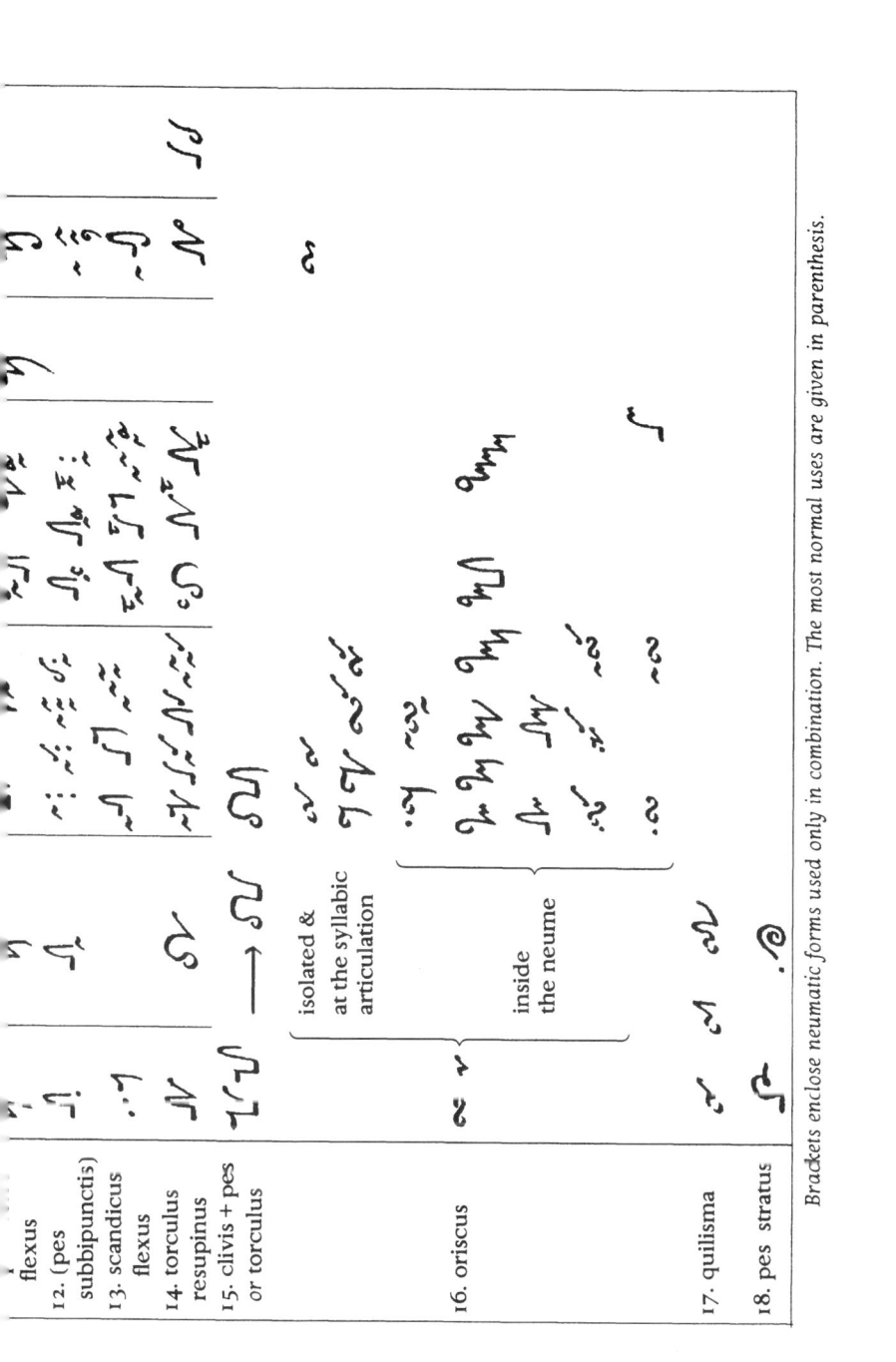

flexus	··	··	··· ·· ·· ··	·· ·· ·· ··	♪♪
12. (pes subbipunctis)	··	··	·· ·· ·· ··	·· ·· ··	··
13. scandicus flexus	···	··	·· ··	··	
14. torculus resupinus					
15. clivis + pes or torculus		→			

16. oriscus

{ isolated & at the syllabic articulation

inside the neume

17. quilisma

18. pes stratus

Brackets enclose neumatic forms used only in combination. The most normal uses are given in parenthesis.

It is practically impossible, and useless besides, to present all of the complex neumes that the St. Gall MSS contain. The symbols shown on this table amply suffice to explain and classify the ones that constitute the system of St. Gall's notation. The principal interest resides in a classification of symbols which, even without corresponding to an absolute logic, nevertheless gives a sufficiently clear concept of the remarkable work of the first copyists.

The concepts will gradually become more clear in the course of the work which we will do on each of these neumatic signs. It is only after this study that we will be able to define the neume itself. At the very outset however, it is necessary to distinguish a sign isolated on one syllable from that same sign in a group, united to others on the same syllable. When a sign is isolated, it is a neume ; when it is in a group, it is only a neumatic element.

V. EXPLANATION OF THE " TABLE OF NEUMATIC SIGNS FROM LAON 239 "

This table is arranged in a way which differs in several respects from the presentation of the St. Gall Table. Here are the principal differences :

Vertically : Numbers 1-4 are classified according to the particular practice of each one of the two schools.

Number 15 gives examples of liaison unknown at St. Gall (clivis joined to a pes or torculus etc.).

Number 16 groups together the various forms of the oriscus found either alone or in combination.

Horizontally : The table counts one less column. L does not use episemas and thus there is nothing corresponding to column C of the St. Gall table.

In addition we have not followed the order in which the meaning of the signs was discovered as we did in the preceding table. Instead it seemed preferable to place first among the differenciated symbols those which are modified in their marking itself and in their grouping. Next comes the addition of letters which are entirely exterior to the neumatic design.

I

ISOLATED NOTES
VIRGA, TRACTULUS, PUNCTUM

The copyists of St. Gall used two signs for writing single notes, the virga and the tractulus. Only the notator of the Cantatorium used a third, the punctum.

I. PALEOGRAPHIC SIGNS

Virga : //
In the first symbol it is easy to recognize the acute accent of ancient grammarians, a rather thin mark drawn upwards and inclined towards the right. This angle of writing characterizes all of the St. Gall notation.

An episema, a small perpendicular mark, can be added to the upper end of the virga. Sometimes, however, it is difficult to tell if the virga is terminated by a deliberate mark or if there was simply a slip of the pen.

Tractulus : — ╲ ╌ ╲ ╌
It is still easy to see the grave accent of the grammarians in the second form, which is rarely used. But in the ordinary sign, it has been reduced to a small horizontal mark, probably to permit faster writing. An episema can be added to both forms. The last symbol, a tractulus with double episemas, is found exclusively in groups and only in a few MSS.

Punctum :
The single punctum is found only in C.. The other St. Gall MSS use it only in symbols of at least three notes, for example the climacus ╱∴ or the pes subtripunctis ╱∴ .

II. MELODIC SIGNIFICATION

1. The melodic relation between virga and tractulus.

In relation to the note which precedes or follows, the virga indicates a higher note, the tractulus a lower note :

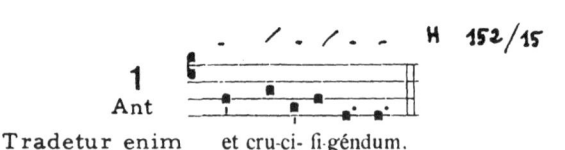

1
Ant
Tradetur enim et cru-ci- fi-géndum.

Regardless of whether one considers the two virgas in relation to the preceding note " ex parte ante " or the following note " ex parte post ", both signify a higher note. The identity of the two relations appears again in the central tractulus ; it is lower than the two notes which frame it. On the contrary, for the initial tractulus and for the one which is carried by the next-to-the-last syllable, only one of the two relations was considered and this sufficed to motivate the choice of the sign. The first tractulus indicates a note lower than the one which follows (ex parte post) and the second, a note lower than the preceding one (ex parte ante). A succession of tractulus always indicates notes in unison.

Here is another case :

2
Ant.
Nativitas glor. ortæ de tri-bu Ju-da,

It seems, at first sight, that after the two notes at the unison, the virga of " tri-bu " indicates a rise in the melody. However, in spite of the virga, the note for " tri-bu " remains in unison with the preceding ones.

ISOLATED NOTES

Here, the virga is explained by that which follows (ex parte post). As the syllable "tri-bu" is on a note which is lower than the three preceding ones, the virga is not trying to say "Raise your voice here", but "Look out! The following note descends."

The contrary can also be found, on the first syllable of the word "Ec-clésiae" for example, where the tractulus takes the place of the virga in order to announce the melodic rise of the following neume.

2 bis
Intr
IN mé- di- o * Ecclé- si- ae

It is in virtue of this principle that the versicle "Os justi..." carries the following notation:

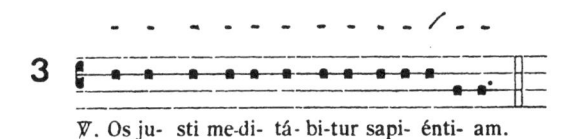

3
℣. Os ju- sti me-di- tá- bi-tur sapi- énti- am.

The virga is explained "ex parte post"; it is a warning which signals the descent of the following note.

This relation "ex parte post" is shown even more clearly in the following example taken from the Gradual "Ad Dóminum dum tribulárer":

4
Gr.
Ad Dom. clamá- vi, et ex-

ISOLATED NOTES

The two cadences are identical[3], but the beginning of the incise which follows is different. In the first case, the first note of the incise is LA; in the second it is a DO. This difference " ex parte post " elicits a different notation for the SI which ends the preceding phrase. In the first case, the copyist used a virga for the SI because the melody descends afterwards to LA. In the second case, on the contrary, he wrote a tractulus because the note precedes a a DO.

Let us first consider the central part of this example.

Even though the syllables " áuferet ju-gum ca-ptivitátis " are in unison one with the other both times, the copyist has alternated tractulus and virga in order to call attention to the melodic descent which follows the virga.

But how would one notate several syllables sung in a descending or ascending succession ? Notice, in the same example, the words " ipse áuferet ". Because of the melodic situation of the notes, the notation of the syllables " *i-pse* " leaves no room for hesitation. The same holds true for " áufe-*ret* " in which the curve of the melody ends on a lower note ; a tractulus is therefore used here. However, the notes on " *áu-fe-ret* " are ambiguous ; both are higher than the note following and lower than the preceding one. Here and in all analogous cases the copyist normally uses a virga[4].

The same is true in an ascending series. Thus, in the preceding example, if we look at the words " captivitátis nostrae ", the tractulus of " ca-*pti*-vitátis " and of " *no*-*strae* " as well as the virga of " captivitá-*tis* " are easy to explain. As for the two ambiguous notes, they are again written with a virga.

It is evident that the notators of St. Gall showed a preference for the virga. Moreover, they often sketched a certain interval with it, as can be seen in the intonation of the antiphon " Cantáte Dómino ".

6
Ant

C Antá-te Dómi- no

Here it is proper to allude to the Laon MS. The Messine notation possesses only one sign for single notes of normal value, a more or less ample curved sign ⁓⁓⁓. Each time that the St. Gall copyists write a virga or a tractulus, for a melodic reason, Laon uses this single sign, disposed in a rather intervallic fashion.

2. *The leaning or grave tractulus*

If a low note, generally written with a horizontal tractulus, is found considerably lower than that which was expected, the tractulus is sometimes written in a leaning fashion ; hence its name, grave.

7
Rcap

Viri sancti co- ró- nas tri- umphá- les

8
Ant

SPí- ri- tus Dómi- ni * replé- vit

3. *The melodic use of the punctum*

The isolated punctum, used only by *C*, replaces the tractulus exclusively, *i.e.* a lower note. When the melodic design demands a virga, a virga is always used. Here are two examples drawn from *C*. We have superimposed symbols from *E* which, ignoring the use of the punctum, constantly writes a tractulus in its place.

E ripe me Ve-rúmtamen justi

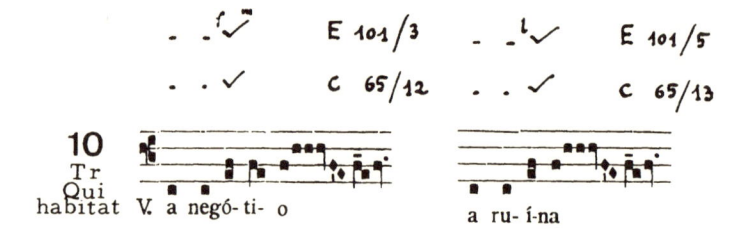

Qui habitat V. a negó-ti-o a ru-í-na

III. INTERPRETATION OF THE SIGNS

1. *The rhythmic relation between a virga and a tractulus*

A certain number of musicologists have advanced the idea that the tractulus and the virga indicate different rhythmic values (— = single value ; ∕ = double value). In order to answer this let us examine the following example, chosen from among many others, in Codex 381 of St. Gall (written around the year 1000) which contains Psalm versicles for Introits and Communions. The example here is the third versicle of the Introit " Verba mea ", p. 82.

ISOLATED NOTES

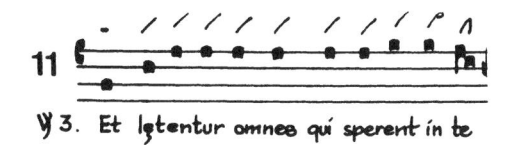

11

℣ 3. Et lętentur omnes qui sperent in te

in ęternum exultabunt & habitabis in e-is

Today, when the second half of a versicle is too long, it is divided with a simple pause in the middle. But at the date of our MS a pes was sung on the accented syllable of the word preceding the caesura. While the notes in unison which precede the pes are written with virgas, those which follow carry the tractulus, because here, the reciting note is lower than the second note of the pes. Now it is manifestly impossible, in this psalmodic recitation, for the notes which precede the pes to be twice as long as those which follow.

Hence we can deduce that the choice of the virga and the tractulus (both representing a single note on one syllable) is based only upon melodic considerations and that there is no difference between the two in the rhythmic scheme.

As for the rhythmic value of the two signs, when they are isolated on one syllable they represent a syllabic beat – a duration essentially related to the text and to its exact pronunciation. In Gregorian chant there is no purely theoretical, *a priori* and absolute rhythm. Gregorian chant being essentially vocal music, the rhythm is realized only in the symbiosis of the text and of the melody and, more precisely, of the syllable and the sound. We will see later that this rule applies equally to neumatic elements and melismas. Here too, the syllabic beat remains the foundation and the point of reference for the rhythmic movement. This syllabic beat is not, however, a beat which is rigorously measured and always equal. It enjoys a certain elasticity as a consequence of the modifications which are imposed upon it by the varying weights of the syllables themselves. It will suffice to simply pronounce the following examples in order to notice the difference in duration of the syllables :

1. Veni Dómine
2. non confundéntur
3. dii eórum — fílii tui

1. Five syllables of normal syllabic beats
2. Five heavier syllables ; the syllabic beat is therefore enlarged here.
3. Five light syllables which produce a more fluid syllabic beat.

This variety in the fundamental duration of the syllables can be developed still further as we will see in paragraphs 2 and 3.

2. *The virga and the tractulus with episemas*

When an episema is added to the simple symbol for the virga or the tractulus the importance of the note is already sufficiently indicated. (The hand of the copyist underlines the neume by this addition.)

a. Episemas in the redundant cadence (*i.e.* repeated cadential note)

Cadences, especially redundant cadences[5], naturally demand a certain enlargement. How do the MSS indicate these cadences ?

12
Ant
QUǽri- te Dóminum, * dum inve-ní- ri pot- est :

13
Ant
SI- on, * no- li ti-mé- re,

ISOLATED NOTES

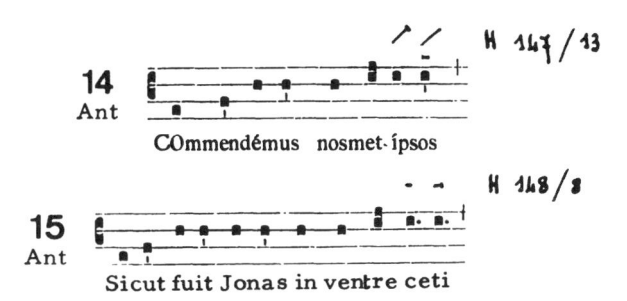

14 Ant
COmmendémus nosmet-ípsos

15 Ant
Sicut fuit Jonas in ventre ceti

(12) The two cadential notes have episemas, which seems normal for us;

(13) Only the second note carries a lengthening sign;

(14) The copyist underlined only the first note, the following incise also beginning on a RE.

(15) Only the second note is lengthened.

This different treatment for the same melodic phenomenon seems illogical to us because our judgement criteria differ from those of the copyist.

The three following examples show the same liberty in the notation of cadences.

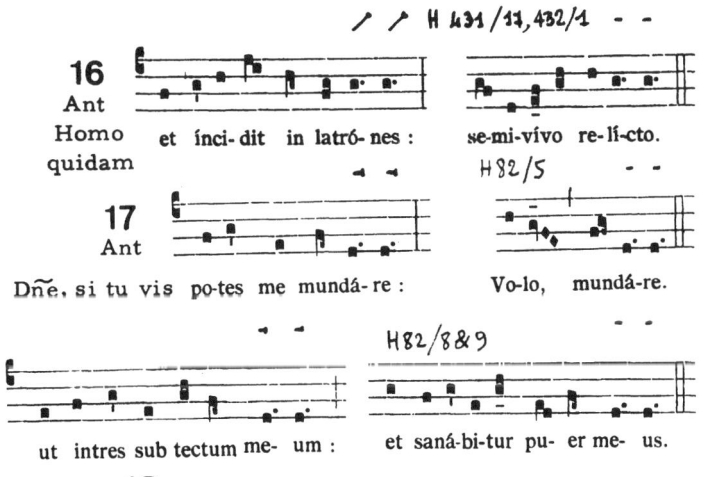

16 Ant
Homo quidam et ínci-dit in latró-nes : se-mi-vívo re-lí-cto.

17 Ant
Dñe, si tu vis po-tes me mundá-re : Vo-lo, mundá-re.

ut intres sub tectum me- um : et saná-bi-tur pu- er me- us.

18 Ant Dne non sum dignus

ISOLATED NOTES

As can be seen, while the two syllables of the median redundant cadences have episemas, those of the final cadences have none. This is quite contrary to our modern logic which would principally underline the final cadences. But in the Middle Ages, the more important or evident a final cadence was, the less it was thought necessary to underline it with episemas. Instead, the copyist called attention to the median cadences in order to prevent them from being neglected.

Needless to say it is difficult to reconcile such facts with a mensuralist concept which sees all episemas as signs which require the strict doubling of single rhythmic values. By what criteria can this theory be supported since, as we have seen, the ancient notators used the episema so freely ? The following examples carry still another argument against this hypothesis.

b. Notes with episemas on important monosyllables

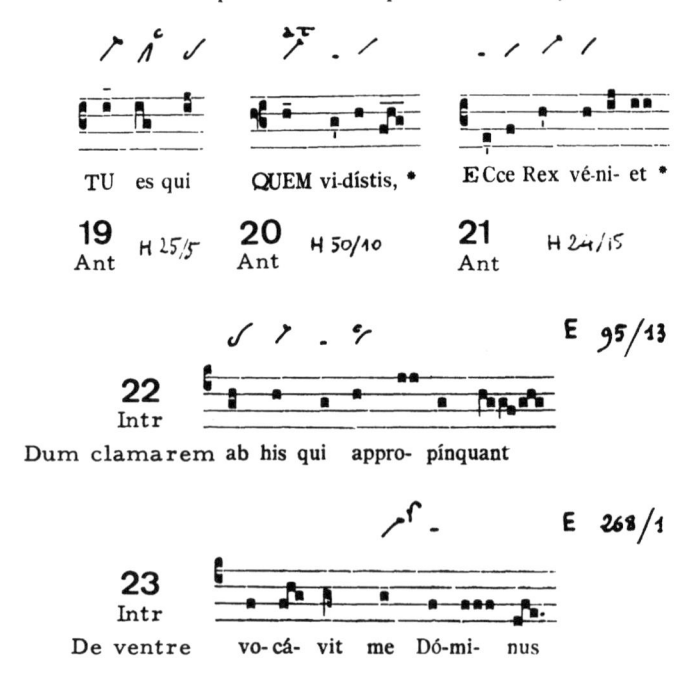

19 Ant — TU es qui — H 25/5

20 Ant — QUEM vi-dístis, * — H 50/10

21 Ant — ECce Rex vé-ni- et * — H 24/15

22 Intr — Dum clamarem ab his qui appro- pínquant — E 95/13

23 Intr — De ventre vo-cá- vit me Dó-mi- nus — E 268/1

ISOLATED NOTES

24 Gr
Omnes de Saba au- rum et thus de-fe-réntes,

In each of these cases, the virga with an episema is found on a word which, without any doubt, has genuine importance and which, by that fact alone, must be emphasized. Contemporary editions do not always reproduce this episema.

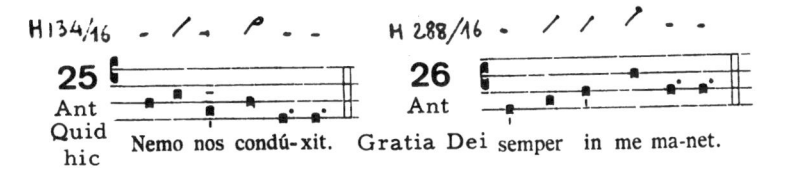

25 Ant
Quid hic Nemo nos condú-xit.

26 Ant
Gratia Dei semper in me ma-net.

In these two cadential formulas the melody already carries by itself a well-defined rhythm. While, in the first instance, the episema on " nos " coincides with the melodic rhythm, the second instance seems to be contrary to it. This shows clearly that the enlargement suggested by the episema is only a light nuance[6].

Finally, here are some more examples drawn from Codex 381 of St. Gall :

60/5 II modo

60/11 VI

119/6 IV
Eructavit cor meum verbum bonum

68/10 I modo

119/12 IV
concupivit rex speciem tu-am

There is here a fact which is even more interesting; in spite of the flow of the psalmodic recitation, the copyist did not hesitate to underline certain important words.

In conclusion, all these examples of monosyllables carrying episemas prove that in no case can the episema be understood as a precise rhythmic indication signifying the doubling of the value of a single neume. They suggest to us instead that the episema was written to invite the singer to emphasize an important word[7].

3. Punctum

We have seen that the syllabic beat can receive a certain lengthening which is due either to the lengthening of a cadential formula, or, occasionally, to the importance of a monosyllable, or of the accented syllable in a longer word (cf. note 7). We will now see that this same syllabic beat can also be made lighter and, hence, a little shorter. The tractulus is then diminished into a dot whose size clearly indicates the lightness of the corresponding syllable.

28 Gr Eripe me ℣. Li-be-rá-tor me- us, C 85/2

The lightness of the first syllables is explained by the fact that, being at the unison, they are in a certain fashion attracted by the accented syllable. Musically, this syllable forms the base from which the melody springs.

29 Gr AUdi, fí- li- a, * et vi- de, C 137/6

The same phenomenon — a light recitation on the unison notes which, together with the following two equally light neumes, draw towards the accent of " *vi*-de ". In both cases, therefore, the notes written with the punctum are light, preparatory notes which lead towards the accent with a certain rapidity.

Nevertheless, even in *C*, the punctum is very rare. Since the St. Gall notation signifies melodic curves with the tractulus-virga relation, the use of the punctum, a light form of the tractulus, is limited to those places where a tractulus could have been used. On the contrary, when a higher note requires a virga, the copyist of *C* necessarily employs this sign, as we already have said earlier. But, and this is interesting, in order to indicate that the virga must be as light and as rapid as the punctum, the notator adds a " c " (= celeriter : rapidly, lightly). This is confirmed by the symbols from *L* :

30
Gr

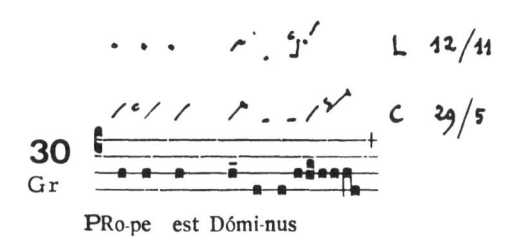

PRo-pe est Dómi-nus

Here we have the same light recitation at the unison just as in the two preceding examples, but in place of the punctum there are virgas since the melody descends after the accent of " Dó-minus ". Laon, which uses an identical sign for all isolated notes of normal value (↗), also has only one sign, the punctum, for the light form and the copyist uses it in a precise and consistant fashion. *C* obtains the same effect by the " celeriter " when he remembers to add it.

Notice the particular placement of the c in this last example. Each time the c is placed *between* two signs, as it is here, it lightens them both (cf. ex. 30 and 33). It is chiefly in the intonation formulas of a particular type (cf. ex. 31 and 34) that the c is used in this way.

ISOLATED NOTES

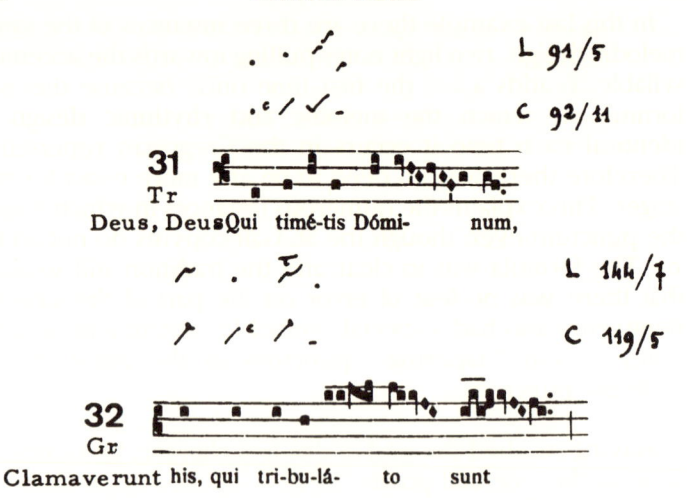

                L 91/5

                C 92/11

31 Tr
Deus, Deus Qui timé-tis Dómi- num,

                L 144/7

                C 119/5

32 Gr
Clamaverunt his, qui tri-bu-lá- to sunt

The copyists of other St. Gall MSS, who did not use the punctum employed in C, had to resort to the addition of a c[8].

                L 98/13

                C 99/2

                E 198/8

33 Tr
Eripe me ℣. Qui co-gi- tavé- runt

L 22/10-12

E 34/10-13

34 Off
IN virtú- te tu- a,   de-si-dé- ri- um   tri-bu- í- sti

In this last example there are three instances of the same melodic design, two light notes pulling towards the accented syllable. E adds a c , the first time only, because this is a formula in which the melodic and rhythmic design is identical each time it occurs in the Gregorian repertoire. Therefore there was no need to be any more exact for the singer. This explains the numerous instances in which L uses the punctum even though the St. Gall copyists do not add a c . The formula was so clear and the tradition still so alive that there was no fear of error on the part of the singers. Benevento also had a special symbol for notating these light notes − the " tapering " punctum in the place of the ordinary punctum.

Having reached the end of this first chapter, let us briefly sum up the essential points.

Three different signs, the virga, the tractulus, and the punctum, were used at St. Gall to write an isolated note on one syllable :

− Melodically there is contrast between :

/ = a higher note, and

− · = a lower note.

− Rhythmically it is necessary to distinguish :

/ − = regular or syllabic beat

- ⁄ ⸱ = shortened beat

/ ⸗ = lengthened beat.

We have nonetheless seen that the manner in which these signs with different values were used does not permit us to apply any rigidly measured rhythmic system to them or to deduce any mensuralist principles[9].

2

CLIVIS

The clivis, or flex, is a two-note neume in which the second note is lower than the first. The symbol is composed of two elements: an acute accent followed by a grave accent.

I. PALEOGRAPHIC SIGNS

1: used regardless of the interval that separates the two notes;
2: indicates an interval of at least a third;
3: carries a horizontal episema;
4: a very rare angular form with an episema;
5: used only in combination, it consists of a virga tied to a tractulus. (In C this tractulus is usually underlined with an episema.)

II. INTERPRETATION OF THE SIGNS

1: ⌒ The rounded top of the sign graphically suggests the lightness of the notes, and this is often confirmed by the addition of a *c* above the clivis near its curve.

CLIVIS 33

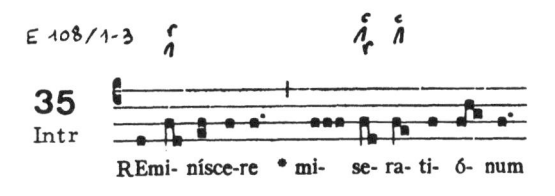

35
Intr

REmi- nísce-re * mi- se- ra- ti- ó- num

et mi- se- ri-cór- di- ae tu- ae,

2 : ⁊ The same light sign with a melodic indication for the second note.

36
Tr

Saepe ℣. Pro- longa- vé- runt

3 : The lengthening indicated by the episema affects both notes. It does not affect the first note exclusively despite the fact that the episema is printed on this note alone in the rhythmic editions. (In some very rare instances, the rhythmic editions do place the episema over both notes, cf. Intr. " Ad te levávi... confí-do ".) The symbols from L clearly prove that both notes are long. L uses the sign ⁊ for the light clivis, and two wavy signs ≈, superimposed one above the other, for the lengthened form. The St. Gall copyists sometimes replace the episema with a τ (= tenete : hold) ; they sometimes even write .

34   CLIVIS

37
Com
Tollite — ad-o-rá-te Dó-mi-num   E 335/12

4 : ⟨ This angular sign, often found with an episema, suggests a more considerable lengthening. In addition, it always involves a disjunct interval of at least a third.

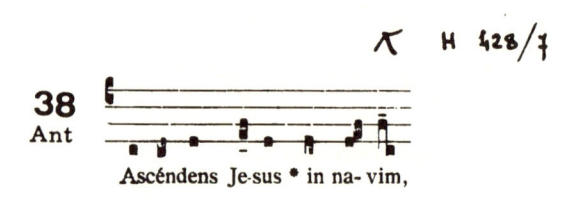

38
Ant — Ascéndens Je-sus * in na-vim,   H 428/7

5 : ⟨ ⟨ The lengthening here concerns only the second note, the first remaining light. This second note is usually in unison with the following note.

                                    C 59/5
                                    E 82/9
39
Tr
De profundis Dómi-ne :

3

PES

The pes or podatus is a two-note neume in which the second note is higher than the first. The designs in the first three symbols are composed of a grave accent and an acute accent. The grave accent, however, is somewhat reduced.

I. PALEOGRAPHIC SIGNS

1 : round pes (pes rotundus) ;
2 : the same sign with an episema on the second note ;
3 : squared pes (pes quadratus) ;
4 : a rather rare sign used for melodic reasons. Sometimes the copyist uses it as a warning that the first note of the pes is higher than the preceding note, or at least in unison with that note if it, too, is relatively high.

Since symbols 5, 6, and 7 include an oriscus, we will return to them when we study that sign. We have added them here only because the Vatican Edition assimilates them to the preceding neumes, using the single sign of the pes ▌ for all seven.

II. INTERPRETATION OF THE SIGNS

1 : ∕ The mark itself suggests the lightness of the group – rapid, cursive writing.

PES

[Example 40: Tr. Qui habitat — V. et re-fú- gi-um me-um, De-us me- us]

This example shows a recitation ornamented by a series of light pes. (The second pes is a liquescent form of the round pes.)

2 : ↗ The episema underlines the importance of the second note. The copyist's hand joins the first note to the second by a light stroke and then pauses to underline this note with an episema.

[Example 41: Ant. Magi — Hoc signum magni Re-gis est]

[Example 42: Gr. Laetatus s. in his quae di-cta sunt mi-hi]

Melodically, the two examples are very clear. After a light leap from a lower note, the melody reaches an important structural note. This process puts into relief a word of the text which needs to be underlined. The melodic line and the rhythmic emphasis both give expression to the same thought[10].

3 : ✓ The angle prevents rapid writing and it gives this neume a certain solidity. To understand the difference in signification, try writing the signs ✓✓✓ and ✓✓ several times. Just as in the epismatic clivis, the two notes of the pes quadratus are equally long.

43 Gr
Probasti ℣. Igne me

44 Tr
Deus, D. m. qua-re me de-re-li- quí- sti?

The two strong pes, side-by-side, underline two important words, " igne " in the gradual for the Feast of St. Laurence and " quare " from the Psalm " Deus, Deus meus ". (The first sign of ex. 43' is a liquescent form of the pes quadratus, caused by the complex articulation of " igne ".)

45 Com
IL-lú- mi- na • fá-ci- em tu- am

46 Tr
AD te le- vávi

The pes quadratus found at the intonation of certain pieces in Mode VII are also quite clear from both the musical and the modal point of view.

47 Intr — PU-ER • na- tus est no- bis, — E 30/1

48 Intr — Ocu-li me- i • sem- per — E 131/6

Lastly, there are some instances in which successive pes quadratus overlap each other, each of them beginning at the unison with the second note of the preceding one.

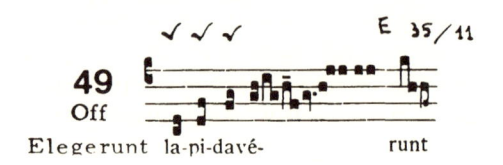

49 Off — Elegerunt la-pi-davé- runt — E 35/11

50 Com — Ego clamá- vi. — E 316/11

51 Com — Illumina et salvum me fac — E 84/7

These signs show quite wonderfully the enhancement that the melodic contour gives to the important words[11].

4 : / The rhythmic value of this sign corresponds to that of the pes quadratus. The notator used this sign in cases where he thought it preferable to point out the melodic height of the first note in respect to the preceding context.

✓ / / B 9ᵛ/19
✓ⱴₑ✓ E 42/12

52
Off

Anima n.   e-répta   est

While *B* writes ✓/ , *E* uses two pes quadratus ✓ⱴ, adding an ℓ (= levate : raise) before the second in order to show that an ascending interval exists between the two pes.

The ℮ (= aequaliter : at the unison) which follows the second pes quadratus of *E* indicates that there is a unison between the second note of this pes and the one that follows.

This sign illustrates the principal of " neumatic breaking " which we will study later. Instead of writing the pes with a single stroke ✓ , the copyist separates the two elements and uses two virga / , a notation which in itself clearly suggests relatively long notes – the pen actually stops and leaves the parchment before continuing the mark.

The copyist of *L* applied the above principle, always writing ⌒ in place of the pes quadratus of St. Gall, and ⌢ in place of the clivis with an episema of St. Gall. In both cases the two signs are separated. The notation of *L* thus gives us obvious proof that, in the long form of the pes and the clivis (✓ ⼻), the two notes have the same value.

THE RELATION OF THE CLIVIS AND THE PES
TO THE SYLLABIC BEAT

Now we are in a position to understand the relation that exists between the syllabic beat written by a virga or a tractulus and the rhythmic value of neumes with two notes : ✓⼻ or ✓⼻ .

For this we refer to the stereotyped melody for antiphons in Mode IV starting on *a* :

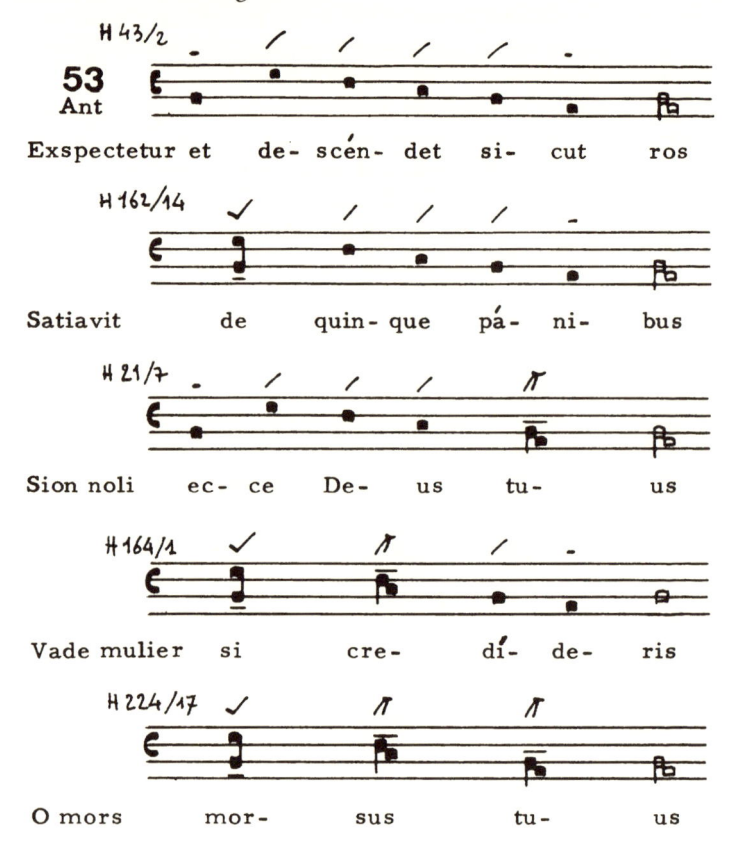

53 Ant H 43/2
Exspectetur et de- scén- det si- cut ros

H 162/14
Satiavit de quin- que pá- ni- bus

H 21/7
Sion noli ec- ce De- us tu- us

H 164/1
Vade mulier si cre- dí- de- ris

H 224/17
O mors mor- sus tu- us

1 : One note per syllable. Each note is worth one syllabic, or basic beat.

2 : As the text has one less syllable, there is a crasis (liaison), or a contraction, of the first two notes on " de ". The two syllabic beats are united by the sign ✓ , pes quadratus.

3 : Here on the syllable " *tu*·us " there is a crasis of the first two notes into a long clivis ⁄𝛾 .

4 : Five syllables in place of the seven in the first example ; therefore two crases on the first two syllables.

5 : The six syllabic beats of the first example are grouped, two by two, on three syllables by means of a pes quadratus and two long clivis.

Keep in mind that we are discussing a stereotyped melody in which the rhythm is invariable. Since, in the place of two syllabic beats, ✓ or ⁄ are found, it is evident that these signs correspond to the value of two syllabic beats.

In addition, just as the common syllabic beat, represented by – and ⁄ can be lightened (. ᵉ ⁄), a group of two common beats written by ✓ and ⁄ can also be lightened. In such cases the signs ✓ and ⁄ are used.

The following examples clearly prove this :

$$E\ 73/8$$
$$L\ 27/7$$

53ᵇⁱˢ
Intr

S Uscé- pimus,

$$E\ 166/3$$
$$L\ 77/9$$

53ᵗᵉʳ
Off

COnfi- té- bor

The two notes of the anacrusis which precedes the accent of " confi-té-bor " were written in L by two punctum, while in E the " celeriter " placed between the tractulus and the virga gives exactly the same indication. Since in the word " Su-scé-pimus ", the accent is preceded by only one syllable, the two light beats are grouped into a round pes (L ♪, E ✓)[12].

4

PORRECTUS

The porrectus is a neume of three notes in which the second note is lower than the other two. The sign is formed by the union of three accents – acute, grave, acute.

I. SIGNS AND MELODIC SIGNIFICATION

1 : The neume begins with the design of a clivis in which the descending stroke forms a sharp angle with the third element, an angle which results from the writing speed and has nothing in common with the square, slanting angle found, for example, in the pes quadratus. The sign is used for all melodic positions. The Vatican Edition prints ℕ.

2 : This sign is hardly ever isolated. It is found chiefly in combination. Only the third note is underlined with an episema.

3 : Two distinct elements : a long clivis and a virga. The Vatican Edition usually prints this sign in the same manner as the preceding one. Only in rare instances does it respect the original grouping (cf. Grad. " Diffúsa est... benedíxit *te* " : ℕ).

4 : A long clivis tied to a virga. It seems, however, that in some instances where this sign is found the copyist wrote it by mistake, uniting the two elements (clivis and virga) instead of detaching them /ʃ/, as did most of the other MSS.

The sign for the porrectus is easy to distinguish. Nevertheless it still leaves room for a melodic problem because its meaning is ambiguous. Actually, /ᴧ/ indicates not only ︶ but also ﬂ▪(unison of the last two notes). This double melodic signification of the same sign is difficult for us to understand today but it is proved by the following arguments :

First argument :

In the MS M, which adds the name of the notes to the neumatic signs, we find :

N   N
lkl   lkk   M 182/8

54
Gr

Dilexisti   et o-di-   sti

The two neumatic symbols are identical : two porrectus. However, under the first, the copyist wrote " lkl " (RE DO RE), while under the second, he noted " lkk " (RE DO DO). This double interpretation is found from one end to the other of the MS.

Second argument :

There are still other instances of unison which do not coincide with the design of the neumatic sign. Let us take, for example, the gradual in Mode V " Christus factus est ". On the word " illum " we find a melodic formula which recurs seven times in the ancient repertoire. Let us compare the different notations in G :

44 PORRECTUS

    Gr. In Deum   ♪   ♪   ␣   50/20

        Christus   ♪   ♪♪   -   70/3

        Exiit   ␣   ␣   -   14/17

        Bonum est   ␣   ␣   -   46/9

55

il-lum,

It is evident that ♪♪, ♪ and ␣ (= clivis + pressus minor) are all equivalent. Now since ␣ undoubtedly indicates a unison of the second and third notes (as we will see when we study the pressus), these same two notes must also be at the unison when the copyist writes ♪♪ or ♪ in the same place. If ♪♪ and ♪ can indicate a unison between the second and third notes despite the fact that here the pen descends and ascends (grave accent and acute accent), the same fact can be verified in the case of the porrectus ␣. The second and third notes are in unison.

Third argument :

The two signs ␣ and ♪(clivis + stropha) are often used equivalently. The same melodic formula is found written in two ways :

c 38/3 & 7

56
Gr

Tecum ex ú- te- ro   V. tu-   os

c 36/15 & 37/4

57
Gr

Hodie vi- dé- bi- tis   V. ap-pá- re

A detailed study[13] has shown that, in C, the added stropha is always at the unison. If, then, a copyist uses ↗, and ⁄𝒱 for the same melodic formula, it is clear that this last sign also indicates the unison.

II. INTERPRETATION OF THE SIGNS

1 : 𝒱 The light form written with a rapid stroke. A c (= celeriter) is often added, especially when several porrectus follow each other on several consecutive syllables.

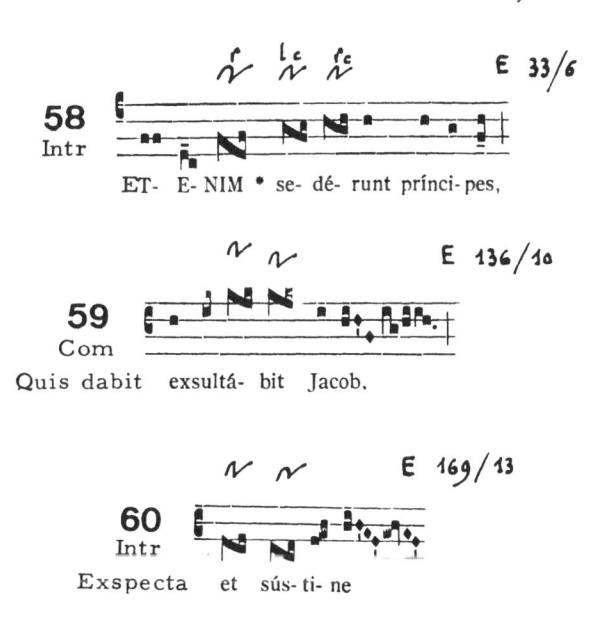

58 Intr
ET- E- NIM * se- dé- runt prínci- pes,   E 33/6

59 Com
Quis dabit exsultá- bit Jacob.   E 136/10

60 Intr
Exspecta et sús- ti- ne   E 169/13

2 : 𝒩 The first two notes are light, the third being the only one underlined with an episema. This mark is almost always used in combination. However :

PORRECTUS

61 Tr
Dñe audivi V. a-ni- má- li- um

62 Gr
Tenuisti as- sumpsí-sti me.

3 : ↗↘ All three notes are long. L confirms this because, while he writes the light porrectus 𝒱, he distinguishes each of the elements of the long porrectus.

63 Com
Honora ut imple- án-tur hórre- a tu- a

As is shown in the above example, the rhythmic editions generally put the episema only on the first note. This error has been corrected in the Monastic Antiphonary, where the episema covers the whole neume.

4 : ↗ See the explanation given above.

5

TORCULUS

The torculus is a three-note neume in which the second note is higher than the other two.

I. SIGNS AND MELODIC SIGNIFICATION

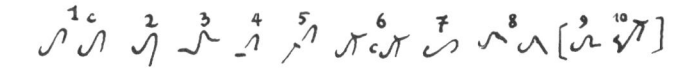

1 : The signs for the pes ✓ and the clivis ∩ are united in one symbol ; a **c** is sometimes added.

2 : The last mark, because of its length, indicates a descent of at least a third.

3 : A crooked sign.

4 and 5 : These signs are rarely found in isolation. The first note is detached from the two following. The two signs differ for melodic reasons. When the first note of the torculus is lower than the note preceding it or in unison with a note approached by descending motion, the copyist begins the torculus with a tractulus. On the other hand, when the first note of the torculus is higher than the preceding note or in unison (cf. ex. 68) with a note approached by ascending motion, some copyists use the virga.

6 : Here the signs for the light pes ✓ and the long clivis /ᛧ are united in the same symbol. The episema can be replaced by a τ (= tenete) ᛧ̄, and a c is sometimes added at the beginning of the symbol.

7 and 8 : The first element begins normally ; the second and third notes are written in different ways.

9 and 10 : These two signs are only used in combination. Number 9 ends with a tractulus (see number 5 of the clivis). As for sign 10, composed of an oriscus and a long clivis, it is actually a pes quassus flexus.

II. INTERPRETATION OF THE SIGNS

1 : ᛧ This light, cursive form of the sign requires an analogous interpretation :

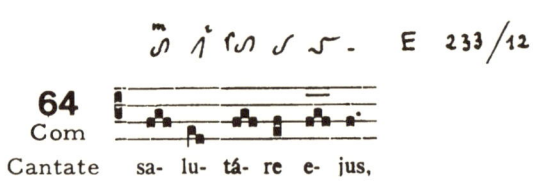

64
Com
Cantate sa- lu- tá- re e- jus,

2 : ᛧ The same light form but with a lengthened extremity in order to call the singer's attention to the descending interval :

65
Com
Hoc corpus quod pro vo-bis tra- dé- tur

3 : ᛧ In making this twisted sign, the copyist could not manage his pen as easily as for the first two signs. This mark signifies a slower movement, thus explaining its frequent use in a great number of cadences.

TORCULUS

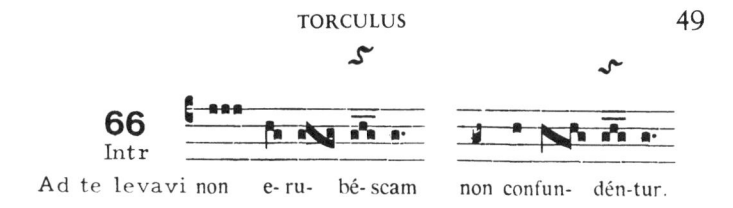

66 Intr

Ad te levavi non e- ru- bé- scam non confun- dén-tur.

In isolation, this sign is seldom found outside of cadences.

E 87/10

67 Com

Introibo ad altá- re De- i,

4 and 5 : The separation of the first note confers a certain predominance upon it which we must take into account in the interpretation. If the composer had not wished to emphasize this detail, he would have written ∽ , *i.e.* the first note tied to the following two.

E 269/12

68 Intr

Multae trib. ómni- a ossa e- ó- rum

There is no doubt that the second and third notes, both light, flow from the impulse given by the initial note.

6 : This mark clearly indicates that, after the first light note, the other two are longer. It is made clear by the addition of an episema or a τ above the sign.

7 : ⌒ The lengthening of the second and third notes is depicted here by the extended symbol for these two elements :

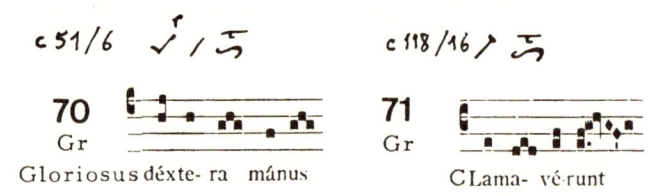

70
Gr

Gloriosus déxte- ra mánus

71
Gr

CLama- vé-runt

8 : ⋏ ⋏ These two signs are equivalent to forms 6 and 7. The symbols themselves indicate the importance of the last two notes.

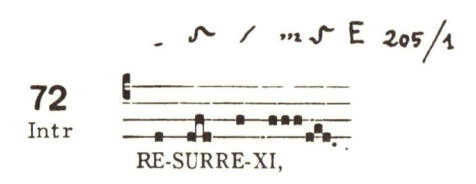

72
Intr

RE-SURRE-XI,

We have given to these last three forms of the torculus the label :

SPECIAL TORCULUS

It would perhaps be more accurate to use the term : " Torculus Initio Debilis ".

Particular problems connected with this form of the torculus call for a closer examination.

All three forms of the torculus initio debilis — *i.e.* torculus with a weak initial note — or special torculus, are characterized by the relative predominance of the last two notes. They are chiefly used in the three following instances — on a final syllable, in intonations, and as a passing element in an ascending melodic movement which generally proceeds by conjunct degrees.

I. THE SPECIAL TORCULUS ON A FINAL SYLLABLE

Let us begin with an example :

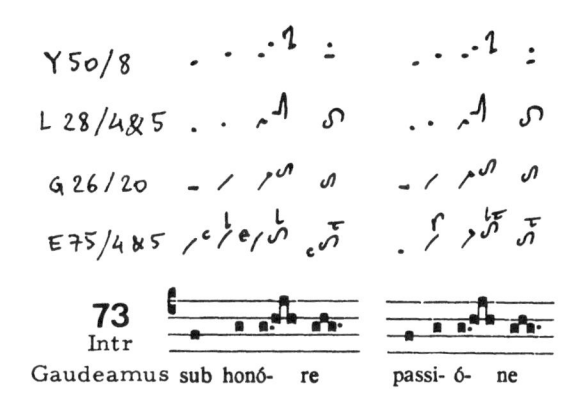

```
Y 50/8
L 28/4&5
G 26/20
E 75/4&5
```

73
Intr
Gaudeamus sub honó- re   passi- ó- ne

The two words carry a special torculus on the final syllable. E and L show this in a very precise way. E clearly writes ✡ᵗ; L writes in place of the normal torculus ↗, a special form ∩. The two MSS express the same reality – a light beginning and the lengthening of the second and third notes. G, on the contrary, has no special indication. Y simply places a clivis on the final syllable, since the first note of the torculus, which is light in E and L, has disappeared.

Other examples show us this type of torculus even more clearly. But, watch out !

Melodic restoration in the Vatican Edition often varies without any precise criteria, sometimes printing a clivis and sometimes a torculus :

TORCULUS

74
Intr
Gaudete pe-ti-ti- ó- nes ve-strae

We have here four torculus. The second and the fourth are found on final syllables. While the first and the third remain the same in all MSS, the second and the fourth vary :
E puts a ᴛ on the two final notes ;
B adds c one time and ᴛ the other ;
G has no special indication, writing the same light sign all four times ;

L writes a long clivis in place of the second torculus and uses a special sign to notate the fourth torculus. The copyist begins this last sign with a special form of the pes (first note light, the second larger), then cuts the symbol, adds an uncinus, and between the last elements adds an ᴀ (= augete), which always augments the two notes between which it is found.
Y and Ben use a clivis in place of the second and fourth torculus where the first notes have disappeared.

The explanation of the two preceding examples should enable the reader to understand the following by himself :

TORCULUS

```
Y 89/9 & 10
L 57/1 & 2
G 44/18
E 125/10 & 11
```

75 Off
Precatus Qua-re, Dómi- ne,   Par- ce irae   á- nimae

```
          Y 59/3
          L 32/1
          G 29/13
          E 82/11
          C 59/7
```

76 Tr
De profundis Fi- ant aures tu-   ae

In this last example, C (which obviously could not include the previous examples) used the sign ℐ.[14]

Finally, here are two examples which will point out the inexact melodic interpretation that the special torculus received in the Vatican Edition :

```
          L 155/8
          E 326/2
```

77 Intr
Inclina Dñe mi- se- ré- re mi-hi, Dó- mi-   ne.

Cum invoc. mi-se- ré- re mi-hi Dómi- ne,

Although two identical examples are involved, the Vatican Edition chose a torculus (miseré-*re*) in one case and a clivis the other, making a melodic error as well.

Conclusion :

In all the cases cited, a torculus is involved which is :
a. on the final syllable of the word ;[15]
b. included in a descending melodic line ;
c. made up of conjunct intervals, *i.e.,* formed with two intervals of a second.

We have noted also that, all too often, the St. Gall MSS were not exact in pointing out the importance of the last two notes of a special torculus.

II. INTONATION TORCULUS

This torculus is found at the beginning of a piece or of an incise :

The second note always regains by means of a leap of a third or a fourth, an important modal tone placed above a half-tone.

TORCULUS

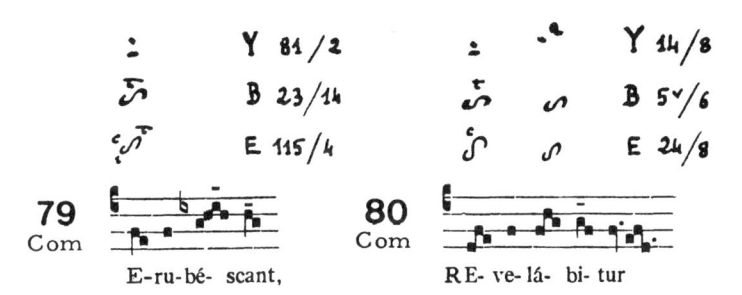

While the Vatican Edition only gives a clivis in the first instance, it gives a torculus in the second. Moreover, in this second example, the MS notation itself seems contradictory, the intonation torculus being written in one MS and by the other. This difference is easy to explain from a musical point of view. One notator chiefly meant to express the relative importance of the second (and third) note by means of. The other, by means of, wished to call the singer's attention to the general movement which must remain light in this intonation.

It is therefore no wonder that most of the copyists prefer the light sign, sometimes with a c, and that, chiefly in MSS from Spain and southern France, the first note tends to disappear completely. In many cases, the Vatican Edition followed this last tradition, as in the two following examples :

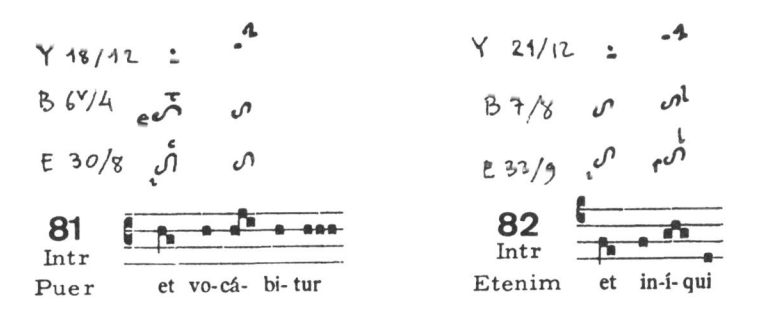

In ex. 81, we see an ⌄ (= inferius : lower) on the first note of the torculus from E, and an ℯ(= aequaliter : at the unison) in B. Since the preceding incise ends on LA, these letters signify that the first note of the torculus is SOL in E and LA in B. This divergence, which appears frequently in the lined MSS from St. Gall proves the weakness and the vagueness of the first note of the special torculus.

III. PASSING TORCULUS

This neume occurs most often when the melody moves from FA to LA. The melody leaves FA and rushes towards LA (the note which carries the accented syllable of the word) by a light passing group, the ornamental torculus, SOL-LA-SOL :

MI-se- ré-ris * ómni- um, Dó- mi-ne, et ni- hil

The copyists from St. Gall did not use a special symbol for this torculus, which is why we only find 𝒩 or 𝒩 . But, here again, there are facts which prove the special character of the group :

First proof: The first syllable of " *ni*-hil " carries the same notes as the first three syllables of " *miseré*-ris ". But in " nihil " the SOL (the first note of the passing torculus : mi-seréris) has become a quilisma, an essentially light passing note.

Second proof: In cases of this type, and when he does not limit himself to the light clivis (ex. 87), L always writes the special torculus :

Third proof: The Aquitaine MSS give only a clivis; the first note of the torculus has disappeard.

Other examples :

84 All — Emitte et cre- a- bún-

85 All — Excita et ve-

First example : The two syllables of " *cre-a-búntur* " carry four notes, an isolated one followed by the three notes of the torculus. Next comes the accent of the word on the third syllable.

Second example : Only one syllable precedes the accent of " *ve-*ni ". It therefore receives the four notes of the melodic formula and the SOL, which was the first note of the special passing torculus in the first example is written here as a quilisma[16].

86 Com Revela sa- lu- tá- bitur

87 Com Viderunt sa- lu- tá- re

How can anyone argue in favor of a rigid rhythmical system in these cases where for the same melodic formula and the same text L writes a torculus (three notes) in one instance and a clivis (two notes) in another ? Does not this use of the clivis prove clearly the weakness of the first note of the special torculus ? Furthermore while in ex. 74 L wrote a long clivis on " petitió-nes " in place of a special cadential torculus, in ex. 87 it is a light clivis which corresponds to the special passing torculus.

Last example :

♪	♪	⁊	Ben 191ᵛ/1
⁒	·♪	⁒	Y 185/8
♪	♪	♪	L 127/2
♪	♪ᶫ	♪	B 56ᵛ/17
♪	♪	♪ᵗ	G 94/2
♪	♪ᵣ	♪̄	E 258/7

88
Intr

AC- cí- pi- te * ju- cundi- tá- tem

Here we have three successive torculus. The first is a passing torculus, the second a normal torculus, and the third a cadential torculus, i.e., coincident with a final syllable.

The St. Gall copyists in no way specify the first, but on the contrary, they all underline the third, indicating the lengthening of the last two notes by an addition. B, moreover, modifies the design.

L distinguishes the two special torculus and carefully transcribes their diversity.

Y, as always, only has a clivis.

But, in all the families of notation, the second torculus conserves its three notes because it is normal. This proves beyond a doubt that a distinction must be made between the various torculus and that not all torculus are " special " but only those which can be included, because of their characteristics, in the well-determined categories presented above.[17]

6

CLIMACUS

The climacus is a descending neume of three or more notes in which the first note is always written with an acute accent (virga).

I. PALEOGRAPHIC SIGNS

We have copied out two series of climacus of three or four notes, certain symbols being encountered only in groups of at least four notes. Most climacus proceed by conjunct degrees.

Only two of these symbols require special mention here :

2 : The last element, a grave accent, indicates a disjunct interval between the last two notes, for example (LA) SOL-FA-RE.

7 : The virga is joined to the first tractulus.

II. INTERPRETATION OF THE SIGNS

1 : ∕∴ All the notes are light ; a c often confirms this.

89
Off
Dextera Dñi non mó-ri- ar,

2 : /⋅ The same group with the melodic precision explained above.

90
Tr

Qui habitat de láque- o   C 65/5

3 : /⋅ The first note carries an episema ; the others are light.

91
Com

DOmi- nus Je-sus,   E 195/10

4 : /= All the notes are long, even if the virga does not carry an episema.(4a, 4c)
— in isolation :

92
Intr

Dns fortitudo Chri-sti su- i est :   E 317/13

— in combination :

93
Gr

Haec dies bo- nus   C 107/10

5 : /= Only the last note is lengthened. The example given here is often found in the versicles of graduals in Mode 5 :

94
Gr   C 96/16

6 : ⁄ Two light notes followed by two more important notes :

95
All

Te Martyrum Dó- mi- ne.

7 : ⁄ Only the first note is light because it is graphically tied to the second. The following ones are broader. See example 97.

8 : ⁄ Here, on the contrary, only the second note is put into relief ; the others are light.

96
All

Dies sanct. il-lúxit no- bis

descéndit lux ma- gna

9 : ⁄ The first two notes are broader than the following ones. The second symbol (a tractulus with a double episema ⁄) underlines the predominance of the second note even more. (In the following example, symbol 7 precedes symbol 9.)

97
Tr

Qui habitat ad lá- pi-dem

We have said earlier that the two symbols, 4a ⁄= and 4b ⁄=, are equivalent. The three notes are long, whether the virga has an episema or not ; therefore ⁄= equals ⁄=.

Now, as we return to the sign /̣. , a difficulty appears. For this form, we have indicated an entirely light interpretation. The virga, in the case of /̣. , represents a lightened note and, on the contrary, in the case of /₌ , it represents a lengthened note. This could seem contradictory if we were to forget what has already been said. The virga, used essentially for melodic reasons, represents a higher note, both in relation to the tractulus (normal beat) and to the punctum (light beat). As a result, when the climacus is written /̣. , the virga represents a light beat because it replaces a rising punctum. On the contrary, in the symbol /₌ , it represents a lengthened beat because it takes the place of a rising tractulus. The value of the virga is thus determined by the value of the second note.

The other symbols prove this fact. A *c* is often added to the simple symbol /̣. . However, when the virga is more important than the following punctum it has an episema. On the contrary, if it is lighter than the following notes, it is rapidly tied to the second note, that is, to the first tractulus. Symbol 5 of the clivis /ᴸ, a light note followed by a second note which is more important, is found once again in climacus 7 /ᴸ̣. After the first light note, the copyist underlines the second note (one which is often important in the modal design) by writing it with a tractulus, which denotes a neumatic break. Then he continues with one or two distinct tractuli /ᴸ̣ /ᴸ̣ (ex. 97) or with two puncta /̣⁻̣ (ex. 96).

It is now clear that :
- /̣. = ͨ/̣. : entirely light ;
- /₌ = /ᴸ̣ : entirely long ;
- /̣⁻ : the first note is lengthened, the others are light ;
- /ᴸ̣ : the first note is light, the others are lengthened ;
- /₌̣ : only the last note is lengthened.

As for the next-to-the-last symbol, we should point out that the last note of a group is never lightened when the preceding one is lengthened. This explains why the sign /⁻̣ does not exist.

7

SCANDICUS

The scandicus is an ascending neume of three or more notes. For practical purposes we can limit our study to the three-note scandicus.

I. PALEOGRAPHIC SIGNS

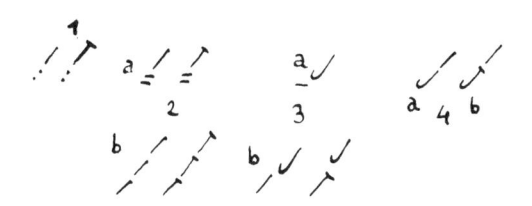

1 : This sign is found only in combination.

2 : The signs 2a and 2b, as well as 3a and 3b, differ by the use of the tractulus and the virga respectively. The difference is of a melodic nature and shows the relation existing between the first note of the scandicus and the preceding one.

3a and 3b : The notes of these scandicus generally proceed by conjunct degrees.

4a and 4b : The first two notes are separated by at least a third. The last two, on the contrary, are conjunct.

II. INTERPRETATION OF THE SIGNS

1 : The fact that this symbol is never isolated indicates that, in all isolated scandicus, one of the notes, if not all three, must be emphasized.[18]

2 : The three notes are long, and this is what the stressed handwriting suggests.

98 Gr — Deus vitam in conspé- tri- bu- lá-

99 Off — BEne-dí- ci-te gen- tes

3 and 4 : It is important to understand the signification of the two following signs whose notes have a different grouping.

3 : The copyist separates the first note from the two following ones : ♩ = ♪. However this does not give any importance whatsoever to the pes, as if the preceding note served as its preparation (pes praepunctis). On the contrary, the purpose of the graphic separation of the first note is the underlining of its rhythmical importance ; the two following notes depend on it, proceeding lightly from the initial impulse.

100 Com — VI- de- o * cae-los

SCANDICUS 65

The vertical episema on the second note, a conventional sign added to the Vatican Edition to indicate the salicus, is erroneous. The true rhythmic signification of this symbol was only understood later and was restored in succeeding publications (Semaine Sainte, 1920 and Ant. Mon., 1934), where it is reproduced as follows :

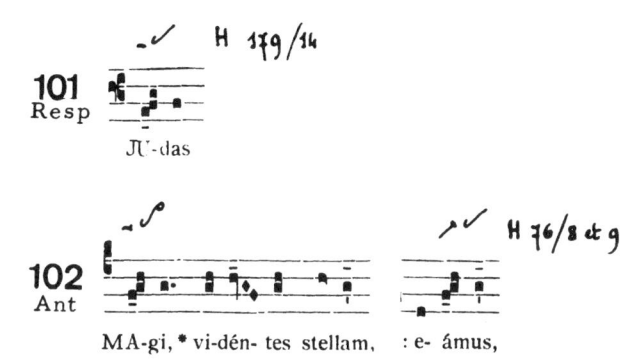

101 Resp — Jú-das — H 179/14

102 Ant — MA-gi,* vi-dén- tes stellam, : e- ámus, — H 76/8 & 9

4 : ♪ ♪ Here the copyist united the first two notes and detached the last. Contrarily to the preceding symbol, the pen quickly tied the first two notes, then stopped before writing the last. This clearly shows the importance of the second note of the group on which the hand of the copyist stopped. The top of the pes is in fact often underlined with an episema. Even without an episema, however, the graphic cutting alone is sufficient to express the rhythmic predominance of the second note.

103 Intr — STá- tu- it * e- i Dó- mi- nus — E 59/13

SCANDICUS

In these last two symbols (3 and 4) the neumatic break depicts the same rhythmic phenomenon : it indicates the importance of the note immediately preceding the break. The symbols correspond very well to the musical meaning. In " Vídeo " (ex. 100) the initial FA is underlined because it gives an impulse to the melodic movement which tends towards SOL, the modally important note, on the final syllable of the word.

In the case of " Státuit " (ex. 103), the melody begins on RE and leaps to LA, which is the principal note of the intonation and which carries an upper ornament.

When the initial leap is not followed by a higher ornament, the musical accent remains on the lower note. This explains the different treatment received by these two intonations on " Factus est ".

104
Com
FActus est Dómi- nus
E 314/7

105
Com
FActus est re-pénte
E 257/4

This phenomenon of an upward leap towards an important note is also found with intervals of a fourth or a third.

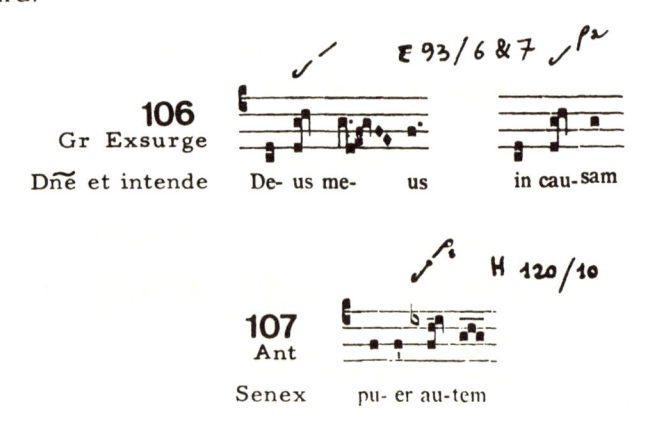

106
Gr Exsurge
Dñe et intende   De- us me-   us   in cau-sam
E 93/6 & 7

107
Ant
Senex   pu- er au-tem
H 120/10

SCANDICUS

Finally, here are some examples of the scandicus with more than three notes :

108
All
Qui timent jú- tor

The two symbols are equivalent and both represent a light ascent. In such cases the copyists preferred the symbol ending with a pes because it allowed them to tie the only two notes capable of being tied.

The light scandicus with four notes is rather often notated ∫. The virga strata which replaces the pes rotundus has a special melodic meaning which we will discuss later in Chapter 14.

There are also some symbols which are either entirely long or in which only the last two notes are lengthened :

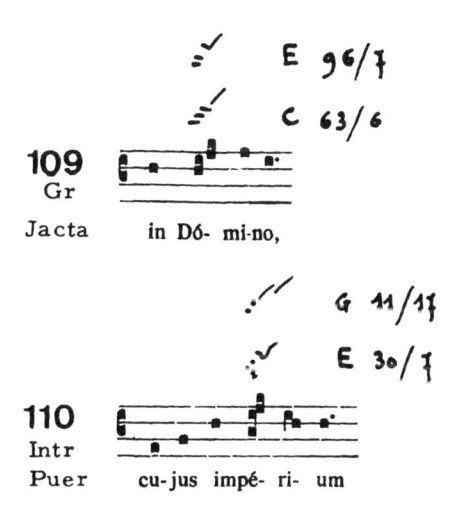

109
Gr
Jacta in Dó- mi-no,

110
Intr
Puer cu-jus impé- ri- um

8

COMPLEX SYMBOLS WITH FOUR OR MORE NOTES

After these chapters devoted to symbols derived from accents, it is necessary to mention those which present a more complex aspect.

PORRECTUS FLEXUS

1 : A simple, light sign which presents the same ambiguity as the porrectus. For as we have already seen, *M* can signify either ⁀ (often written as ▪▪) or ▪▪ :

111 Intr — Eduxit Dó- mi-nus (E 220/8)

112 Com — Data est al-le- lú- ia : (euntes) (E 222/10)

One often finds two separate clivis *ʎʎ* in place of the porrectus flexus *M*, but as we shall see further on, they are always one and the same neume.

2 : These two symbols indicate the lengthening of the third and fourth notes :

113 Off — Portas cœli alle- lú- ia. (G 80/2)

3 : Here again, the separation of the first note underlines its rhythmic importance ; the three light notes which follow depend on this initial impulse.

114
Intr

Viri Galilæi alle- lú-ia,

PES SUBPUNCTIS

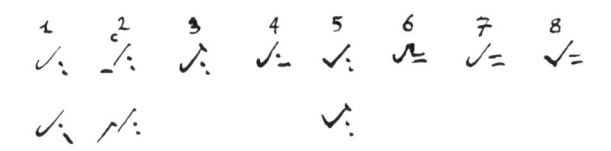

The pes can be followed by two, three, or four descending notes. We will confine ourselves here to the pes subbipunctis.

In this four-note group, the first, second or fourth notes can be underlined (singly or together), but the third can never be emphasized alone since, as we have already said, the last note necessarily participates in the lengthening of the preceding one. This rule always applies.

70   COMPLEX SYMBOLS

1 : ✒ All four notes are light ;

115
Intr

Esto mihi quó-ni- am firmaméntum me- um,

2 : -✒ As its graphic separation indicates, the important first note is the rhythmic source for the three light notes which follow. Unhappily, the Vatican Edition almost never points out this important initial cutting.[19]

116
Intr

HO- di- e sci- é- tis,

3 : ✒ An episema underlines the second note.

117
Com

Inclina ut é- ru- as nos.

4 : ✒ Only the last note is long. (The leaning tractulus from symbol 1b does not indicate a lengthening but an interval of at least a third between the last two notes.)

118
Gr

Ex Sion De- us

5 : ✒ The first two notes are lengthened ; the next two are light. This symbol is used most often in cadential formulas.

PES SUBBIPUNCTIS

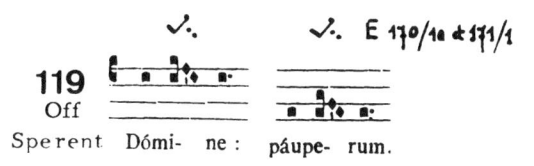

119 Off
Sperent Dómi- ne : páupe- rum.

6 : ◡ = Two light notes followed by two enlarged notes.

120 Com
Tu es Petrus aedi- fi- cábo

7 : ◡ = The last three notes are long. (Actually this amounts to symbol 4 of the climacus, preceded by one light note. The horizontal episema of the rhythmic editions ought to cover the second note also.)

121 Ant
Stella ista Ma- gi e- am vi-dé-runt,

8 : ◡ = The four notes are lengthened equally.

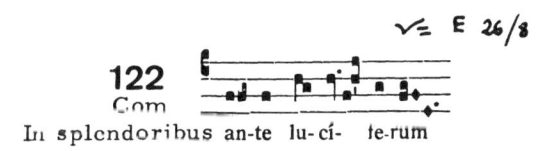

122 Com
In splendoribus an-te lu-cí- fe-rum

Finally, we have an example in which there are two successive symbols of the same design in combination, symbols 6 and 8. (The dot added after the fourth note of each group does not exactly correspond to what the paleographic signs express.)

72   COMPLEX SYMBOLS

123
Gr

Constitues eos prín-ci- pes

C 123/9 et 13

fi-   li- i :

SCANDICUS FLEXUS

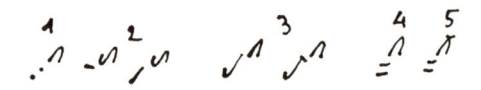

1 : ♪ An entirely light symbol.

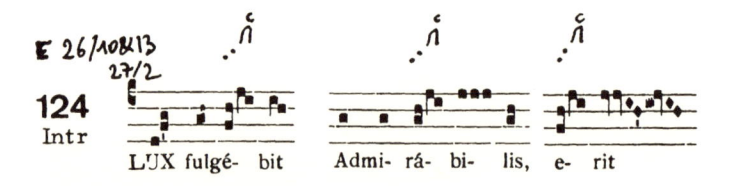

E 26/108&13
27/2
124
Intr

LUX fulgé- bit   Admi- rá- bi- lis, e- rit

2 : ♪ As always, the initial cutting points out the particular value of that first note on which the three following light ones so closely depend. This commonly used neume characterizes the intonation of Tracts in Mode VIII.

SCANDICUS FLEXUS

125 Gr — Oculi omn. et tu das il- lis

126 Tr — C Anté- mus

3 : ♪♩ This symbol is found only in combination. The second note, often (but not necessarily) underlined with an episema, is the principal one.[20] Ex. 128 shows a formula which appears frequently in the Tracts of Mode VIII.

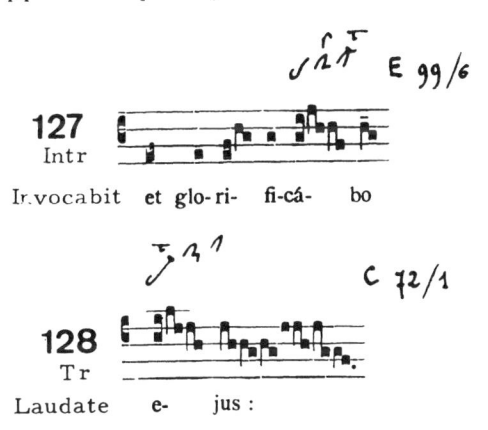

127 Intr — Invocabit et glo-ri- fi-cá- bo

128 Tr — Laudate e- jus:

1 · ♩ Two long notes followed by two light notes.

129 Tr — Dne audivi De- us

74   COMPLEX SYMBOLS

5 :=⊼ All four notes are long.

130
Intr

Os justi ju-dí- ci- um:

E 56/1

TORCULUS RESUPINUS

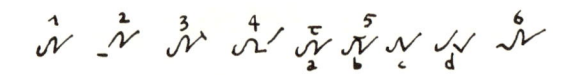

1 2 3 4 5 6
(a b c d)

1 : 𝒩 All the notes are light.[21]

131
Intr

Suscepimus in mé- di- o

E 73/11

The last note is often at the unison with the preceding one, as has been illustrated in the study of the porrectus.

132
Off

Perfice gres- sus me- os

E 86/6

2 : ℳ The first detached note is the rhythmic source of the light movement of the three following notes.

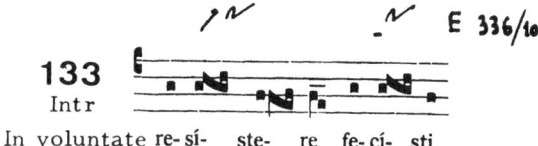

133 Intr

In voluntate re- sí- ste- re fe- cí- sti

(In the first excerpt of ex. 326, notice how E notates this typical cadence for the deuterus (Mode II).

3 : ℳ The first three notes are light and they move towards the last note which is the rhythmically important one. This symbol is usually found in combination.

134 Gr

Adjutor ℣. Quó- ni- am non

4 : ℳ Two light notes followed by two longer notes. The last note shares in the lengthening of the preceding one.

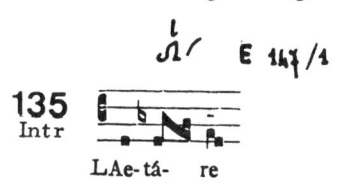

135 Intr

LAe- tá- re

6 : ℳ The four notes are long. This rather rare symbol is usually found in combination.

136 Gr

Adjutor Dó- mi- ne.

137 Gr — Tenuisti pedes,   C 90/5

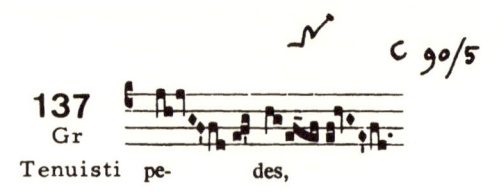

5 : ẘ ẘ ẘ ẘ The four symbols have an identical rhythmical signification and they are therefore used interchangeably. The following examples illustrate this. The light first note leaps rapidly towards the following three which are always long. These different symbols are reproduced here in a rather stylized way. In reality, the different St. Gall writers (and even individual writers) show a certain inconsistancy in the use of this sign. They do not always use an identical or perfectly regular symbol.

In place of the various forms of ex. 5 found in the St. Gall MSS, L uses only the symbol ∫ɾ✓ (light pes + long pes), with or without letters, which corresponds perfectly to sign 5d ✓✓ from St. Gall. This tends to prove the equivalence of the various St. Gall signs.

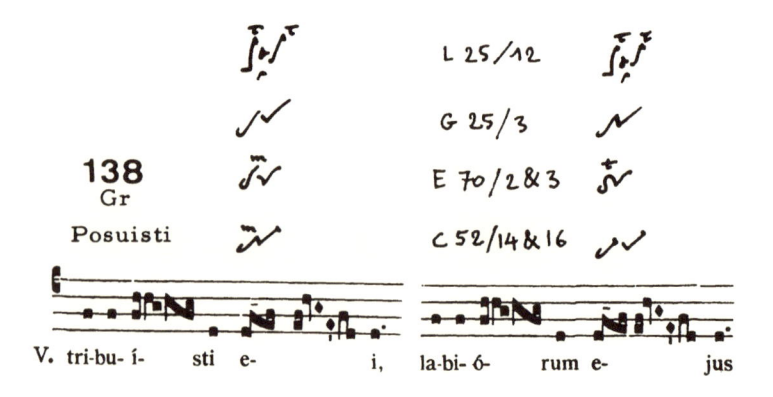

138 Gr — Posuisti

	L 25/12	
	G 25/3	
	E 70/2 & 3	
	C 52/14 & 16	

V. tri-bu- i- sti e- i, la-bi- ó- rum e- jus

TORCULUS RESUPINUS

In these two utterly identical formulas, it is to be noted that only at one point did two St. Gall MSS use the same sign – E and G in the first example. All the other signs are used without any distinction and are thus found to be perfectly equivalent. It is interesting to point out the interchanging of the symbols ⁄⁄ and ⁄ in C and G. Clearly, the second sign is the same as the first but done in a single mark. E on the contrary, uses a different form the second time.

As for L, in both examples the copyist writes two separate pes, adding a τ on the second note of the light pes in order to underline its importance. (We know however that this addition of a τ as well as C's addition of an episema on the fourth note of the first example or the second and fourth notes of the second example was not absolutely necessary. In C, the break in the writing which follows the second note of the light pes in the second example and the fourth note of each group – a pes quadratus in the second example, suffices to underline these notes. If the second note had been light, the copyist would have tied it to the following note, not by an angular symbol but by symbol 4 : ⁄⁄.) This formula is found several times in the ancient repertoire.

A final example :

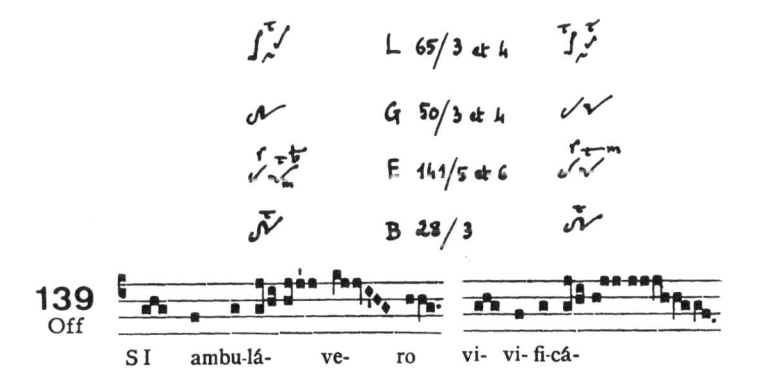

Instead of C, which does not contain this piece, we have used an example from B and we find the same diversity. All the MSS repeat a similar sign for the two formulas, but G changes it the second time. The Vatican Edition uses two pes, while in the preceding example, it gave two torculus resupinus.

The discussion of the torculus resupinus, and more precisely, the study of this last form, ⋎⋎, brings to a close the examination of the fundamental symbols, that is, of those which are composed of accents and which can be distinguished and classified with precise terminology. We are now reaching a point which is completely beyond the limits of the generally received definition of the neume. In the preceding chapters we have already seen several symbols composed of two sections which correspond to simpler independent neumes ; for example, the modification of a porrectus ⋎ into a clivis + a virga ⌐, the scandicus ⋰ into a tractulus + a pes ⋎ or into a pes + a virga ⋎⋎, of the porrectus flexus ⋎⋎ into two clivis ⋏⋏ or into a virga + a torculus ⋎⋏, etc. The examples which we have just studied present a similar phenomenon. Apart from the fact that the symbol ⋎⋎ is found only in combination, we find that it is actually composed of two elements i.e. two pes, even though it corresponds exactly to the three forms which are written by a single stroke of the pen ⋎⋎⋎.

More and more instances of this type appear as the neumes become more complex. Classification and terminology are incapable of expressing all the various divisions which correspond, as we have seen, to diverse and well defined performance practices. There is thus little point in continuing a study of longer neumes by the use of a nomenclature which must inevitably prove to be inadequate. The facts themselves lead us to see in each of the various symbols studied above, as well as in the longer melisma, a unique neume composed of several neumatic elements.

9

THE NEUMATIC BREAK

We have already affirmed and we must now once again emphasize that the St. Gall notation used chironomic signs – signs which fix the gestures of the conductor onto the parchment. Chironomy gave rhythmic and expressive cues to singers who already knew the melodies by heart. This explains why an identical melodic design may be represented by many different symbols. Moreover, in addition to those forms in which a single trace already expresses the lightness or the importance of the sign, we have encountered others which involve the separation of one of the notes of the group ; for example, the torculus, the porrectus flexus, the scandicus or even, and the pes subbipunctis.

Now, since there are various symbols for tying the diverse elements in each of these neumes, there must be a special reason when one of the elements is graphically separated from the others. The copyist's hand, and the conductor's hand as well, stops on a note in order to show its importance. Notice that in examples 68, 101-102, 114, 116, 125, 126, and 133 the first note is always separated. On the contrary, in examples 103-107 and 135 the last note is separated. Moreover, in examples 138-139 we find a separation in the middle of a four-note element, so that the group, normally called a torculus resupinus, is drawn instead as two successive pes in the separated form.

As we consider next some of the more developed neumes, we must logically expect to find that there too the phenomenon of neumatic breaking (Neumentrennung) ('coupure neumatique') has a special signification, entailing definite consequences in the interpretation. As we shall see, the manner of grouping the sounds in the writing was in no way left to the fantasy of the copyist. It is the melody itself which determined the choice of the symbols. The melody existed long before anyone wrote it down, and when the copyists finally fixed it onto the parchment, they had to respect the relative value of the notes.

Let us begin with simple examples, starting with the already cited cases of separation of the initial note of a group. The figure ◡ can be prolonged by the addition of notes onto the end of the symbol. But the first note still remains the principal one, and the following notes proceed lightly from this initial impulse :

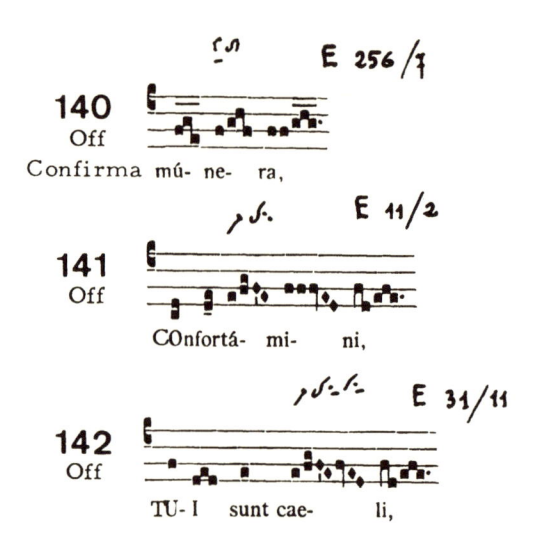

140 Off — E 256/7
Confirma mú- ne- ra,

141 Off — E 11/2
COnfortá- mi- ni,

142 Off — E 31/11
TU- I sunt cae- li,

Moreover, when the development of the symbol precedes the initial note of a given configuration, this note continues to be the most important note of the melodic motive.

143

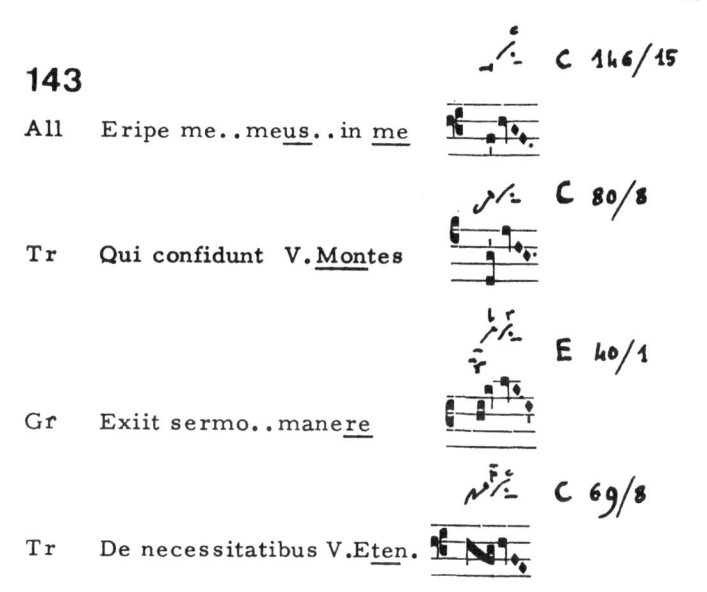

All   Eripe me..meus..in me   C 146/15

Tr   Qui confidunt V. Montes   C 80/8

Gr   Exiit sermo..manere   E 40/1

Tr   De necessitatibus V.Eten.   C 69/8

Here are additional examples showing the antecedent development of a porrectus flexus with an initial break. The motive can be preceded by one or by several notes, but these notes invariably lead to the same important note. (In the light of the analogous cases superposed in ex. 144, the signs in the rhythmic edition appear defective and illogical. When these signs were established in 1908, people were unaware of the facts which research has since permitted us to learn.)

144

Com   Revelabitur   E 48/5

All   Laetatus sum..in domum   3/10

Off   Ave Maria gratia   — 12/6

All   Laetatus sum..Domini   — 3/10

Intr   Ex ore..inimicos tuos   — 42/2

Let us pause on this last example. The melody gives us the following notes.

If we were to make an abstraction of the exact pitch of the notes, we would have simply a succession low-high-low-high, etc. This melodic design could be written by the symbol ෴ which unites all the notes with one quick, easy mark. There is as a matter of fact, just such an instance in the Offertory. Benedíctus... Dó·mi·nus.

෴   B 44/8

But, in the preceding example (Intr. " Ex ore ") the symbol is very different in all the MSS. This unanimity on the part of the copyists in transcribing an identical low-high-low-high succession can only be explained by a particular rhythmic situation. In this melodic succession, the notator distinguished two important notes that he wished to emphasize through his symbol. In this he undoubtedly imitated the conductor who, in his gestures, indicated not only the shape of the melody but also its rhythmic and expressive structure. The conductor's hand (and the

NEUMATIC BREAK

copyist's pen) stopped on certain notes, separating them from the following ones, while the other notes were tied as much as possible.

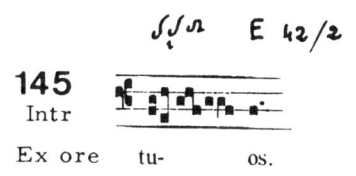

145
Intr

Ex ore tu- os.

It is quite probable that our modern notation would tend to group these notes in a very different way. Let us suppose, for example, that we had to notate the two following melodies in which the important notes are circled :

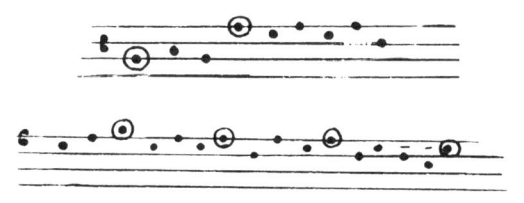

How would we group these notes in our current system ? Probably in such a way that each important note would be the first note of a group, because the principal rhythmic beat would fall at that point. Perhaps a sign similar to an episema would be added to stress this note.

The copyists of St. Gall grouped the notes in a different manner. They wrote :

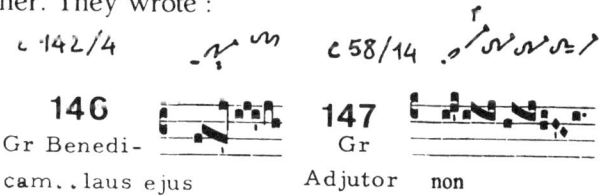

146
Gr Benedi-
cam..laus ejus

147
Gr
Adjutor non

Another very instructive example :

Today, we would write :

If all the notes had been equally light, the St. Gall copyists would have written. (N.B. The little dots express nothing but a succession of light notes.) But since this symbol became inadequate as soon as there were notes to be underlined, they all wrote :

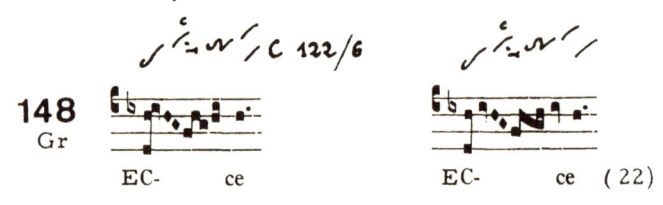

148
Gr

EC-   ce   EC-   ce   (22)

Each time that the pen arrives at an important note, it stops after having written it and it cuts it, ipso facto, from the following notes. Thus the break takes place *after* the important note and not before it, as would be the case in modern notation.

The neumatic break which reveals the particular expression of the preceding note is called an " expressive cut ". The MSS often add an episema to the important note which precedes this cut (cf. ex. 147). This episema, however, is not necessary ; the simple fact that the notator broke the line when he could have continued it already indicates sufficiently the importance of the note. The episemas confirm and emphasize a phenomenon which is already expressed clearly by the simple grouping of the signs.

Obviously, a long melisma cannot always be written with just a single line. Some subdivisions and separations are inevitable. In a certain sense, these also have the advantage of grouping the notes in a way that makes them easier to read. Consequently, it can be asked whether every break has the same purpose. Must every note which precedes a break be emphasized ?

Let us return to a case already cited :

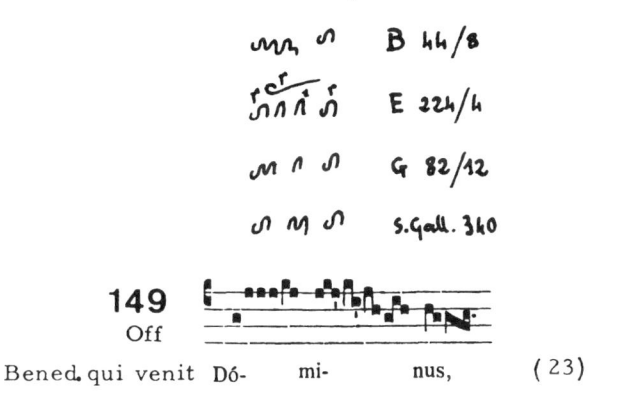

How does one explain that the notators, who were unanimous in the preceding examples, are now so different from each other, cutting the same neumatic group so arbitrarily ? Either there was uncertainty and divergence in the interpretation of this melisma or the copyists had complete liberty to tie or not to tie the neumatic elements. Their unanimity in the preceding examples makes one pause before admitting any uncertainty on their part.

And actually, it can be observed that the notators who cut the melodic design always did so at the same place — after one or another of the low notes and never after a high note. It is also interesting to note that the symbols agree once again in grouping the last three notes into a single element. All the MSS write a torculus here ; not a single one wrote ♪♪ for the last five notes of the neume. The importance of the fourth note before the last is unanimously underlined by the break which separates it from the following three.

And thus we see that there are several kinds of neumatic breaks. These can be reduced to the four following figures. In order to understand the rules for the cutting of neumes, it is not enough to look at the note preceding the break. In addition it is necessary to take into consideration the melodic context. We have therefore placed, above each one of the formulas, a design indicating the exact situation on the melodic line of the note followed by the neumatic break.

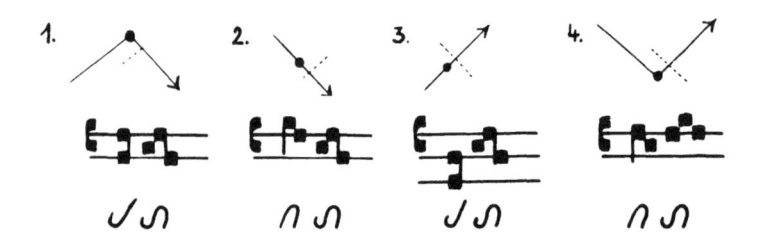

1 : *a break after a high note :* The first neumatic element ends on a note that is higher than either the preceding or following note.

2 : *a break at the descending mid-point :* The first neumatic element ends on a note that is lower than the preceding one but higher than the following one.

3 : *a break at the ascending mid-point :* The first neumatic element ends on a note that is higher than the preceding one but lower than the following one.

4 : *a break after the lowest note :* The first neumatic element ends on a note that is lower than either the preceding or following notes.

The corresponding neumatic symbols are added under the notes.

In the first three instances, the cutting is expressive and functional. It expresses the importance of the preceding note. If this note had not required a particular expression, the copyist would have written :

The symbol in the fourth example, on the contrary, could not be modified without underlining some note by that same deed. The grouping /V^, for example, would put the third note into relief by a break at the ascending mid-point. Only the symbol /1^, with a break at the low note, adequately represents the lightness of the five notes.

Here are some examples.

Column A : Groups of five light notes, followed by two long notes in line 1 and preceded by one important note in line 3.

Column C : In the groups of five notes, the first two are both important but the second is the most important of all because it is followed by an expressive break ; at a melodic high point in ex. 1 ; at the descending mid-point in ex. 2 and the ascending mid-point in ex. 3.

Column B : Here we find the same expressive breaking as in column C, but now, it is preceded by a light note.

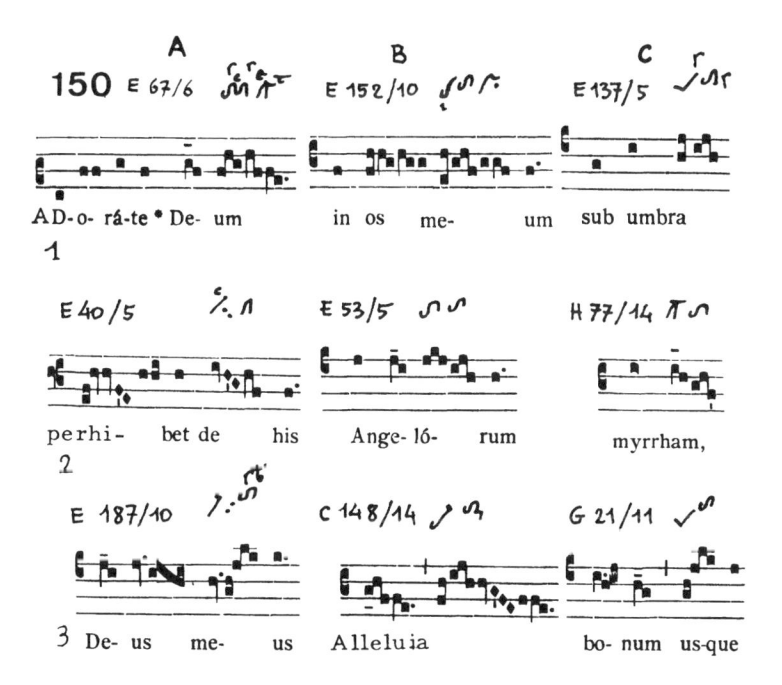

150

A	B	C
E 67/6	E 152/10	E 137/5
AD-o- rá-te • De- um	in os me- um	sub umbra

1

E 40/5	E 53/5	H 77/14
perhi- bet de his	Ange- ló- rum	myrrham,

2

E 187/10	C 148/14	G 21/11
De- us me- us	Alleluia	bo- num us-que

3

These examples differ among themselves from a melodic point of view as well, because the notes of a neume cannot be rearranged indifferently by just any break. The neumatic cutting is determined by the melody itself and is not left to the arbitrary judgement of the copyist or performer. Musical analysis of each example gives evidence to prove this fact.

We must now explain the purpose of a break at the bottom of a melodic element.

We have seen that, except for an occasional error, the copyists mark without fail the expressive breaks. They are unanimous in indicating them and they often even underline them with the addition of signs. On the contrary, for the break after a low note they frequently differ among themselves, tying the various neumatic elements or separating them, according to the possibilities. Moreover, the same copyist will sometimes modify the grouping of the notes for the same melodic formula :

This formula (the final cadence of the versicles in the Tracts of Mode VIII) recurs about ten times. The same copyists indifferently employ the liaison or the break at the lower note, between the two clivis.

This fact allows us to affirm that in this case, that is, after the lowest note of a melodic curve, the break does not have the same function as in the other instances. In other words, the low note which precedes a separation in the design does not necessarily and automatically have the same importance as the notes which elicit a neumatic break at any other point of the melodic line. We can thus conclude that, in a light context, a break at the lowest note, compared to others, is, in a certain sense, neutral as to its rhythmic signification. It is " inexpressive in itself ". If this were not the case, the copyists would not have used it with the liberty which we can observe once again in the following examples:

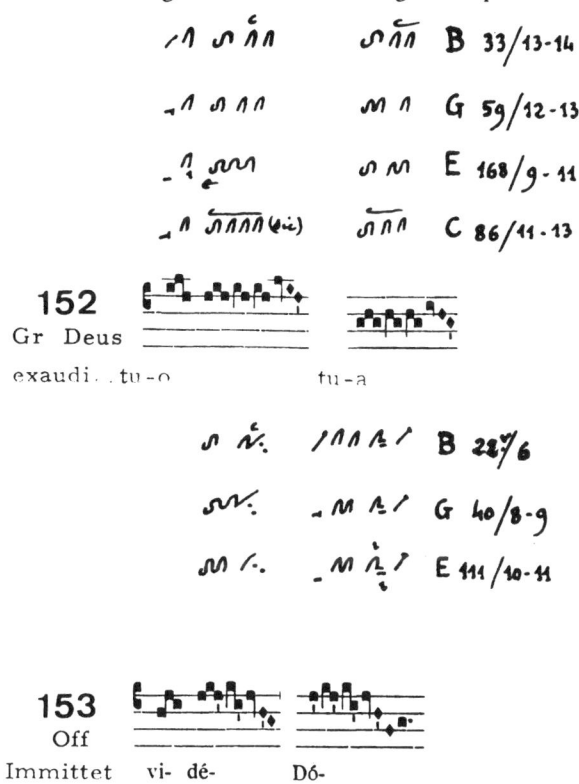

[neume examples with references B 33/13-14, G 59/12-13, E 168/9-11, C 86/11-13]

152
Gr Deus
exaudi..tu-o   tu-a

[neume examples with references B 28/6, G 40/8-9, E 111/10-11]

153
Off
Immittet   vi- dé-   Dó-

We have deliberately said that the break at the low note " compared to others " is " in a certain sense " neutral. In actual fact, the manner of writing even a light group is not always indiscriminate. Sometimes the distinction between the tying and the detaching of each of the neumatic elements in a light melisma is made deliberately.

Moreover, in a light design it is often possible to discern certain articulated notes − these also evidently light − which indicate phrasing in the melodic structure, phrasing which is executed almost unconsciously when one understands the particularities of the melodic structure. The following example can be explained in this way :

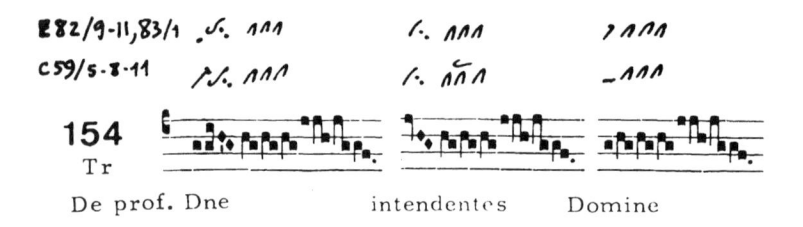

E82/9-11,83/1 ./. ∩∩∩   /·. ∩∩∩   ⁊∩∩∩
C59/5-8-11   ⁊/·. ∩∩∩   /·. ∩͂∩∩   _∩∩∩

154
Tr

De prof. Dne   intendentes   Domine

This formula of three successive light clivis (varying only in its antecedant context) turns up again five times in the authentic repertoire. Neither C nor E ever tie any of the clivis. This fact becomes all the more interesting if it is taken into account that this formula belongs to the same Tracts from Mode VIII from which we have taken ex. 151. In that example, the same copyists indifferently tied or cut the four notes into two clivis ; here, they always cut them. (The first and third parts of ex. 154 demonstrate by the sign used to indicate the initial SOL, that this note is indeed the principal structural note of the formula ; the LA is only an ornament.)

On the other hand, when the lowest note of a melodic curve has special importance, the copyists generally indicate it, either by the addition of a sign or by a modification of the outline, depending upon whether the symbol is tied or detached.

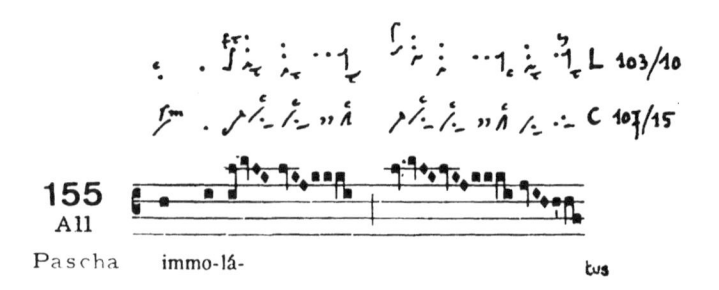

155
All

Pascha   immo-lá-   tus

The lengthening of such low notes was sometimes considered to be so obvious that certain copyists did not even think it necessary to point it out.

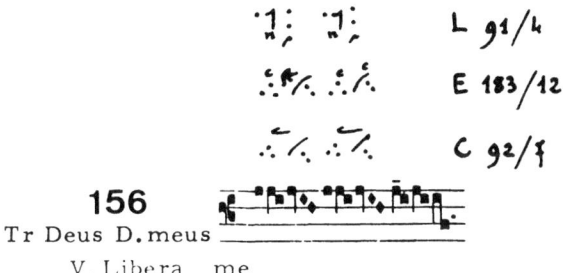

L 91/4
E 183/12
C 92/1

156
Tr Deus D. meus
V. Libera me

A brief musical motive is repeated ; C and E write a light climacus both times, while L uses the uncinus twice for the lowest note, thus indicating a certain broadening of the last note of each climacus.

Here, we have only briefly mentioned certain aspects of the principle of neumatic cutting. Because of the rich signification of this phenomenon, we will return to it at the end of each of the following chapters.

10

STROPHA

The sign ՚ which is called apostropha, stropha or strophicus, was originally used by ancient grammarians. It indicated the elision of a vowel (can't – can not) as it still does today in various languages.

The copyists of St. Gall adopted this sign to represent a musical fact : one or more light notes.

The last stropha of a group of strophicus often has an episema ՛ .

I. GROUPS OF STROPHICUS

The strophae are most often combined into groups of from two to five or six notes in unison.

1. Melodic use

The DISTROPHA, a group of two strophicus, is almost never to be found isolated on one syllable ; in such a case, at least one stropha precedes it on a lower note[25]. Strictly speaking, however, this is not a distropha but a tristropha which begins on a lower note.

In combination, on the contrary, the distropha can mark the beginning of a neume.

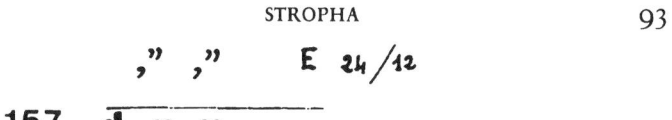

STROPHA

157 Intr
Dominus dí- xit ad me:

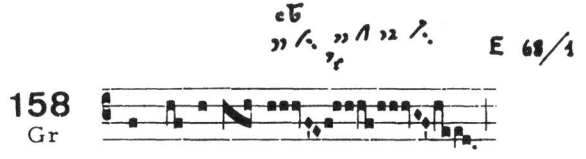

158 Gr
Timebunt et vi- dé-bi- tur

The TRISTROPHA, a group of three strophicus, is often found in isolation and even more often in combination with other signs.

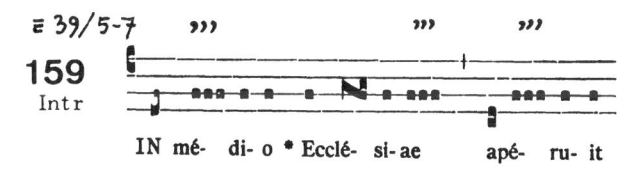

159 Intr
IN mé- di- o * Ecclé- si- ae apé- ru- it

Groups of four strophicus or more are found less frequently.

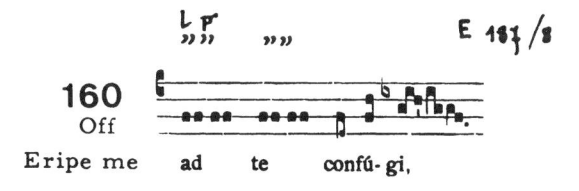

160 Off
Eripe me ad te confú- gi,

161 Off
Portas caeli pa-nem Ange-ló- rum

162 Gr — Eripe me vo- luntá- tem

2. *Interpretation of the signs*

The very form of the sign tells us that it cannot indicate heavy notes but light, delicate ones. This is confirmed by L's notation which lacks a special sign corresponding to the St. Gall stropha and which writes simple dots instead.

While the typography of the Vatican Edition does not differentiate the tractulus and the punctum from the stropha, the Monastic Antiphonary uses a special sign which makes it possible to recognize the strophicus:

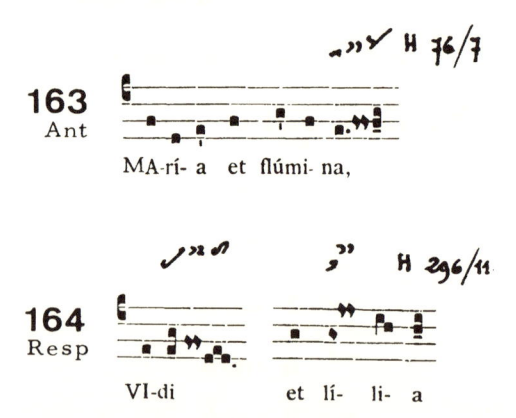

163 Ant — MA-rí- a et flúmi- na,

164 Resp — VI-di et lí- li- a

The lightness of the strophicus persists even at a melodic summit; an objective interpretation must not neglect this indication.

165
Gr

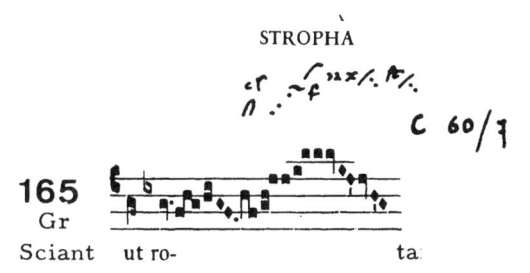

Sciant ut ro- ta

Although there is no doubt concerning the light interpretation of the various groups of strophicus, there is still much discussion with regard to their practical performance. Must they be chanted all melted together into one single, long sound or should there be a light repercussion on each strophicus?

Let us try to resolve the problem from the following examples:

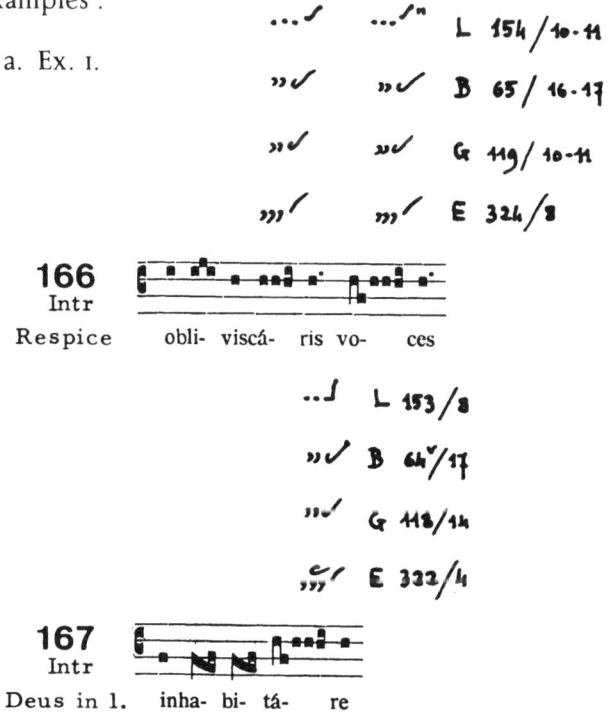

a. Ex. 1.

166
Intr

Respice obli- viscá- ris vo- ces

167
Intr

Deus in l. inha- bi- tá- re

There are here three instances of three notes in unison followed by one higher note. The Vatican Edition writes two notes in unison + a pes beginning on the same degree. The MSS, however, present two different versions. One (*G* and *B*) corresponds to the grouping of the Vatican Edition and other (*E*) separates the three notes in unison from the last one. *L* sometimes writes like *G* and *B* and sometimes like *E*. Relying on the Vatican Edition, the traditional methods teach us to execute the four notes in two groups of two, that is, one note held for two beats and a repercussion on the third note (the first note of the pes). According to the symbols from *E*, however, it would be necessary to sing one note for three beats and then the last note. Now it is highly unlikely that some sang 2 + 2, while others sang 3 + 1, and that at *L* they sang in two different ways. But if the second and the third stropha are sung with a slight repercussion, the practical execution does not vary and the difficulty disappears.

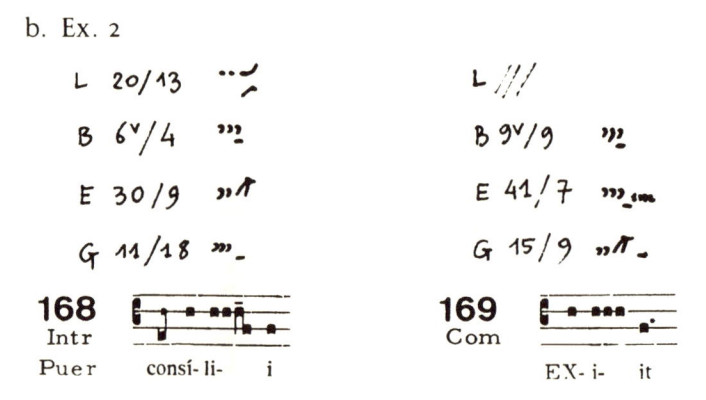

b. Ex. 2

L 20/13

L

B 6ᵛ/4

B 9ᵛ/9

E 30/9

E 41/7

G 11/18

G 15/9

168
Intr
Puer consí- li- i

169
Com
EX- i- it

The same phenomenon in a descending melody. (In the first example, the Vatican Edition prints one additional note for the last syllable, as in many other instances in which two vowels of the same timbre follow each other. *G* also does the same thing in the second example, but this has little bearing on our present subject.)

Whereas, in ex. 166 and 167, each of the MSS preserved its symbol in all three instances (E writing always ⟩⟩⟨, G always ⟩⟩⟨), we can observe here that the same MS uses different groupings (2 + 2 or 3 + 1). Does this imply different rhythms and different practical execution ? It would seem not. Instead we have here additional evidence for the repercussion of each stropha ; the performance remains identical regardless of the grouping.[26]

c. Ex. 3.   ♪··⌣   L 19/13

              ♪⟩⟩   E 28/3

170
Off

Deus enim pa- rá- ta

According to today's system, the two symbols each indicate a different subdivision. *L* appears to underline the first of the three notes at the unison while the St. Gall MSS underline the second note! However, if the singer pulsates each DO, the two symbols agree (at least with regard to the figuration of the three unison notes which are equally light in both notations).

d. Ex. 4.

The following formula is found seven times in the graduals of Mode III :

171

C
⎧ ·⟩⟩ ⟩⟩ ⟩⟩   v. g. 75/11   4 fois
⎨ ,⟩⟩⟩ ⟩⟩⟩   - 48/3   2 -
⎩ ,⟩⟩⟩⟩⟩⟩   - 47/16   1 -

L   ♪·····   - 60/8

Cha   ·······   - 37/8

98 STROPHA

How were the six unison notes of this formula sung? It is obvious that there are four different groupings! Were they performed as one six-beat tone? Do the three different ways of writing these notes in C signify that in one instance they sang a single six-beat note, in two others, two three-beat sounds, and in four others, three two-beat sounds?

The only possible solution is that the six notes were individualized by a slight repercussion. C's frequent presentation of the stropha divided into groups was intended to facilitate the reading of the total number of notes, but is does not signify a different execution of the notes each time.

e. Ex. 5.

This formula recurs about 16 times in the Tracts of Mode II.

Cha, *M* and *Ben* also invariably write an individual group of five notes. It is therefore not a matter of a single sound held for five beats but of five repercussed notes, which are made more readable by the graphic division of *G* and *B*.

There are also other instances : two successive distropha or tristropha in which the last strophicus of the group has an episema.

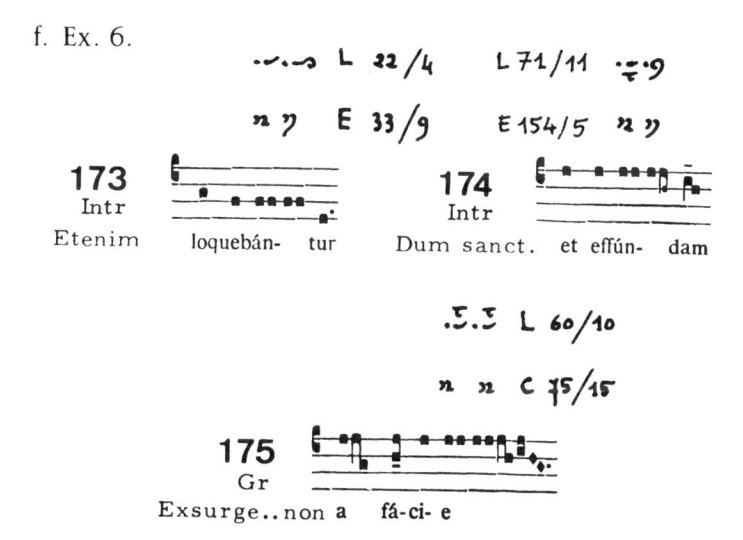

f. Ex. 6.

173 Intr — Etenim loquebán- tur

174 Intr — Dum sanct. et effún- dam

175 Gr — Exsurge..non a fá-ci- e

These examples are quite different. In the cases previously cited the strophae were notes of equal value and their grouping was left to the choice of the copyist. In these examples the MSS unanimously separate the groups from one another.

We are generally taught to chant these notes as two sounds of two beats each. But how can one reconcile this practice with the symbols in the MSS which, on the contrary, clearly underline the second note with an episema or a τ ? A single sound of two beats is unjustifiable here. It is therefore necessary to admit as an established paleographic fact the repercussion of the second stropha which is even enlarged in its relation to the first.

The following example is the only case in which there are two successive tristropha in combination with the same rhythm as the preceding – the two first notes are light and the third has an episema :

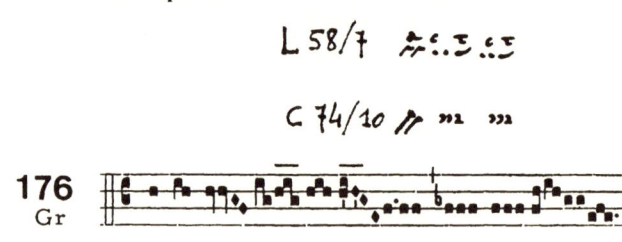

176
Gr

Dum tribul. Dómi- ne,

If one simply sings a single, three-beat sound twice, what do the indications in L mean by the c on the first two notes and the τ on the third ?

g. Ex. 7.

In order to further prove the repercussion, we can cite numerous instances in which, in the place of one stropha at the unison, certain MSS use a symbol which implies a lower half-step :

177
Intr

Respice in me- um

178
Off

Precatus pó-pu-lo

In this situation the Vatican Edition prints the unison stropha but elsewhere it often follows a later tradition which pitches the first strophicus a half-step below the second :

STROPHA

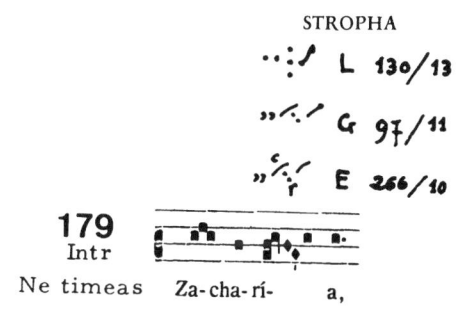

179
Intr

Ne timeas Za-cha-rí- a,

It seems easy to explain the use of the half-step in the place of a stropha at the unison by the fact that the repercussion was performed clumsily, giving the copyist the impression that in ex. 177, the second note rose a half-step (according to E), while in ex. 178, the third note descended from the same interval (according to G).

All of the examples cited make it obvious that the repercussion of the stropha at the unison corresponds to the original practice, whereas their performance by sounds that are held for two or three beats contradicts paleographic facts.

Let us complete this paragraph by examples of neumatic cutting after a distropha or a tristropha.

180
Off
Jubilate

E 58/1

ju-bi- lá- te

This example is self-explanatory. The expansive melodic ascent begins with four small motives which all end with a lightly lengthened stropha. The melody then starts out from the lower second and takes a new leap. In addition to the episema, E adds an **x** (= expectate : wait) three times.

STROPHA

The following formula is characteristic of the stereotyped melody for alleluias in Mode II :

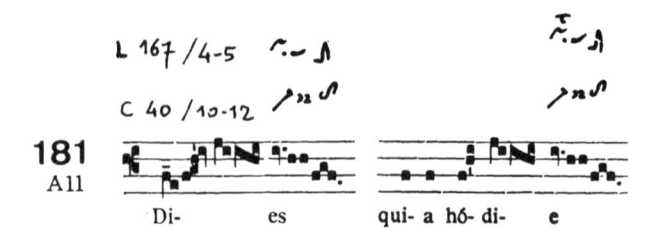

181 All
Di- es qui- a hó- di- e

The melody moves from RE to SOL and then returns to RE after underlining the second FA which is lightly repercussed and lengthened. This last stropha is in fact followed by an expressive break (" high " in relation to that which follows) and the importance of this break is, with only one exception, always confirmed by an episema in C. In addition, an initial break underlines the first note of the neume – the SOL, represented by a virga with an episema (in one instance L adds a τ). Therefore, this note is also important. If the melody had not required these two rhythmic particularities, the copyists would have tied the notes two-by-two ⌢⌢ or would have even united all four, putting SOL-FA-FA-RE in the same syllable, ⌢ a porrectus flexus with the two middle notes at the same pitch.[27]

There are also some groups of strophicus in which the last note of the neume has an episema in order to facilitate the correct articulation of one syllable before passing to the next. L and Cha always lengthen the last note in such cases.

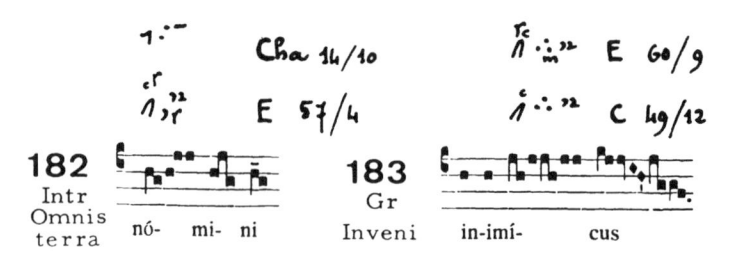

182 Intr Omnis terra
nó- mi- ni

183 Gr
Inveni in-imí- cus

II. APOSTROPHA

The stropha is never found in isolation but always in combination with other neumatic elements. In most cases a single stropha precedes other strophic groups or another sign implying notes at the same pitch. If, on the contrary, the stropha is placed next to any other symbol, it is in unison with the preceding note.

1. *apostropha at the beginning of a neume or in an ascending melodic line*

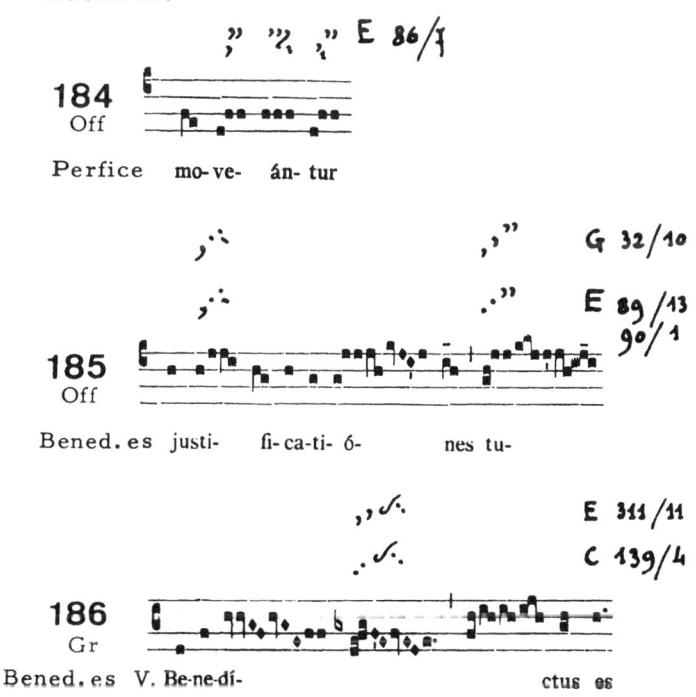

184 Off

Perfice mo- ve- án- tur

185 Off

Bened. es justi- fi- ca-ti- ó- nes tu-

186 Gr

Bened. es V. Be-ne-dí- ctus es

The fact that in so many cases a stropha is interchangeable with a punctum clearly indicates that both signs are of equal lightness.

2. *apostropha at the end of a neume*

In the chapter dealing with the porrectus it was stated that in certain instances the sign ∕∕ does not signify ⬛ but ▬⬛(unison of the last two notes). It was precisely the comparison of the symbols ∕∕ and ∕↓ in C which gave indisputable proof of this. Let us now examine other examples of the apostropha added to a clivis or to a torculus.

Ben 43ᵛ/1-3

Y 40/3-5

G 22/18-20

E 63/8-11

187

Com — Feci et Dómi- ne, ó-mni- a di- ri- gé- bar, hábu- i.

Ben and Y clearly show that the apostropha of apposition is always in unison with the preceding note. The melodic restitution of these neumes in the Vatican Edition seems illogical. ∕↓ is rendered by ⬛ and ▬⬛, but the two instances of ∕↓ are transcribed by ⬛ and not by ▬⬛. The Vatican Edition thus mixes the authentic tradition with a later one.

H also uses the porrectus or the clivis + apostropha indifferently, even in the same formula. Thus, in the cadential formula of the versicles for Responsories in Mode IV ∕∕ is found 66 times and ∕↓ 27 times.

In every case where C writes ∕↓ , Ben places the last two notes at the same pitch. Consequently, in all these cases, it is necessary to explain ∕∕ by ∕↓, and not the reverse.

In the cadences for responsories in Mode IV H writes ∕∕ or ∕↓ . The responsory " Dum ambuláret " contains a crasis on the word " Galilaé-ae " which is noted as a torculus + pressus major. This proves the repercussion of the two unison notes. If things were otherwise, it would not be possible to unite the second FA to the clivis FA-MI in this instance where there is a succession of two syllables with the same timbre (ae-ae). (This also proves the repercussion of the pressus.)

3. *apostropha between two neumatic elements*

When the apostropha is found at the center of a neume, its function is very different from the function exposed in the preceding paragraphs. There, we observed that the apostropha was essentially a light note. But here it acquires a particular importance and it becomes a note of punctuation.

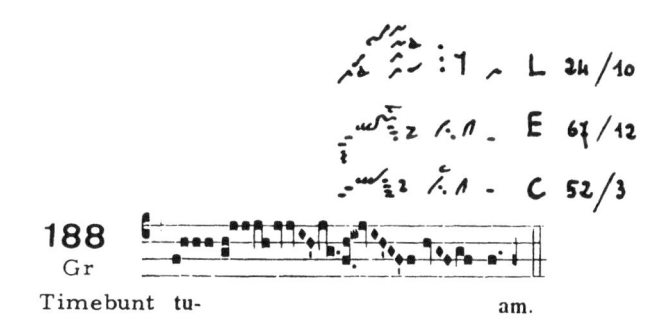

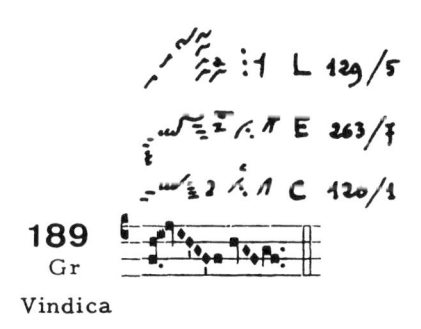

188
Gr

Timebunt tu-   am.

189
Gr

Vindica

The ample descending movement of the climacus concludes with an apostropha and the melody continues with the light, ornamental cadence. The copyist of E always used the special epismatic form ⌐ ; C uses either the simple form or the epismatic form ⌐ .[28]

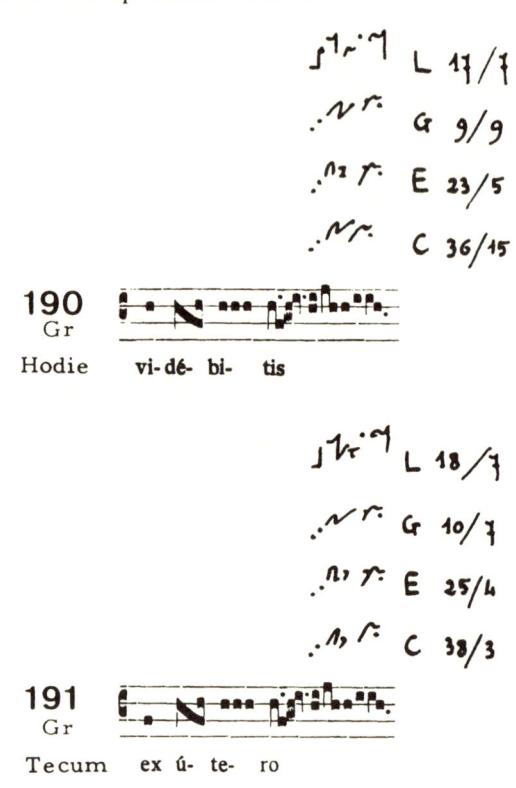

L 17/7
G 9/9
E 23/5
C 36/15

190
Gr

Hodie   vi- dé- bi- tis

L 18/7
G 10/7
E 25/4
C 38/3

191
Gr

Tecum   ex ú- te- ro

In these formulae from the Graduals of Mode II, the apostropha at the center of the neume has a role which is analogous to the one which it had in the two preceding examples. After the light scandicus flexus, the apostropha underlines the importance of DO, contrasting it with the double RE of the pressus major which follows. Some copyists add an episema to the stropha, others do not[29].

In the two following examples of a cadential formula, the apostropha underlines the preceding note, doubling it with a repercussion. But it is the apostropha which is the more important of the two unison notes because it is followed by an expressive cut, high in relation to the following note.

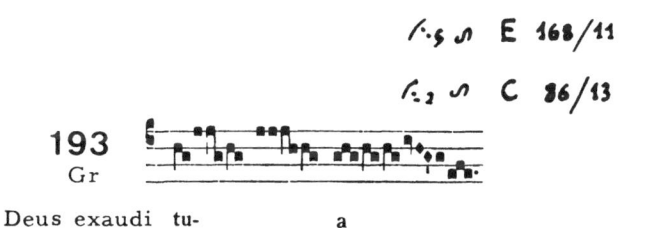

192
Intr

Terribilis cae-li :

193
Gr

Deus exaudi tu-　　　a

We will see later, however, that in these formulae, the oriscus would be more appropriate than the apostropha, and this is illustrated by the way in which G writes in ex. 192 and E in ex. 193.

II
TRIGON

Before it was used in musical notation, the sign for the trigon ∴ ∵ ∵ was used for punctuation or for abbreviation (q ∴ = quæ). Thus there is nothing in the sign itself to indicate the melodic relation of the three notes. It is a stereotyped symbol which varies from one MS to another.

I. MELODIC SIGNIFICATION

The melodic signification of the trigon is the first problem which confronts us. The Vatican Edition transcribes the trigon either as ▪▙ or, less frequently, as ▪▙. Here is one of the most typical examples. The following formula occurs three times in the same piece:

The first of the two successive trigons is preceded by a long note ; the second is formed of four notes with the last two lengthened. (The light St. Gall form is ∴ .) What does this indicate ? To begin with, the symbols in C and E show clearly that the initial note (tractulus) of this formula is lower than the first note of the trigon. L confirms this and also proves that the first two notes of the trigon are in unison.[30] *Ben* and the Aquitaine MSS also indicate the lower position of the initial note and the unison of the first two notes of the trigon. The Vatican Edition, on the contrary, writes ♩♪♫, evidently accepting a later tradition. The authentic melodic design of the first group is certainly ♩♪ (the first two notes of the trigon in unison), and this is accepted by the Vatican Edition for the second trigon of the formula.

A formula taken from Graduals of Mode III furnishes another proof of the unison of the initial notes of the trigon :

195

Below is a complete table of the eleven instances where this formula is found in the authentic repertoire. How are these five notes in question written there ?

The perfect correspondence between ∴" and "," clearly proves the unison of the first two notes which are sometimes written as a trigon and sometimes as strophae. For these can be no doubt about the fact that the distropha are at the same pitch.

In addition, this equivalence and interchangeability of the signs proves that the first two notes of the trigon, notes in unison, must be individuated by a repercussion. In effect, the repercussion of the distropha, and of strophic groups in general, logically requires a similar execution for the trigon, since it can take the place of a distropha.

It is also interesting to note that in all of these instances, neither the later MSS or the Vatican Edition ever transform the unison into a torculus as above, but correspond perfectly with the oldest symbols. The reason for this is that the trigon is situated here on the upper degree, not of a half-step (DO or FA), but of a whole step. When the trigon is on DO or FA, the weakness of the lower degree more easily draws down the first of the two unison notes.

Here is a final proof of the initial unison of the trigon :

196
Off

Laetentur sa- lu- tá- re (V. 2)

The example is taken from the second versicle of the Offertory of the first Mass for Christmas. This formula, which interests us here because of the trigon, appears earlier in the Offertory itself, as well as at the end of the first versicle. The symbol for the two formulas is, however, modified.

197
Off

Laetentur et exsúl- tet V. 1: o- mnis

TRIGON   III

The complex articulation of the two words " ex*súl*-tet "
and " *om-nis* " caused the copyist to choose, instead of the
simple sign of the trigon, the liquescent form ⸻ consisting of
two strophae with a prolongation of the second one. This
modification indicates a third light sound at a lower pitch.
Since there is no doubt that the two strophae are in unison,
the two first notes of the trigon on " *salutá-re* " must also be
sung in the same way – that is, at the unison.

II. MELODIC USE

The trigon is never isolated on one syllable. It is almost
always preceded by at least one note which can be either
light or long.

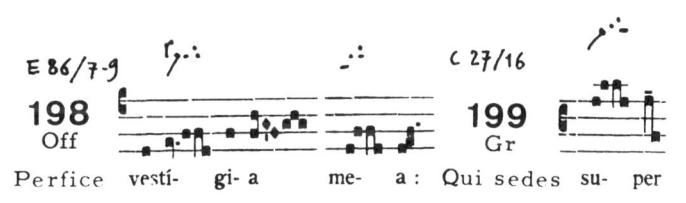

198 Off — Perfice vestí- gi- a me- a :   **199** Gr — Qui sedes su- per

It is only very rarely that the trigon coincides with the
attack of a syllable :

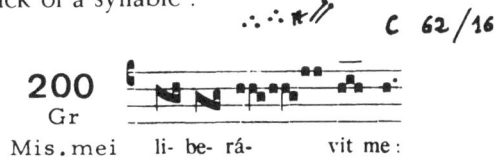

200 Gr — Mis. mei li- be- rá- vit me :

Most often, it is preceded or followed by several notes,
either light or long :

201 Gr — Custodi Dó- mi- ne,

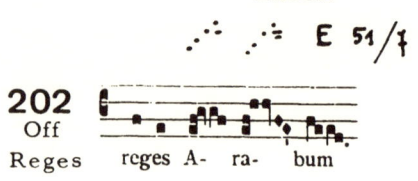

III. INTERPRETATION OF THE SIGNS

In general the trigon is a light neum and its written form conveys this lightness. It is usually found in light contexts:

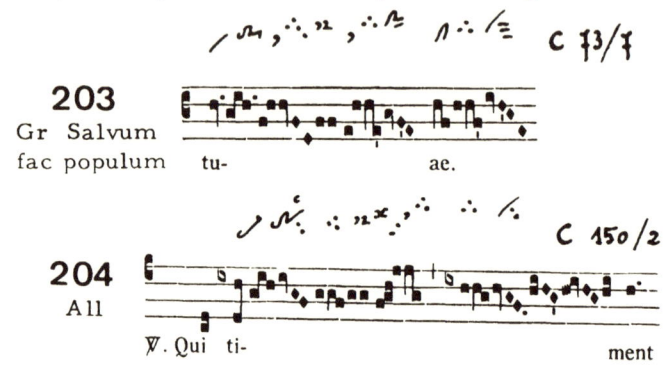

The trigon even preserves its lightness at the top of a melodic curve. Here are two examples of this fact (205 and 207). They are contrasted with parallel cases in which the same culminating notes have a greater importance, indicated by the use of different signs:

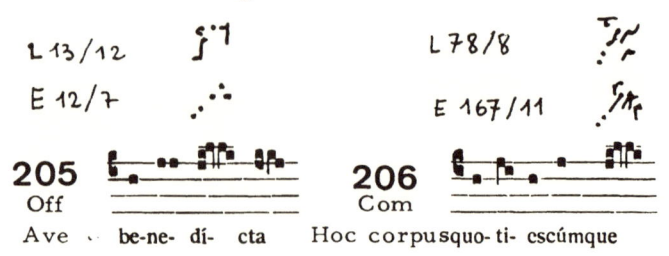

TRIGON

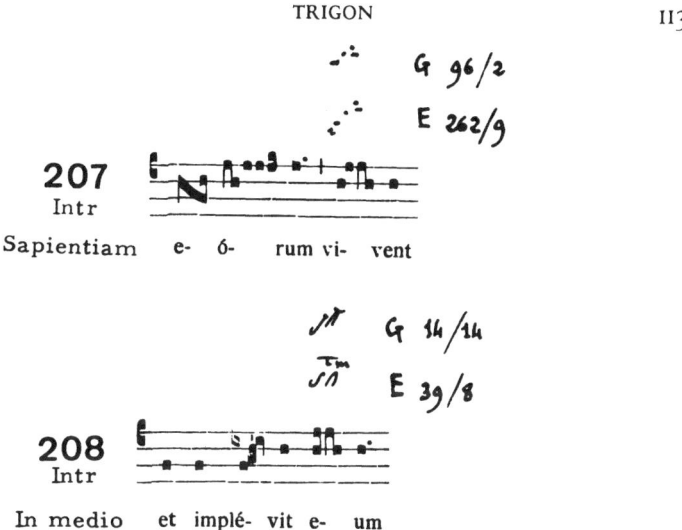

207 Intr
Sapientiam e- ó- rum vi- vent

208 Intr
In medio et implé- vit e- um

There are nevertheless some cases in which the first two notes of a trigon (and quite exceptionally the first alone) are light while the rest (as well as the following notes in the case of the elongated trigon) is long :

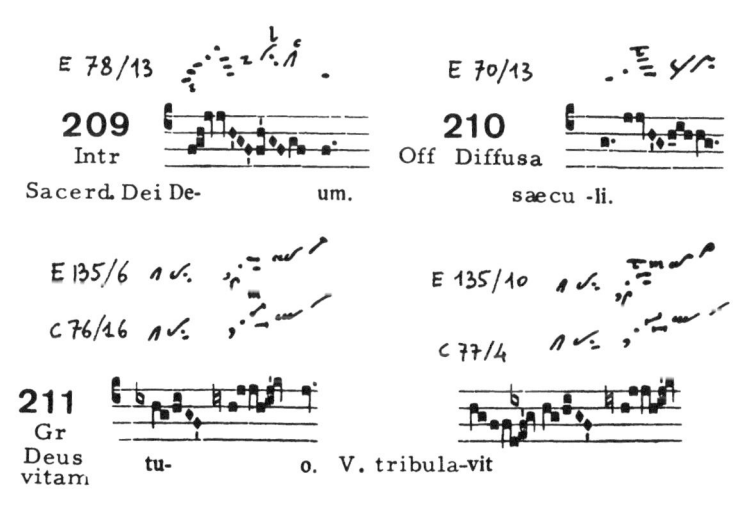

209 Intr
Sacerd. Dei De- um.

210 Off Diffusa
saecu -li.

211 Gr
Deus vitam tu- o. V. tribula-vit

IV. NEUMATIC BREAKING AFTER A TRIGON

When the trigon is found at the descending mid-point of a melodic line, its last note, followed by a neumatic break, is underlined because of its position and must therefore be somewhat lengthened. To illustrate this clearly the following examples are cited and beneath each one appears the notation which would have been employed if the melody had contained no important notes to emphasize.

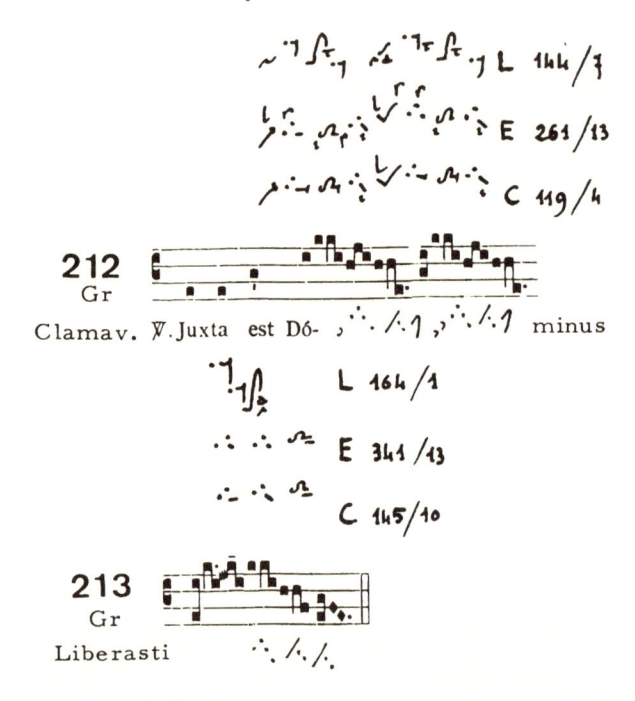

212
Gr
Clamav. ℣. Juxta est Dó- minus

213
Gr
Liberasti

Example 212, more complex than the following one, is particularly interesting. Each time RE occurs in the melody it is underlined, first by an initial break at the beginning of the melisma and next by the two breaks in the course of the melodic descent, after the trigon, and after the torculus. The same melodic motive is immediately repeated, but this time it begins with a long pes whose second note, followed by a break in the course of the melodic ascent, corresponds to the virga of the first motive.

C indicates the lengthening of the last note of the trigon ⌐ both times ; E does so only the first time ; L, on the other hand, adds the letter τ the second time only. Now we must repeat what we already said in Chapter 9 ; even when the copyists write the entirely light form of the trigon, its last note must nonetheless be lengthened, for the grouping of the notes sets the trigon off from the neumatic element which follows, and this alone indicates sufficiently the importance of the trigon's last note. If this note were not important, the copyist would have grouped together all the notes found before the low DO∴ as we have done in the example given above, and the cutting would then not be, in itself, expressive.

The form ∴ indicates a melodic descent of at least a third. (See symbol 2 of the climacus ⁄∴ in Chapter 6.) This inclined mark (gravis) does not signify a lengthening. Its signification is of a melodic nature.

When a trigon appears on a syllabic articulation, its last note is sometimes underlined, as we have already noted when studying the stropha (ex. 182 and 183) ; this slight lengthening is simply the normal consequence of good pronunciation.

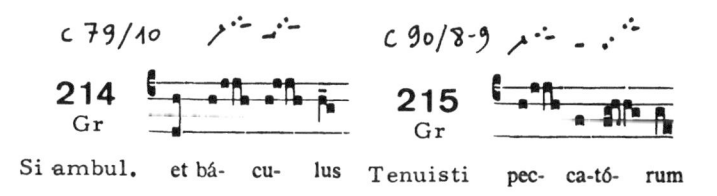

c 79/10

214
Gr

Si ambul.   et bá-   cu-   lus

c 90/8-9

215
Gr

Tenuisti   pec-   ca-tó-   rum

BIVIRGA · TRIVIRGA

I. SIGNS AND MELODIC USE

In St. Gall MSS, a double punctum (bi-punctum) at the unison is never found on the same syllable. The virga, on the other hand, may be repeated once or twice to form a bivirga or a trivirga. The horizontal position of the virga // (and not // or /\ ) indicates that the two or three notes were sung in unison. A majority of the most ancient St. Gall MSS always add episemas to the bivirga and trivirga : // and ///. These episemas underline the importance of the neume and indicate that the second and third notes are equal to the first. A bivirga in which only the first note has an episema // is never to be found.

E usually writes the bivirga without episemas. It seems to reserve the episema to indicate special nuances, such as the predominance of the accented syllable over the other syllables of a word.

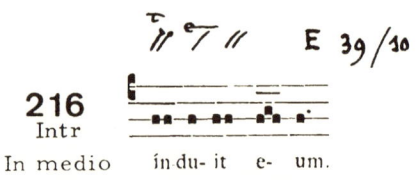

216
Intr
In medio   ín du- it   e-   um.   E 39/10

Two consecutive syllables in unison, side by side, can each receive a bivirga. This is even an excellent way to underline an important word :

BIVIRGA-TRIVIRGA

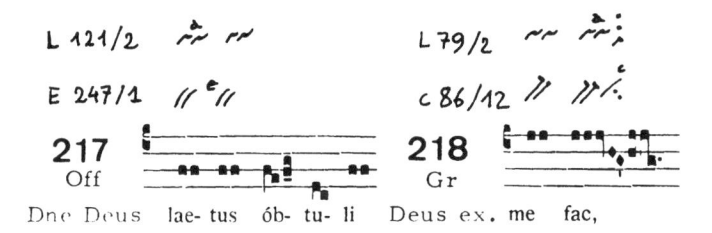

217 Off — Dne Deus lae-tus ób-tu-li

218 Gr — Deus ex me fac,

L is not acquainted with the bivirga but writes two uncinus in its place. In ex; 217 it also underlines the predominance of the accented syllable by the addition of an a(= augete : swell).

The bivirga, isolated or in combination, is used much more frequently than the trivirga. It is often encountered in the Graduals of Modes II and V, at the beginning of a more or less long unison recitative, and always on an important degree, FA or DO :

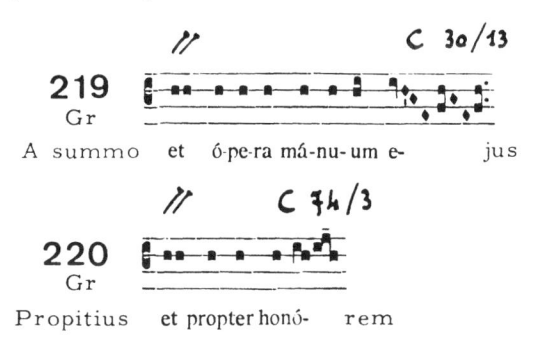

219 Gr — A summo et ó-pe-ra má-nu-um e- jus

220 Gr — Propitius et propter honó- rem

A bivirga can also underline the first verbal accent of a piece or of an incise :

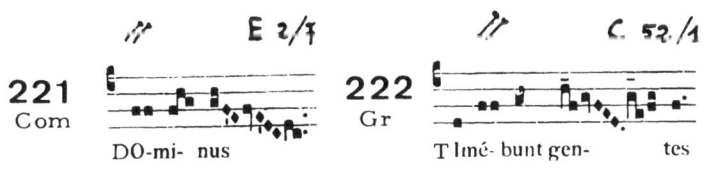

221 Com — DO-mi- nus

222 Gr — Timé- bunt gen- tes

223 Off
DE-si-dé- ri- um

The isolated trivirga is only found on exceptional occasions :

224 Off
Repleti et de- le- ctá- ti su- mus.

225 Ant
Dns veniet De- us, fortis,

It is rather rare even in combination. It is found most often in the final melisma of Mode VIII Tracts.

226 Cant
Cantemus

This final formula (cor-de) is also found several times in Modes I and II.

227 Off
Laetamini re- cti cor- de.

BIVIRGA-TRIVIRGA

More than three successive virgas are never found on the same syllable. The opposite is true of strophae which are often more numerous.

There also are some expanded forms of the bivirga; for example:

— Bivirga preceded by a light note which is tied to the first virga.

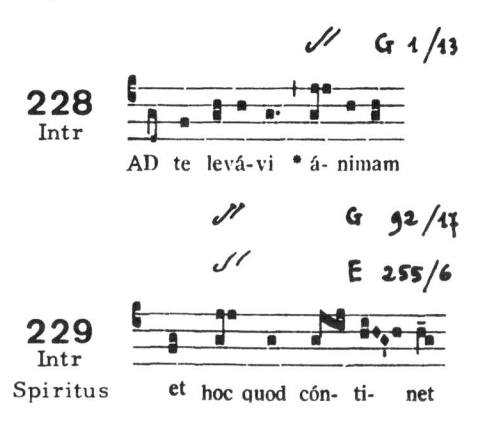

228 Intr
AD te levá-vi * á- nimam

229 Intr
Spiritus et hoc quod cón- ti- net

— A bivirga preceded or followed (bivirga subpunctis) by two light notes :

230 Off
Sicut hó- di- e,

231 Intr
Esto mihi in De- um re- fú-gi- i,

— A light melodic succession between two bivirga :

232 Com — Pascha í-ta-que

233 Intr — O mnes

Often an important note attracts a whole series of notes by means of a bivirga :

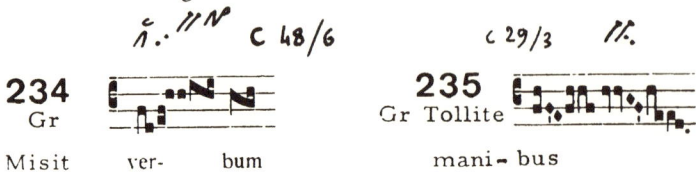

234 Gr — Misit ver- bum

235 Gr Tollite — mani- bus

II. PERFORMANCE PRACTICE

A bivirga is commonly sung today as a single sound of two beats. But this does not seem to have been the original practice. This can be illustrated by the following cases :

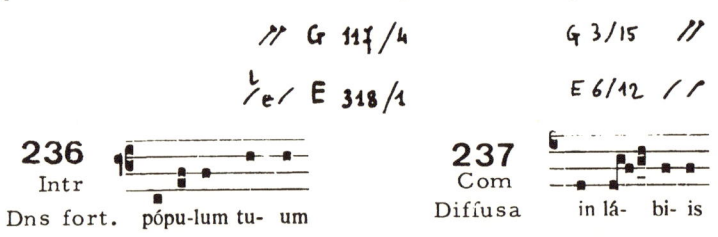

236 Intr — Dns fort. pópu-lum tu- um

237 Com — Diffusa in lá- bi- is

The above examples present a succession of two identical vowels. In both cases E places an isolated virga on each syllable whereas G writes a bivirga. Now since it is evident beyond a doubt that the two notes in the first notation are to be sung distinctly, why should not the same hold true in the second ?

238 Tr — Eripe lá-bi-is

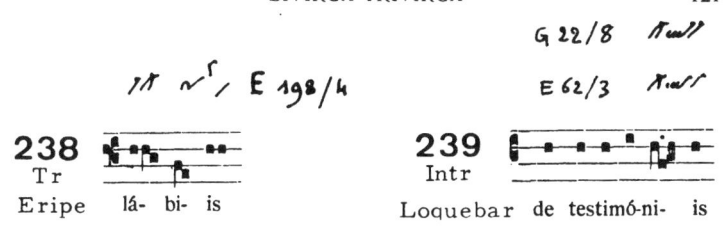

239 Intr — Loquebar de testimóni- is

A comparison of the Vatican Edition with the ancient MSS reveals the same phenomenon. In the first example, the MSS write the first note of the unison on the syllable " Lábi-is " and the second one by itself on the final syllable, while the Vatican Edition groups together the two unison notes on this last syllable. This is not proof that, originally, two very distinct sounds were sung on the two syllables " lábi-is " and that they were later represented, in the MSS followed by the Vatican Edition, by a single sound of two beats on the last syllable. The entire problem disappears if we admit a repercussion[31]; the same reasoning applies to the other example.

The following examples, along with many analogous instances, provide a solid argumentation in favor of the repercussion of the virga at the unison.

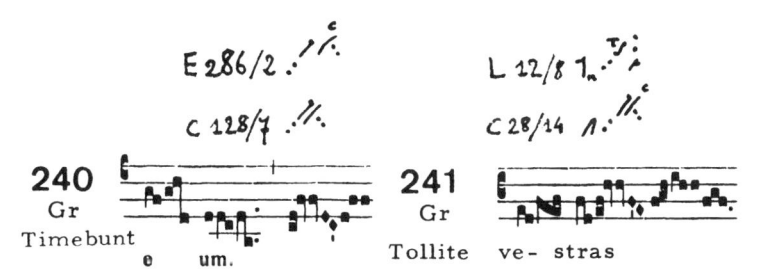

240 Gr — Timebunt eum.

241 Gr — Tollite ve- stras

If, at the date when the MS was written, a single sound of two beats was to have been sung, it would be impossible to account for the episema on the first virga and the addition of c on the following virga which introduces the light movement of the climacus.[32]

Last of all, there are instances in which, even in the best MSS, a pes quadratus starting one half-step below replaces the bivirga. If the bivirga had been sung as a single, two-beat note, the copyists would not have been given the impression of two sounds on two distinct pitches and they would never have written a pes quadratus. See, for example :

242
Intr

Omnia quae fe-císti no- bis, Dó- mi- ne,

243
Intr

Esto mihi et re-fú-gi- um me- um

In other instances, only the later MSS (but already G !) give a bivirga in place of the pes quadratus of the earlier MSS :

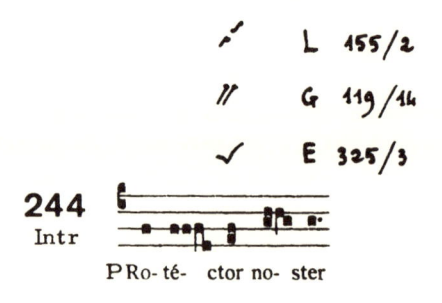

244
Intr

PRo- té- ctor no- ster

		L 76/9-10
		G 58/1
		E 164/4-5

245
Intr

Judica me me- us, et forti- tú- do

The Vatican Edition follows the MSS without any criterion, sometimes printing ▪▪ and sometimes ▪.

A well-known formula for Alleluias in Mode VIII contains a rather serious error of this type. Here, the Vatican Edition clearly contradicts the most authentic tradition.

	Ben 1/2
	L 166/3
	G 1/20
	E 1/3
	C 26/5

246
All

Ostende tu- am

It must be added however that this tendency to transform a group of two ascending notes into a bivirga takes place only when these two notes cover an interval of a half-step. A pes quadratus of a whole-step always remains intact, even in the latest MSS.[33]

13

PRESSUS

The following five chapters concern symbols which include the oriscus : ∼ ⁊ ⌐ .

The sign for the oriscus was commonly used in litterature to indicate a contraction, as in Dñum, Dñe. It still has this fonction today in French and in Spanish.

It would seem logical to begin with the oriscus itself, but the particular function of this sign will be more apparent after the study of the pressus and the virga strata.

I. PRESSUS MAJOR

1. the sign and the melodic signification

The sign of the pressus major ⌒ is composed of three elements : virga, oriscus and punctum. Melodically, the first two notes of the pressus are always in unison. In other words (and this also holds true for the pressus minor), the characteristic note of the pressus, the oriscus, is always in unison with the preceding note. The last note is always at a lower pitch, but usually not lower than a second or a third. When it unexpectedly descends further, the addition of an ↙(= inferius, iusum : lower) or an inclined tractulus (gravis), or even the two signs together underline the fact.

247
Ant

Urbs   et   antemu-rá- le :

248 Off
Eripe.. Deus et ab insurgén- tibus

The pressus is found both on low and on high notes and it can be used either in isolation or in combination.

2. *interpretation of the signs*

For a long time it was commonly held that the pressus was a group of heavy notes (" pressus " from " premere " : to press). But a detailed examination demonstrates that it can express a variety of nuances. Thus, it is necessary to enumerate the different types separately.

a. ⌢ = three syllabic beats

249 Ant
Stans a d. candí-di- or,

Ant
Euge serve fi- dé- lis,

Ant
Super muros Je-rú-sa- lem,

All three examples involve the same cadential formula.
– In the first instance, the three notes are distributed over the last three syllables : a virga or a tractulus (according to the rule which governs the choice of one or the other sign), oriscus at the unison, and then the final tractulus.
– In the second instance there are only two syllables for the three notes ; the virga and the oriscus are joined to form a virga strata.

— In the last instance, all three notes form a pressus major on one syllable. Hence the conclusion that this pressus is the equivalent of three syllabic beats.

When this form of the pressus major is found in isolation it is usually a cadential group :

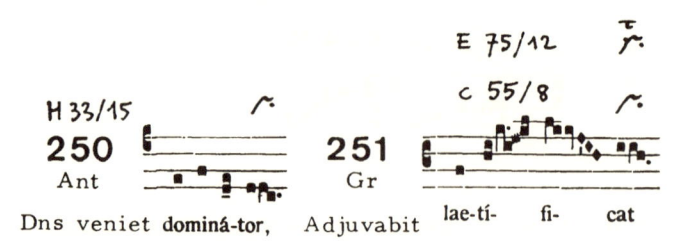

The copyist of E carefully adds an episema to the first note and a ⌐ over the other two notes. C on the other hand makes no addition, since the correct way of performing this neume was evident to him. It should be noted that the dot always remains the same, even when the last note is long. ⌐ is inexistent. On the contrary, ⌐ is the liquescent form of the pressus when it is followed by a complicated syllabic articulation.

We must also mention the so-called " displaced " cadences in which the last neume descends an extra degree lower than the customary melody in order to create a smooth connection with the first note of the following incise.

253
Resp
Surgens di- xit : * Pax Dómi- no, al- le-

In this type of cadence, the pressus major replaces the long clivis of the normal formula. There is, however, a rhythmic difference between the clivis and the pressus major. The clivis conducts the melody quite normally to the cadential note, whereas the pressus major emphasized this note with a double, repercussed sound and then, on its last note, descends one additional step. This gives an unfinished character to the cadence and prepares the next melodic section.

The isolated pressus major with three syllabic beats is also found outside of cadences.

254
Com
Posuerunt pu- ni- tó- rum.

E underlines only the first note but G's symbol indicates that the second and third notes are equally long.

This same form of the pressus major is also found in combination, most often at the beginning of a neume :

PRESSUS

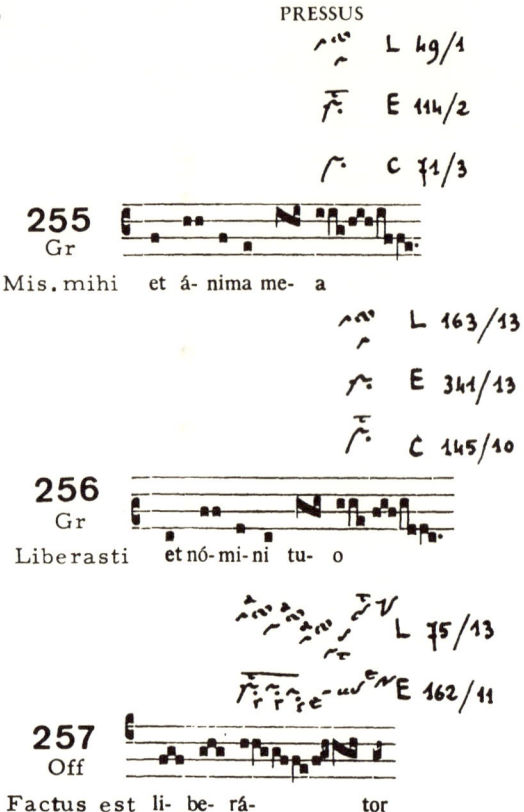

255
Gr
Mis. mihi et á- nima me- a

256
Gr
Liberasti et nó-mi-ni tu- o

257
Off
Factus est li- be- rá- tor

In the last example, an entirely long pressus major is followed by two pressus minor. E indicates the lengthening of the pressus major by the addition of an episema and a letter, but in L (in ex. 255 and 256) the neume alone is already quite clear : ⁓ = uncinus, ʘ = oriscus whose importance is emphasized by a separation from the following note (in place of ♍). And thus, with or without the addition of an a, ⁓ and ⁓ are equivalent.

b. ⁓ = the first note long and the others light

This form of the pressus major is only rarely found in isolation.

PRESSUS

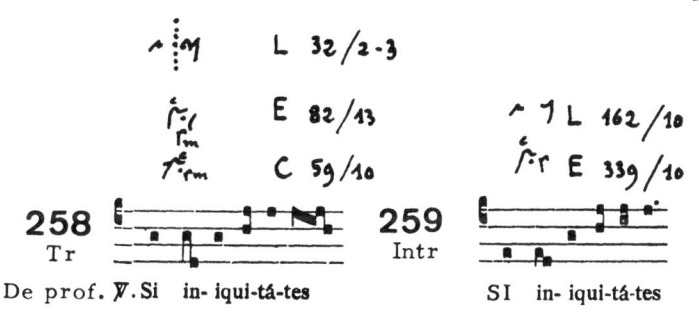

258 Tr — De prof. ℣. Si in-iqui-tá-tes
L 32/2-3
E 82/13
C 59/10

259 Intr — SI in-iqui-tá-tes
L 162/10
E 339/10

Because of the two successive *i* vowels, the two St. Gall MSS join the three notes of the two syllables into one single pressus. C puts an episema on the first element and places a c over the other two. E and B only add the c : G contents itself with the initial episema. L, which distinctly separates the signs for the two syllables, writes an uncinus on the first and, on the other, a light clivis whose first element, in ex. 258, is an oriscus. (In this example, the two symbols used by L are separated because of a change of lines.) L's notation indicates that the first two notes are in unison and this corresponds perfectly to the pressus of the St. Gall MSS.

This rhythmic form with emphasis on the first note is often found in combination :

L 9/5
E 3/5
C 7/8

260 Gr — Ex Sion ℣. Congre-gá- te

C's indications are clear. The elongated ⌒ in E does not contradict the particularities pointed out by the other MSS ; E simply seeks to underline the essential lightness of the whole neume.[34] As for L, it corresponds perfectly to C even though it does use different symbols. By grouping the first six notes into two porrectus, it indicates the importance of the third and sixth notes (a neumatic break at a melodic high point) and further emphasizes this by the addition of a τ. The first note of the second and third neumatic elements is an oriscus which indicates a unison with the last note of the preceding symbol.

In the above examples it must be noticed that L is more precise than St. Gall. The St. Gall copyists had to resort to additions (episemas, τ or c) in order to express the lengthening or the lightness of the elements of the pressus, – and these additions are always in danger of being forgotten. In L on the contrary, the neumatic design in itself accurately contains all the necessary indications.

c ⌢ = three light notes.

This form of the pressus major is also rarely isolated.

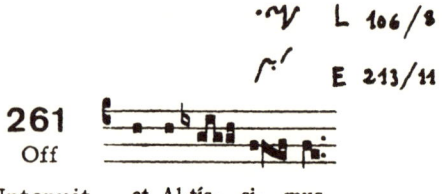

261
Off

Intonuit et Al-tís- si- mus

Here we have an example of the pressus major resupinus. The symbol in L denotes lightness: it consists of a dot followed by a light porrectus whose first element is an oriscus.

In composition, the pressus with three light notes appears frequently as, for example, in this formula for Tracts in Mode II.

262
Tr
Dne ex.

a me :   ad me   cor me- um :

The pressus major appears in an entirely light context. As in the preceding example, the symbol from L is especially precise and clear.

d. Pressus major with two light notes followed by a long note

This type of pressus major is found only in combination.

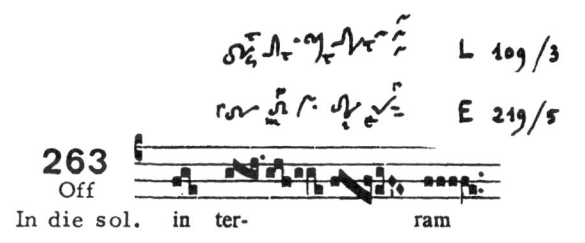

Here again L shows proof of keen precision, clearly writing two light notes and a third note with the addition of a τ.

II. PRESSUS MINOR

1. the sign and the melodic signification

The pressus minor ⌐ is composed of two elements, the oriscus and the punctum. It is never isolated, but is found only in combination with other neumatic elements. Its first note is always in unison with the preceding note :/·⌐ ⌐. When the oriscus comes after a clivis or a torculus, it is sometimes tied to these symbols :/⌐ /⌐. Because of the rapidity of the handwriting, /⌐ became /⌐ or /⌐ in a few of the latest MSS. However, this sign never denotes a clivis + pressus major ; only four notes are involved.

Although it is possible, from a graphic point of view, to consider separately the pressus minor, it is always dependent, melodically, upon the preceding note with which it is in unison.

2. *interpretation of the signs*

Like the pressus major, the pressus minor and its preceding note can receive various rhythmic nuances.

a. the preceding note and the pressus minor : three long notes.

There is a typical example of this in the intonation of the "O" Antiphons:

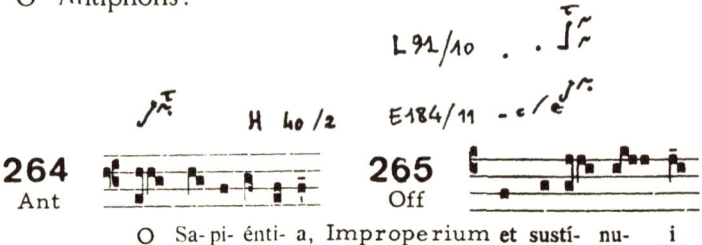

264 Ant — O Sa- pi- énti- a,

265 Off — Improperium et sustí- nu- i

After the first light note which launches the melody upwards, there are two broadened notes : the second note of the pes (a neumatic break at a melodic high point, reinforced by an episema) and the oriscus. Both these notes are on FA, the principal degree. The last note, the second of the pressus minor, is one half-step below. It too is broadened despite the fact that it is written as a dot. (The τ affects the two notes of the pressus minor.) L writes two superimposed uncinus − a long clivis − in place of the pressus minor used by St. Gall.

Let us return to an already cited example in order to complete it.

266 Off — Factus est li- be- rá- tor

PRESSUS   133

in e-   um

The syllable " liberá·tor " begins with three long neumatic elements : a pressus major and two pressus minor. E shows this lengthening by using a ⌐ crossed with a horizontal line which covers all three of the elements. The symbols in L, which are already clear in themselves, as we have already noticed in ex. 255, 256 and 257, carry three ª affecting the first six notes.

In the second part of the example, the syllable " in e·um " also begins with a long pressus major followed by an equally long pressus minor whose rhythmic value is specified by L alone, since E has omitted the addition of a⌐ here. These two pressus, like the three on " liberá·tor ", are inserted in a descending line like overlapping bricks, the final point of the first element being at the unison with the following note and so on. Consequently each time, there are three long notes in succession : the dot of the pressus major + the pressus minor, whose dot (in the case of " liberá·tor ") is in turn a long note in unison with the last pressus minor. As for the second pressus minor of " e·um " at the lowest point of the melisma, it alone is long, the two preceding notes being light. There is thus a unison here between a light note (the second of the clivis) and an broadened note (the first of the pressus minor). On the other hand, the third pressus minor follows a pes subbipunctis whose last two notes are lengthened. This pressus minor is equally long, as the neumatic symbols in L and the letter ⌐ in E indicate.

b. a long preceding note, a light pressus minor

This form of the pressus minor is found in a melodic formula common to almost all of the versicles of the Graduals of Mode II:

L 12/10
E 337/5
C 144/12

267
Gr
Dne ref. ter-   ra

C writes two light pressus minor which are both preceded by a long note at the same pitch (/- and ル). In the pressus major at the center of the formula only the first note is long. E separates the elements of this pressus major, writing an epismatic virga + a pressus minor.

L, writes both the first pressus minor and the pressus major of E and C as a porrectus starting with an oriscus. (It joins the low note, the last element of the two pressus, to the note which follows.) This confirms that the two notes of each pressus minor in the St. Gall MSS are light and each preceding note is long. Therefore, the horizontal episema which the rhythmic editions place over the last pressus minor is an error.

L 89/11
C 90/1

268
Gr
Tenuisti   Isra- el De-   us

The same phenomenon : two light pressus minor (the second in *C* contains a melodic indication) preceded at the unison by a long note (*C* adds the letter **x** as well as the episema to the distropha). Here again the episema of the rhythmic editions is erroneous, and this mistake reccurs in many other cases where a pressus minor follows a distropha.

c. a light note preceding, a long pressus minor

We have already pointed out one instance of this type in ex. 266 ; here is another example :

269
Gr

T Enu- ísti   * ma- num

A pressus minor which is joined to a light clivis.
This formula for Alleluias in Mode IV also belongs to this group:

270
All

V. Excita   AL-le- lú- ia.

L writes an **a** between the oriscus and the tractulus : *C* adds nothing here but sometimes writes more clearly, in the same way as *E*. See for example the Alleluia " Laudáte Dóminum " : (*C* 48 ; *E* 302).

d. the note preceding and the pressus minor : three light notes

The following example illustrates the exceptional use of a succession of three light pressus minor :

271
Gr
Mis . mihi Conturbá-ta

The addition of c twice in C and the unbroken sign in L are equivalent. The same light pressus is also found in the eighth-mode tract formula :

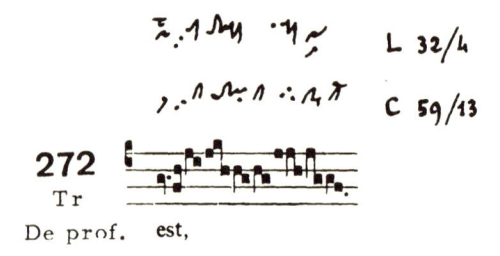

272
Tr
De prof. est,

e. the last note of the pressus minor is long

Here is a rhythmic peculiarity which cannot be deduced from the St. Gall notation alone. As we have already noted, the copyists of this school invariabily use the punctum to notate the last note of the pressus. (The only exception is the inclined tractulus.) L alone, in the first example, points out the lengthening of this last note by the addition of ⸱ ; C indicates the same thing with the × in ex. 274.

PRESSUS

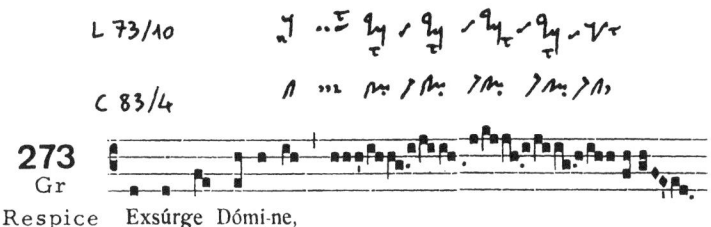

273 Gr

Respice Exsúrge Dómi-ne,

274 Gr

Diffusa et mansu- e-tú-di-nem

The melodic curve of the short musical motive pauses on the last lengthened note of the pressus minor before entering into a new progression with the following isolated virga.

III. DEVELOPED FORMS

On very rare occasions, notes are added to a pressus major in a downward progression.

275 All

Multifarie AL-le- lú- ia.

This Alleluia is a rather recent composition.

The pressus minor, on the other hand, is more often to be found in this form.

276 Ant

Tu es páupe- res

277 Ant

Sac. et P. pó-pu-lo :

278 Gr
Vidérunt ter- ra.

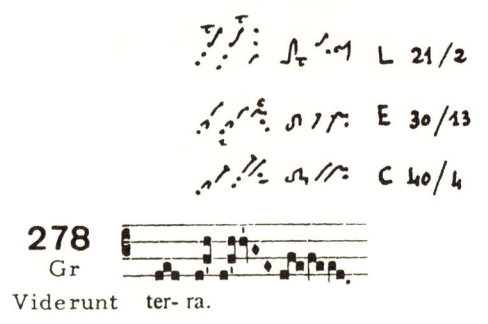

In this last example, the pressus minor, which only E notates, indicates to the singer that the first note of this symbol is in unison with the preceding note. The other St. Gall MSS and L write a climacus. E itself, on other occasions, indifferently uses the pressus minor or the climacus (when this formula appears in other graduals).

Sometimes the pressus is followed by a higher note (pressus major or minor resupinus) :

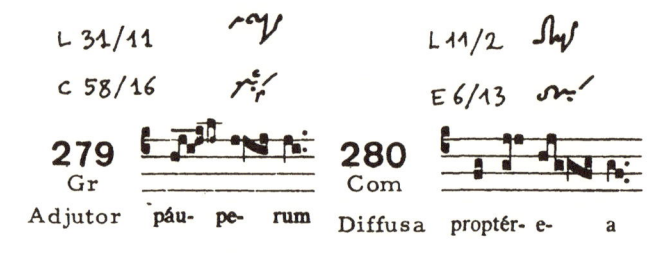

279 Gr
Adjutor páu- pe- rum

280 Com
Diffusa proptér- e- a

IV. REPERCUSSION OF THE NOTE AT THE UNISON

It is a commonly held opinion that the unison notes of the pressus form one sound of double length.[35] Let us cite a few of the numerous examples which refute this theory.

First argument :

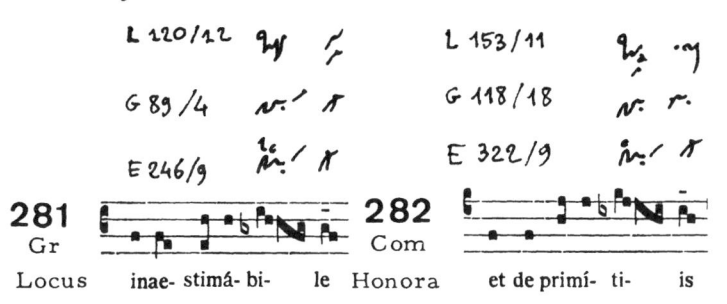

```
L 120/12                    L 153/11
G 89/4                      G 118/18
E 246/9                     E 322/9
```

281 Gr — Locus inae- stimá- bi- le   **282** Com — Honora et de primí- ti- is

Here is a well known cadential formula. In the Gradual " Locus iste " the notes are distributed over two syllables (inestimabí-le). On the word primiti-is in the Com. " Honóra ", on the other hand, the repetition of the same vowel sound in two adjacent syllables makes it possible to distribute the notes differently. E retains the same symbol in both instances, but G and L, in ex. 282, unite the antepenultimate note with the two following ones to form a pressus major. Either the rhythm of the formula is distorted in this way or there is repercussion of the two unison notes of the pressus. In this second case, the two signs are rhythmically identical.

Second argument :

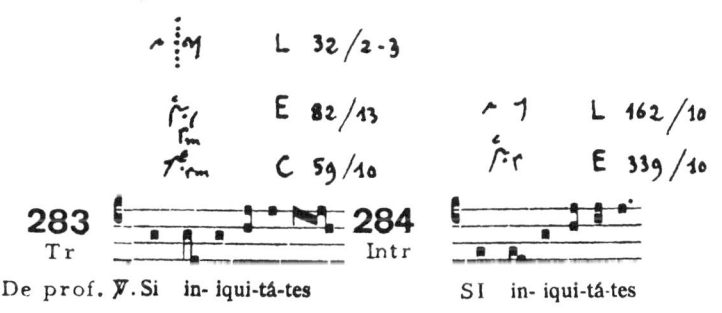

```
        L 32/2-3
        E 82/13              L 162/10
        C 59/10              E 339/10
```

283 Tr — De prof. ℣. Si in- iqui-tá-tes   **284** Intr — SI in- iqui-tá-tes

As we have already pointed out, L writes the two notes of the first two syllables separately (even placing them on two different lines in the first case). C and E, however, group the three notes into a single pressus major. Either there was a difference in the manner of singing the syllables (L repeating the vowel and C and E singing only one) or C and E also sang the two unison notes with a repercussion. This is the only explanation of the episema on the first note and the letter " c " on the second in C. With these additions there is correspondence to the notation of L. How is it possible to sing a single long tone with two beats of different value ?

It is to be kept in mind here that the various categories of pressus classified above are differentiated by rhythmic indications affecting the two unison notes. These indications generally call for a separate execution of the two notes. What point would there be in adding these indications in the MSS if no one was to respect them in actual practice ?

Third argument :

The formula is found twenty times in final cadences of Mode II responsories. In nineteen of these instances the vowels of the last two syllables differ. In one case, however, the word " meae " offers the possibility for an elision, and H writes.

The same thing occurs in the versicles of Mode III responsories. Seventy times the final cadence is writen But in the case, once again, of the word " me-ae " H writes.

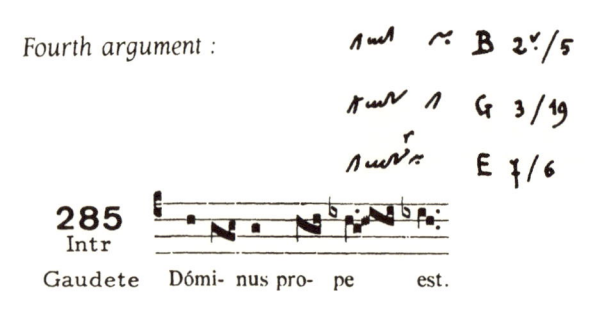

Fourth argument :

285
Intr
Gaudete Dómi- nus pro- pe est.

The Vatican Edition follows G's notation. B joins the last note of the quilismatic group to the following notes, thus forming a pressus major, and E, which places a single neume over the two syllables " pro-pe est ", because of the conjuncture of the two identical vowels, keeps the virga in the preceding group and adds a pressus minor. Must we conclude from this that, according to E, " propest " was sung and, according to B and G, " propre est ", with a different rhythm ? Here again, if we admit that the unison notes were repercussed, everyone necessarily sang in the same way.

Fifth argument :

We too, although we may not always notice it, often make repercussions in places where the MSS write a pressus. Even those who, because of their theories, defend the performance of the unison notes by a single sound of double duration, often practice the repercussion. Let us refer to the two examples already cited :

286
Gr

Tenuisti Isra- el De-   us

C 90/1

We have already established (cf. ex. 268) that the episemas added to the clivis in the rhythmic editions are mistakes. But according to common usage, the first note of each clivis, even without the episemas, would receive a repercussion intended to maintain the rhythm.

The same situation occurs in this formula from Graduals in Mode II.

287 Gr
Tollite e- jus?

Here again, the episema of the rhythmic editions does not correspond to the paleographic signs. Since we continue today to perform the repercussion between the distropha and the pressus minor, why shouldn't we do the same thing beforehand, between the climacus and the pressus minor, as well as on the pressus major?

Sixth argument :

There are many who see solid proof for the fusion of the pressus in the cō (conjungere : join) which sometimes is found on the pressus. The following case makes it possible to determine the real meaning of this indication :

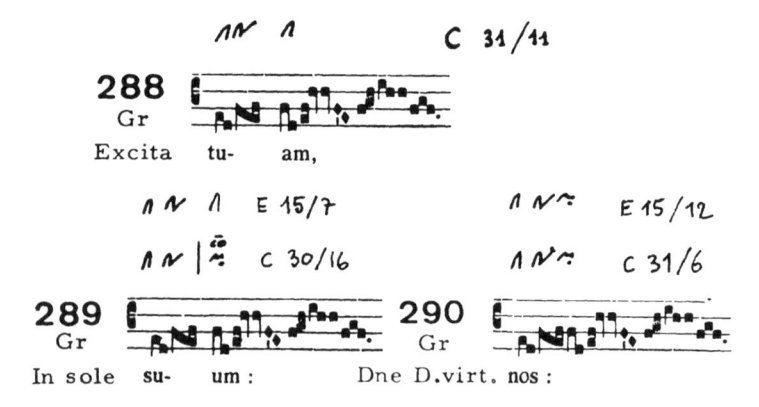

288 Gr
Excita tu- am,

289 Gr
In sole su- um :

290 Gr
Dne D.virt. nos :

This is a stereotyped formula for Graduals of Mode II. In the first instance the melody is distributed over two syllables, as always in this formula. On one occasion however there is no second syllable, and all the notes are grouped together on one syllable (ex. 290). According to the usually accepted theory, the two notes form only one sound which, obviously, alters the rhythmic structure of the formula. There is one other case (ex. 289) where, because of the crasis (*su-um*), C writes a pressus minor and adds c̄o there (the two syllables are separated by a change of lines). Although in the other instances this c̄o is invoked by some as solid proof of the fusion of the unison notes, these same persons prefer to neglect this indication here and sing two separate and distinct notes ; in this instance they make the repercussion.[36]

What, in conclusion, is the particular value of the pressus and its characteristic meaning ?

It would certainly be an exaggeration to attribute too much expressive importance to the pressus. To prove this it is sufficient to recall example 54 where one can see the equivalence between /ᴍ , /ᴍ/ and /ᴧ . On the other hand the pressus cannot be considered as a simple graphic variant of the clivis. It has a melodic specification (the unison between the oriscus and the preceding note), and also indicates a special relation between the last two notes (oriscus and punctum) – a fixed melodic direction. The oriscus always leads to a lower note. This relation between the oriscus and the following note will appear even more clearly as we study of the virga strata.[37]

14

VIRGA STRATA

The virga strata ⌒ is composed of two elements : virga + oriscus. It differs from the pressus major only by the absence of the dot. Nevertheless, just as in the pressus, the oriscus conserves here its characteristic function – always leading on to a lower note on the following syllable (or on the following neumatic element, in the rare cases when the virga strata appears in combination), and conserving a close connection with that note. The virga strata can thus be considered as a diaeresis of the pressus. However, while the first two notes of the pressus are always in unison, the virga strata can signify (I) two unison notes or (II) a group equivalent to a pes. In either of these instances, the oriscus, second note of the virga strata, is followed by a lower note.

I. THE VIRGA STRATA SIGNIFYING TWO UNISON NOTES

(Ex. 249) Ant   H 442/9
Stano ad candí-di- or,

Ant   - 384/1
Euge serve   fi- dé- lis,

Ant   - 420/5
Super muros   Je-rú-sa- lem,

The example which is in the center groups together into a virga strata on the accent of the paroxytone " fi-*de*-lis ", the two unison notes which appear in the proparoxytonic cadence " can-*di-di*-or ". Here, the virga strata evidently represents two symmabic beats. Many paroxytones receive this same melodic treatment, chiefly in the cadential formulas of first-mode Antiphons :

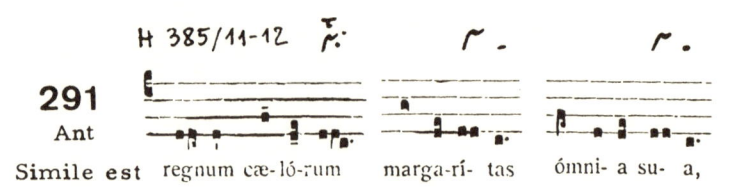

291
Ant

H 385/11-12

Simile est regnum cæ-ló-rum marga-rí- tas ómni- a su- a,

The phrase or the melodic incise ends on the virga strata and the tractulus which follows.

But the use of the virga strata is not limited to cadential formulas. The isolated virga strata at the unison is often a neume of melodic liaison :

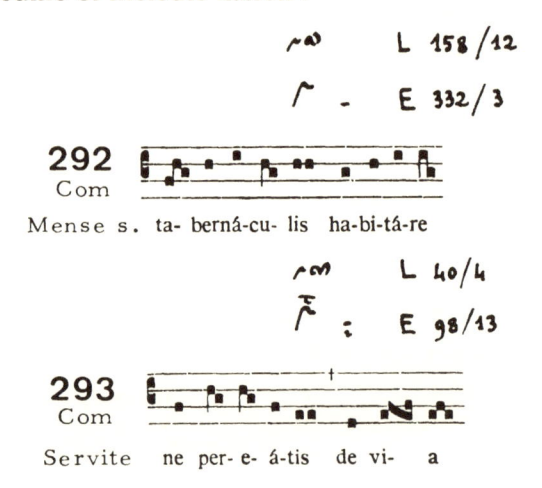

L 158/12
E 332/3

292
Com

Mense s. ta- berná-cu- lis ha-bi-tá-re

L 40/4
E 98/13

293
Com

Servite ne per- e- á-tis de vi- a

On the one hand, the melody has reached a verbal caesura on the notes DO and SOL and the virga strata concludes the short fragment with the two unison notes ; on the other hand, because of its close affinity to the lower note which follows, the virga strata binds together the two consecutive incises, and unifies the melodic-verbal phrase.

L writes uncinus + oriscus on a horizontal line, and thus gives the double indication of two syllabic beats and of notes in unison.

The same phenomenon is found in certain stereotyped formulas in which two unison notes, normally distributed over two syllables, are grouped on a single syllable and designated by a virga strata.

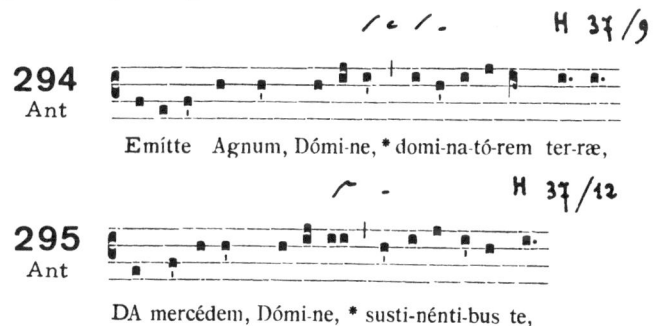

294
Ant

Emítte Agnum, Dómi-ne, * domi-na-tó-rem ter-ræ,

295
Ant

DA mercédem, Dómi-ne, * susti-nénti-bus te,

Even the two following examples justify the use of the virga strata, although at first sight, they appear to contradict what was said above.

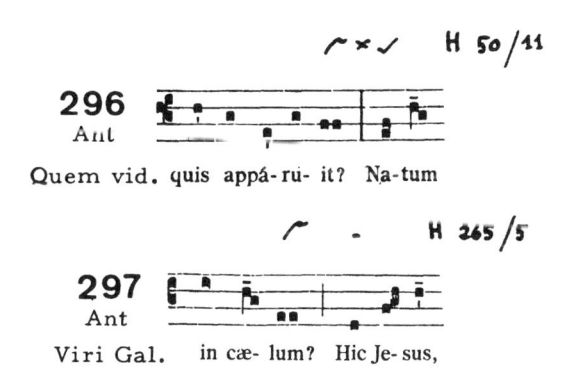

296
Ant

Quem vid. quis appá-ru- it? Na-tum

297
Ant

Viri Gal. in cæ- lum? Hic Je- sus,

Here, the virga strata is found at the end of an incise, and hence it is *not* immediately followed by a note to which it must be tied directly. This apparent contradiction is easily explained. From a purely musical standpoint, the virga strata here brings to a close an independent melodic fragment. But there is continuity in the text. Both instances involve questions which require answers. The virga strata makes the continuity between the two phrases of the text obvious, underlining it despite the apparent melodic independence of the incises.

The same thing appears again in the following example. In addition to the melodic bond that is indicated by the virga strata, we have here an obvious proof of the repercussion of two notes at the unison.

298
All
In die re- sur-re- cti- ó- nis me- ae, di- cit

The copyist notates the two identical vowel sounds in the word " me-ae " with a virga strata. (Here the Vatican Edition has been modified according to the MS.)

One final example proves once again the repercussion of the virga strata at the unison.

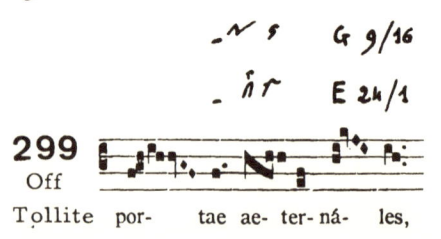

299
Off
Tollite por- tae ae- ter- ná- les,

We have here corrected the Vatican Edition, restoring the oriscus (a second DO) on " aeternáles ", which it omitted. Once again, there are two similar vowel sounds in succession. While E indicates the grouping which the Vatican Edition follows, separating the tractulus on

" por-tae " from the two following neumatic elements and placing the clivis and the virga strata over " ae-ternáles "), G reunites on " por-tae " the tractulus and the clivis to which it joins the first of the two notes at the unison, thus leaving only the second note, the oriscus, on " ae-ternáles ". Here again, either the rhythm differed between E and G or else the manner in which the two notes were grouped was of no importance because of the repercussion of the virga strata.

II. THE VIRGA STRATA SIGNIFYING A PES

The virga strata is often used in place of a pes. It is necessary, first of all, to distinguish between the case found most frequently and which presents itself as normal, the half-step pes, and a much rarer case, the whole-step pes. Regardless of the interval, however, the second note of the virga strata, the oriscus, is always followed by a lower note.

1. virga strata used as a half-step pes

a. isolated

This form of the virga strata is the equivalent of a light pes.

As we have already said, when the second half of a psalm verse was too long, it was divided by a pes on the accented syllable of the word which today would simply have its last note lengthened. The Versiculary SG 381 always uses the light pes ✓ . There is, however, one constant exception ; the virga strata is used in preference to the pes in versicles of Mode III. Since the pes indicates a whole-step in all of the other psalm-tones, it is obvious that the use here of a special neume – the virga strata – must indicate a different interval, the half-step. And, as a matter of fact, that time the recitation note for the versicles in Mode III was si and not do as it is today. This is also illustrated by the general movement of the melody.

300 Domine de-us salutis me-ae

in di-e clamavi et nocte coram te.   E 115/11

The virga strata is also found as a light, half-step pes at the beginning of the second incise of each versicle in second mode Tracts. The melody is modified each time by the number and the nature of the syllables which precede the first verbal accent:

301
Tr

Qui hab. ti-bi au- tem   pró-tegam e-

in pro-tecti- ó- ne   et sub pennis e-

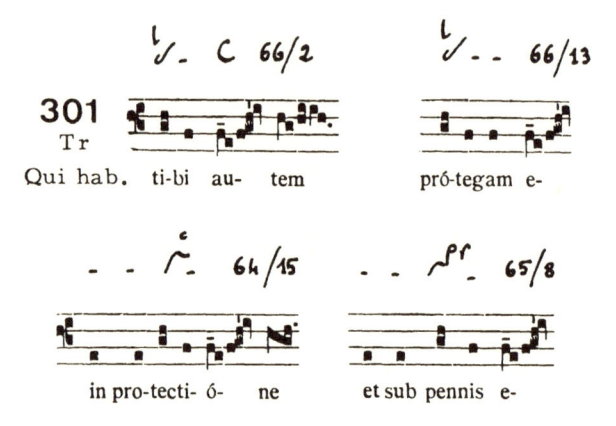

The last example carries a virga strata with an augmentative liquescence because of the complex articulation on " pennis ".

In the first two instances, and in all similar cases, the Vatican Edition made an error in putting the light pes on MI-FA. *Ben* proves that this pes represents a whole-step, RE-MI. MI-FA with a virga strata is only found when the group is preceded by one or two notes. Therefore, each time that the first syllable is accented, we ought to have:

ti-bi au- tem   pró-tegam e-

VIRGA STRATA

In the Tracts of Mode VIII, the virga strata is also found on the half-step, SI-DO.

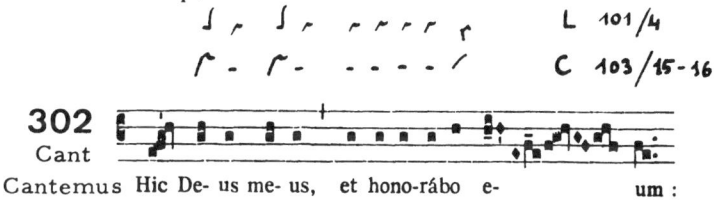

302
Cant
Cantemus Hic De- us me- us, et hono-rábo e-   um :

Here, *L* writes a light pes. Elsewhere, it employs the sign ·ω (= punctum + oriscus) which equals a light pes but which is at the same time more precise with regard to the subsequent melodic context :

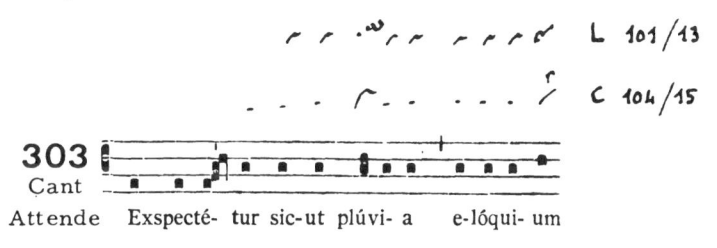

303
Cant
Attende Exspecté- tur sic-ut plúvi- a   e-lóqui- um

In ex. 302, we have corrected the Vatican Edition, putting the recitation back on SI. This is what the most authoritative manuscripts and the use of the virga strata, which would otherwise be unexplainable, clearly call for. The virga strata necessarily requires that the following note be lower and this is confirmed by the use of the tractulus on the syllable which follows.

Other examples of the virga strata :

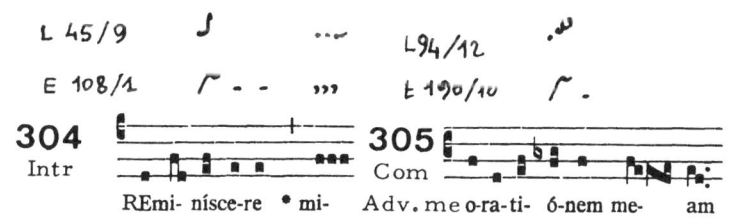

304
Intr
REmi- nísce-re • mi-

305
Com
Adv. me o-ra-ti- ó-nem me-   am

In ex. 304, we have once again corrected the Vatican Edition. In the first instance, L uses a light pes and in the second ·ω , and both signs indicate the lightness of the two notes.

b. in combination

The virga strata can also be found at the end of a neume, taking the place of a half-step pes when the melody descends afterwards. This situation gives to each of the two notes the value of one syllabic beat ; thus the virga strata is equivalent here to a long pes.

306
Gr
Oculi

in tém-po- re

307
Gr
E ripe   ex- altá- bis me :

308
Gr
Beata gens Verbo Dó-   mi- ni

In the first and the third examples, C put an episema over the virga strata ; L writes a long pes whose value is emphasized even more by an a in ex. 306. The copyist of E gives no special indication concerning the rhythmic value of the virga strata, and the letter c which he adds in the first example even proves that he considered this neumatic element as a light pes of a half-step.

VIRGA STRATA 153

In the second example, G separates the oriscus from the virga, which it ties to the torculus in order to form a torculus resupinus. But the expressive break which follows the virga, and the added fact that this same virga carries an episema, throughly prove that both the notes are long. As for the m (mediocriter) added to the virga strata by C, it probably suggests that this group should not be excessively lengthened.

The variety of the neumatic writing in these examples shows that delicate nuances are involved. In ex. 306 and 308 the melodic movement resembles that of a cadence, but the cadence is still some distance away.

2. *Virga strata used as a whole-step pes*

a. in isolation

The virga strata can also replace a whole-step pes. The examples are much less frequent, less systematic and less logical. It is undoubtedly nothing more than the extension of the original usage.

309
Intr
Oculi   et mi-se-ré- re me-   i,

E writes a light pes. The virga strata which G prefers indicates both lightness and the return to the low note which follows.

b. in combination

We should also mention the formulas " Veni ", " ecce ", etc. which look like scandicus with four ascending notes followed by a drop onto a lower note, and which, in some MSS, were actually notated in this way :

VIRGA STRATA

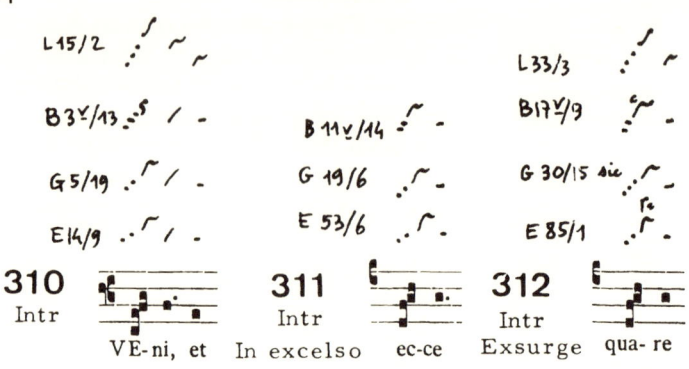

310 Intr — VE-ni, et

311 Intr — In excelso ec-ce

312 Intr — Exsurge qua-re

The neume is light. Puncta precede the virga strata in E and G. In B it is difficult to tell whether there are dots or small tractulus, a problem which occurs throughout this MS. In any case, the addition of a c in the third example explicitely shows the lightness of the virga strata.

L writes twice a light scandicus. In the first example, B notates three dots + an oriscus; but, given the tendency of the St. Gall copyists to tie all light notes capable of being tied, the form ⌐ is more normal.

Very rare indeed are the other instances in which the virga strata is used as a whole-step pes.

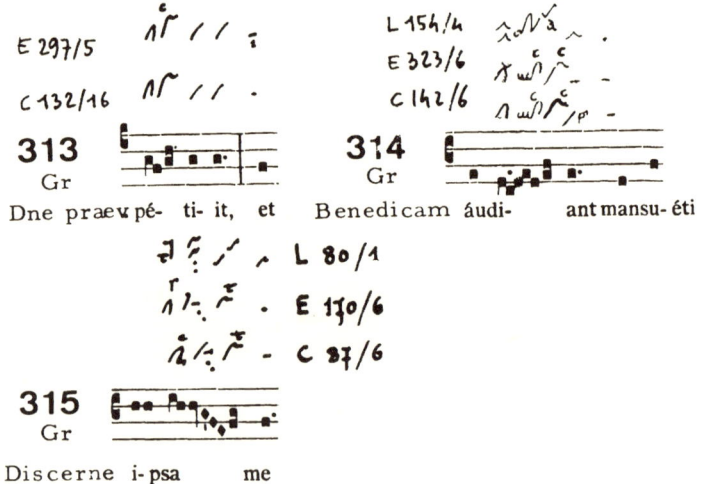

313 Gr — Dne praev pé- ti- it, et

314 Gr — Benedicam áudi- ant mansu- éti

315 Gr — Discerne i-psa me

15

ORISCUS

The detached oriscus (isolated or in apposition) is drawn by a vertical wavy line ς. Its melodic use however remains the same as in the pressus and the virga strata.

I. ISOLATED ORISCUS

The isolated oriscus is found in two particular instances.

1. A diaeresis of the pressus major

We have already seen that the notes grouped into a pressus major can, depending on the number of syllables involved, be distributed over two or even three syllables. The oriscus is then isolated, but its melodic situation and its role are the same as in the pressus: situated on the same pitch as the preceding note, it leads to a lower note on the following syllable.

Ant — Stans a d. candí-di- or,   H 442/9

Ant — Euge serve fi- dé- lis,   384/1

Ant — Super muros Je-rú-sa- lem,   420/5

It is, at present, the first of these three instances which particularly interests us : it represents the complete diaeresis of the third case.

There are numerous examples of this in the Antiphonary :

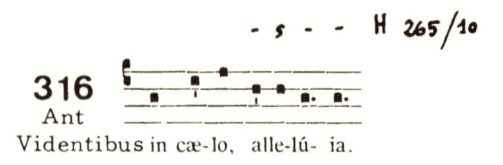

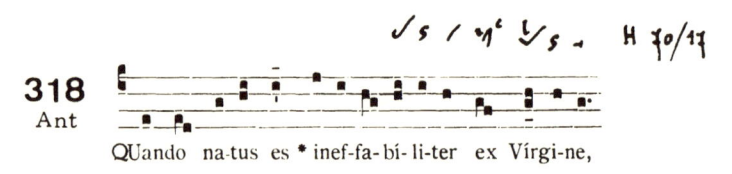

316 Ant
Videntibus in cæ-lo, alle-lú- ia.

317 Ant
Sancti tui sic-ut lí-li- um, al- le-lú- ia :

318 Ant
QUando na-tus es * inef-fa- bi- li-ter ex Vírgi-ne,

2. *Succession of two identical vowels*

Since the signs ⁄ and ⌇ represent the diaeresis of the virga strata (which, at the unison, is repercussed), it is quite normal to find them when an identical vowel is represented in succession :

319 Tr
De nec. qui te exspé- ctant,

320 Tr
Jubilate i- pse est De-

The tractulus which follows the oriscus in ex. 320 confirms that the melody has to descend after the oriscus.[38] And so, the Vatican Edition's reconstruction of this melody is faulty; it ought to read :

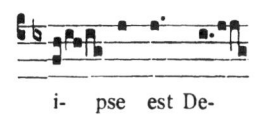

i- pse est De-

II. THE ORISCUS IN APPOSITION

Here the oriscus brings back to mind the melodic situation and the role which it has in the virga strata. In the virga strata, the oriscus was either in unison with the preceding note or higher – when it took the place of a pes. Similarly, the oriscus of apposition can be in unison with or higher than the last note of the preceding neumatic element.

1. oriscus in unison with the preceding note

When used in this way the oriscus in apposition can be found either at the end or in the center of a neume.

a. oriscus in apposition at the end of a neume

This oriscus is often found at the end of a stereotyped formula in the Antiphons of Mode I :

321 Ant Exiit inter fratres quod discípulus

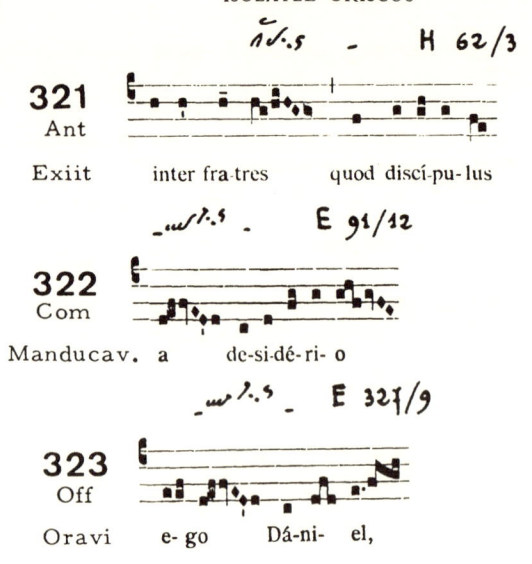

322 Com Manducav. a desidério

323 Off Oravi ego Dániel,

The following instance proves the repercussion of the oriscus at the unison :

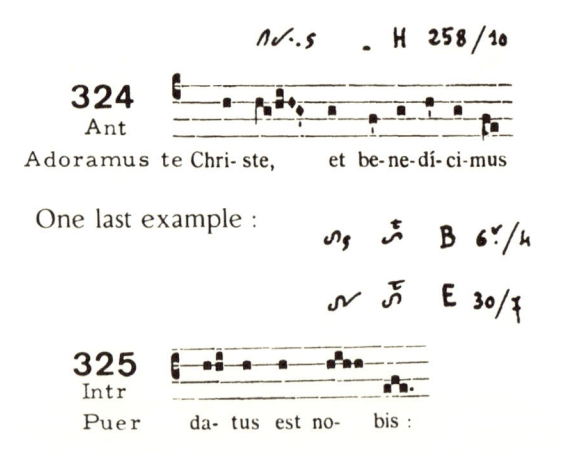

324 Ant Adoramus te Christe, et benedícimus

One last example :

325 Intr Puer datus est nobis :

The melody descends on " no-*bis* " ; *B* shows this by the use of an oriscus ; *E*, who could have done the same thing, writes a torculus resupinus.

ISOLATED ORISCUS

When the melody does not descend, the oriscus is never used. One finds instead ⟋ or ♩ :

326
Com
Jerus. quae ascendé- runt   Dómi- ne.

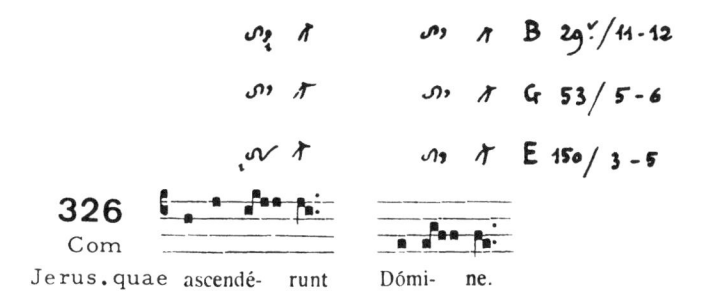

b. The oriscus in apposition between two neumatic elements.

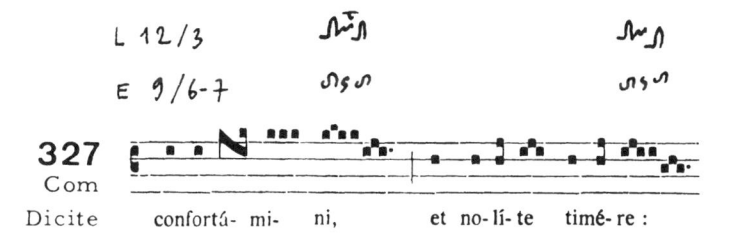

327
Com
Dicite confortá- mi- ni,   et no-lí-te timé-re :

The oriscus appears between two torculus. All of the symbols are elements of the same neume. Once again, the oriscus is in unison with the last note of the first torculus and above the first note of the second. Because it is more important than the preceding notes, this second unison note is emphasized by the expressive break which follows it. The ʈ found in L confirms, in the first instance, the importance of this break. The lower position of the second torculus and the link which exists between the two torculus, suggest to the copyist, but do not impose, the use of an oriscus.

In the following example we can see the freedom with which copyists either used or did not use this possibility :

ISOLATED ORISCUS

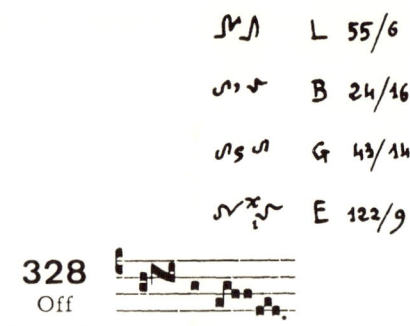

    L 55/6

    B 24/16

    G 43/14

    E 122/9

328 Off

Mis . mihi Dó- mi-ne

This formula is analoguous to the one in ex. 327. G notates it in the normal way – with an oriscus. B uses a stropha. This is not incorrect, but it is melodically less precise as to the position of the following note. Exceptionally, E writes ⁓, but uses an ✗ to confirm the value of the last note which is already emphasized by the neumatic break, and he then indicates the melodic descent by adding an ⌄ in front of the first note of the second torculus. L uses the same notation as E and not a torculus with an oriscus, ⌢, as it does elsewhere.

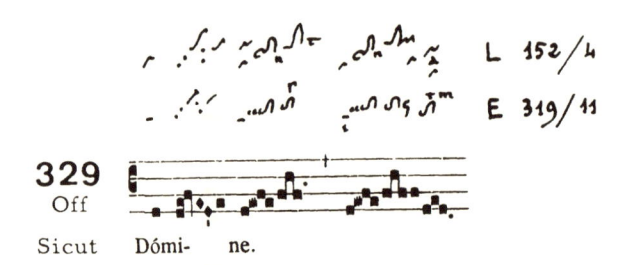

    L 152/4

    E 319/11

329 Off

Sicut Dómi- ne.

This interesting formula underlines well the importance of the unison oriscus as a note which concludes a neumatic element and links this same element to the following one. The first melodic curve on " Dómi-ne " ends on LA. The melody then repeats the same notes, and before passing from LA to the final cadence on FA, it underlines the former by a break after the oriscus.

ISOLATED ORISCUS

According to present day theories, the two motives should be sung in an identical fashion; on ♪ the last note is held for two beats and on ♪ the two notes form one sound of double value. But how, in this case, can one explain the different notation indicated in the MSS?

2. *oriscus higher than the preceding note*

Because it corresponds to the diaeresis of the virga strata – which sometimes represents a pes – the oriscus can be found above the note which precedes it. Just as in the case of the virga strata (cf. ex. 302), the majority of those instances where there should in fact be a half-step need to be corrected in the Vatican Edition. See, for example, the previously cited intonation from the versicles of the Tracts or Canticles of Mode VIII where the Vatican Edition notates the recitation on DO:

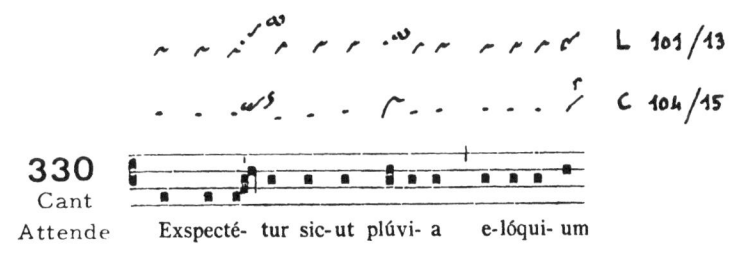

330 Cant
Attende Exspecté- tur sic-ut plúvi- a e-lóqui- um

L 101/13
C 104/15

Other examples of the oriscus above the preceding note:

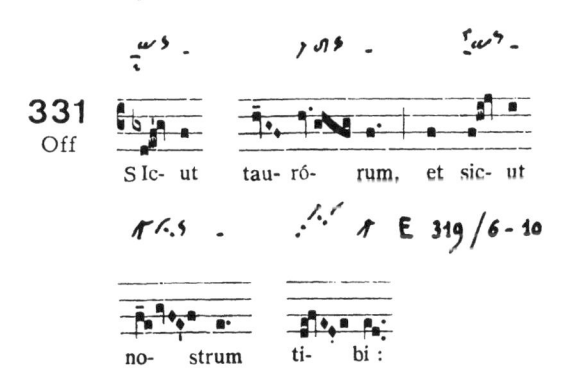

331 Off
SIc- ut tau- ró- rum, et sic- ut

E 319/6-10

no- strum ti- bi:

On the other hand, the oriscus is never used if the following note is on the same degree. This was already visible in the last formula of the example above ; here is another instance where, on the same line, the copyist has been careful to differentiate his signs :

332
Intr
Salus ad me, e- os :

16

SALICUS

The salicus is a neume with at least three ascending notes in which the next-to-last is an oriscus.

I. SYMBOLS AND MELODIC SIGNIFICATION

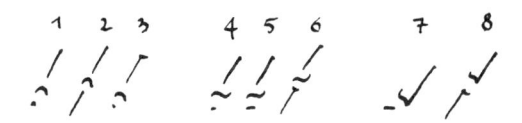

The second group (4-6) retains the original form of the oriscus (a double curve) while those in the first group are graphically shortened (a simple curve). Symbols 7 and 8 are formed with either a tractulus or a virga + a pes quassus, *i.e.* an oriscus tied to the following virga.

The use of the initial virga in symbols 2, 6 and 8 was motivated by melodic considerations. The melodic functions of the salicus are rather diverse. Even though it can be formed with one or two conjunct intervals, it can also be found in a succession of disjunct degrees encompassing the interval of a fifth. In addition, there are numerous instances of the unison salicus − with the first two notes on the same degree ; in this case, the last note never rises more than a second (half-step or whole-step).

II. INTERPRETATION OF THE SIGNS

In current pratice, the next-to-last note of the salicus, the one corresponding to the oriscus, is generally lengthened. Because of the special sign used for this note, it has been considered as the principal note of the group. It is, consequently, the one which stands out in the rhythmic editions, thanks to the vertical episema placed under it .

Paleographic facts, however, demonstrate that the oriscus is not the principal note of the salicus (or of the pes quassus). Semiological study of the various forms of the salicus and a comparison of parallel symbols in the principal MSS show that the principal importance belongs to the note which immediately follows the oriscus. As for the oriscus, it is a sign which indicates a kind of melodic tension towards the following note. This affirmation rests upon the following arguments :

1. proof of the importance of the note which follows the oriscus

The first argument is based on the the St. Gall symbols themselves, which clearly show the primacy of the note which follows the oriscus. Musical analysis also confirms this fact.

The second argument presents certain St. Gall signs of the isolated salicus in which the melodic tension towards the summit is evident.

The two other arguments are based on the notation of L as well as on variations in the symbols from St. Gall MSS.

a. salicus at the beginning of a neume

The stereotyped melody from the Graduals of Mode II furnishes the first example :

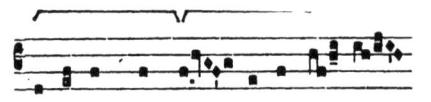

SALICUS

This melodic fragment, which is found both at the end of the Gradual and the versicle consists of a formula which normally begins with LA on the penultimate verbal accent. The incise itself begins on FA and on the second syllable the melody already reaches the LA, either by a light pes or a salicus (cf. " us*que* ad " in ex. 334 and " ut *sal*vos " in ex. 335). When the text is long, the melody, which has attained LA, remains there for the recitation of the syllables preceding the penultimate accent. The concluding formula is then introduced by a solid stress on the LA, and this note is lengthened in the rhythmic editions by the addition of a dot.

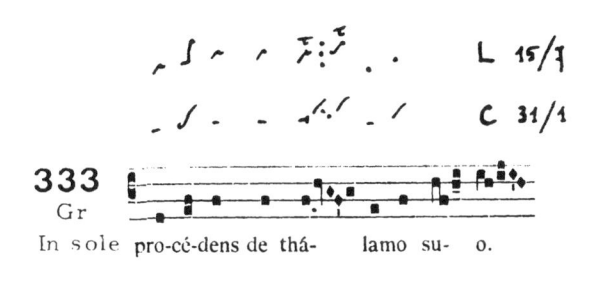

333 Gr
In sole pro-cé-dens de thá- lamo su- o.
L 15/3
C 31/1

334 Gr
A summo usque ad sum- mum e- jus.
L 15/4
C 30/10

335 Gr
Excita ut salvos fá- ci- as nos.
L 15/12-13
C 31/13

336
Gr

Dne D. virt. et sal- vi é- ri- mus.

337
Gr

Tecum gé- nu- i te.

In these five examples, the texts become progressively shorter. In the last example the notes, which were originally spread out over five syllables, are grouped on one single syllable which carris both the initial, preparatory movement from FA to LA and the introduction of the final formula with its stress on that same LA. In the first three examples there is no doubt that the LA (which receives a dot each time in the rhythmic editions), is the key note. The preceding syllables lead up to it, and it then becomes the point of departure for the cadential formula. How then can it be explained that, in the two last examples where the notes are grouped together into one single neume, this same LA has lost all of its importance in favor of one of the preparatory notes ? Here, not only has the LA lost its dot. In addition, it is the second note of the salicus, the SOL, which now appears to be the principal note and the melodic curve of the final cadence seems to start from there, before reaching the LA, which has become a simple passing tone.

What do the MSS indicate ? In the last two examples, C puts an episema on the third note of the salicus, the LA. In the same examples, L, which does not make use of the oriscus, replaces it with a simple dot and writes the third ascending note as a long virga whose importance is confirmed with a τ in ex. 337.

Thus, both MSS underline the LA and not the SOL. The rhythmic signs of the current editions, which generally serve today as the basis for interpretation, are in complete opposition to the melodic movement and to the MSS themselves. On the other hand, the musical analysis and the precise paleographic indications are in perfect accord with one another.

Other examples also prove the predominance of the note which follows the oriscus:

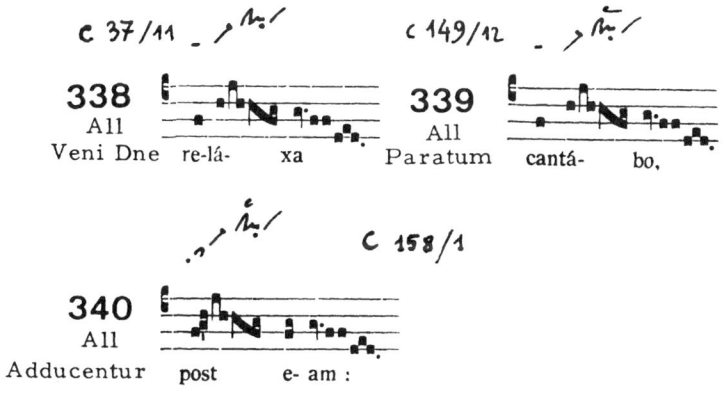

338
All
Veni Dne re-lá- xa

339
All
Paratum cantá- bo.

340
All
Adducentur post e- am:

In the first two instances, the MSS have only a tractulus on the first syllable. The Vatican Edition has a pes, and this has been corrected here.

In ex 338 and 339, the melody starts on FA and leaps immediately to LA, which is underlined by an expressive initial neumatic break as the key note and source of the neume which follows. In the last example, the melodic passage from FA-LA occurs on one single syllable by means of a salicus. The vertical episema, which the rhythmic editions place under the SOL in this instance, underlines a note which does not even exist in the first two examples. But C's notation, which places an episema over the LA here just as in the other instances, confirms that this note has lost nothing of its value as key-note.

341
All
Eripe

et ab insurgén-   ti- bus

SOL is the melodic-verbal accent towards which the melody progresses in the first incise, and it is evident that this note conserves the same importance at the return of the motive.

A melodic formula borrowed from the Alleluias of Mode II :

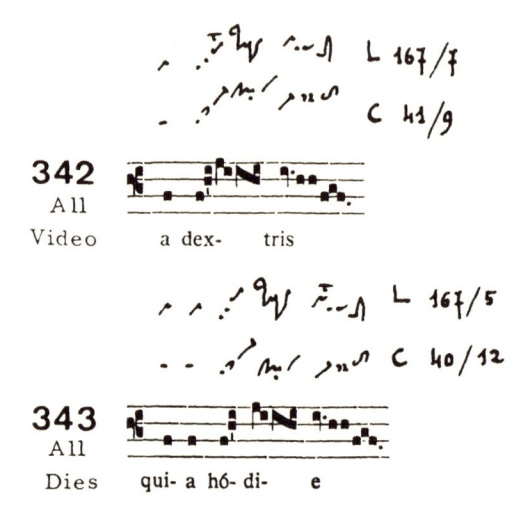

342
All
Video   a dex-   tris

343
All
Dies   qui- a hó- di-   e

A short, rising melody leads from RE to SOL, the principal note of the incise. The SOL is at first lightly ornamented by the clivis and the pressus minor resupinus. Then, at the beginning of the descending melodic curve, it is emphasized by an epismatic virga. There is no comparison between the evident value of this SOL, on a stable degree, and the passing note, FA, which is the oriscus of the salicus. C writes a salicus, but, as always in this formula, it places an episema on the third note. L omits the oriscus and lightly passes from RE to SOL which is written as a virga plus a ␛. It is no wonder then, that, in ex. 343 where the same formula is spread over two syllables, C again puts the episema on the SOL, the third note of the isolated salicus.

b. Isolated salicus with an episema on the virga

The isolated salicus is normally written without an episema on the virga but, in spite of this, there are some instances in which E (and more rarely C) underlines this last note with an episema, for example :

— on the final syllable of a word :

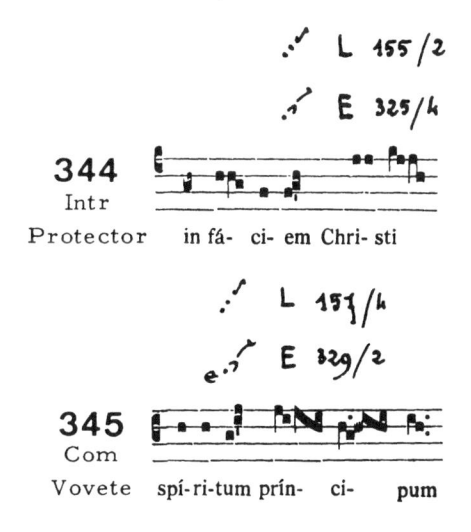

L 155/2
E 325/4

344
Intr
Protector   in fá- ci- em Chri- sti

L 157/4
E 329/2

345
Com
Vovete   spí-ri-tum prín-   ci-   pum

— on a monosyllable :

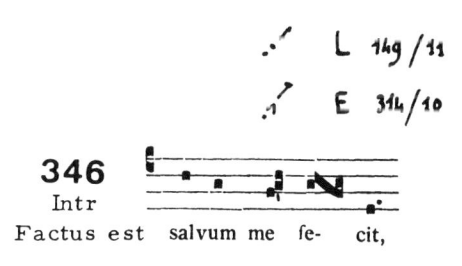

L 149/11
E 314/10

346
Intr
Factus est   salvum me   fe-   cit,

347
All
Posuisti de lá- pi-de   E 366/11

— inside a word :

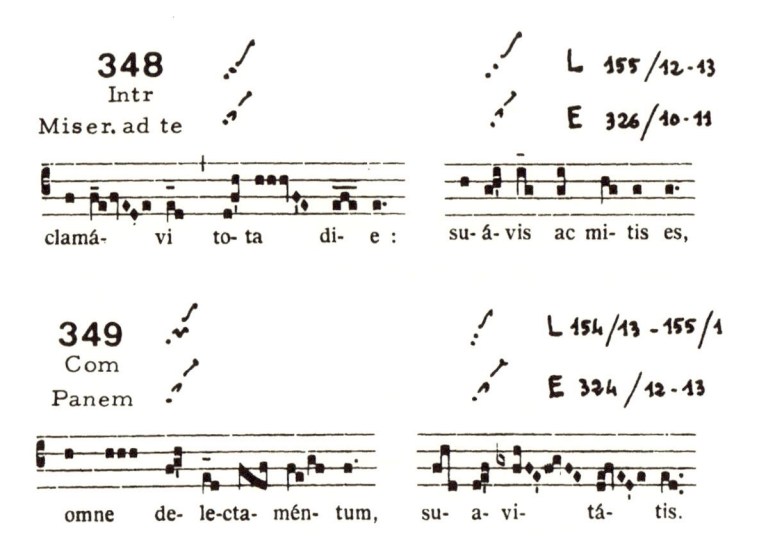

348
Intr
Miser. ad te
clamá- vi to- ta di- e :

L 155/12-13
E 326/10-11
su- á- vis ac mi- tis es,

349
Com
Panem
omne de- le-cta- mén- tum,

L 154/13 - 155/1
E 324/12-13
su- a- vi- tá- tis.

c. *L*'s notation

L has its own special symbol for the salicus, , but in about half of the instances in which the St. Gall copyists used a salicus, *L* writes only a light scandicus . The two first notes have an identical dot, and nothing indicates a predominance of the second note. This can be seen in a majority of the instances already cited. Moreover, when *L* writes a salicus it often adds a c to the oriscus.

350 Off — LAeténtur

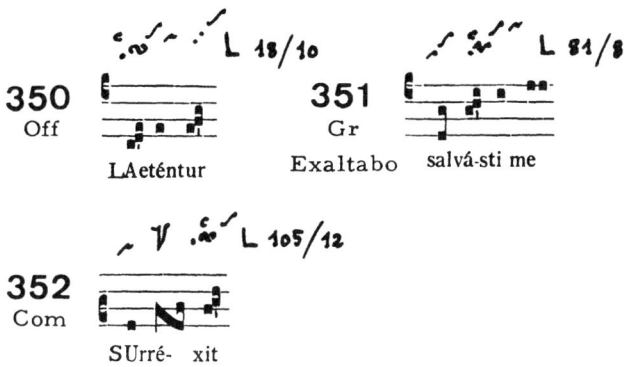

351 Gr — Exaltabo salvá-sti me

352 Com — SUrré- xit

We will see later on that L even more frequently adds a c to the oriscus of the unison salicus.

d. Variations in the notation of the St. Gall MSS

L is not the only MS that sometimes writes a simple scandicus with a long terminal virga in the place of a salicus. The copyists of St. Gall themselves do it too, although rarely, as the two following examples show :

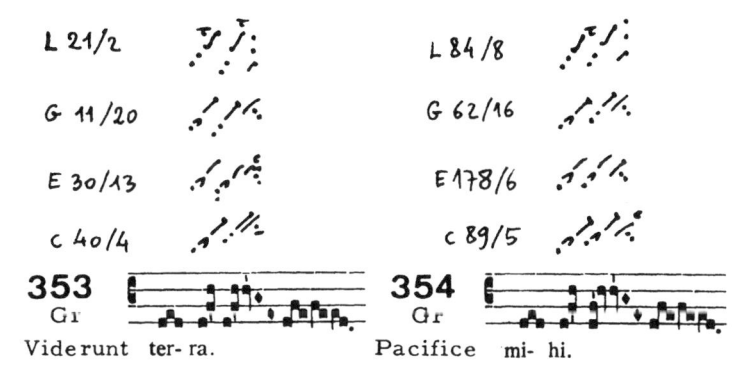

353 Gr — Viderunt ter- ra.

354 Gr — Pacifice mi- hi.

In ex. 353, C and G omit the oriscus of the second salicus ; in ex. 354, G alone omits it.

On the contrary, copyists occasionally put a salicus in places where there usually is a scandicus.

SALICUS

355 All VIII — AL-le- lú- ia.

C	E	L
26/3	1/1	166/2
111/9	223/4	111/4

Of the four St. Gall signs, E writes the salicus once. L, however, writes the oriscus both times. (The sign ℘ is the liquescent form of the virga.)

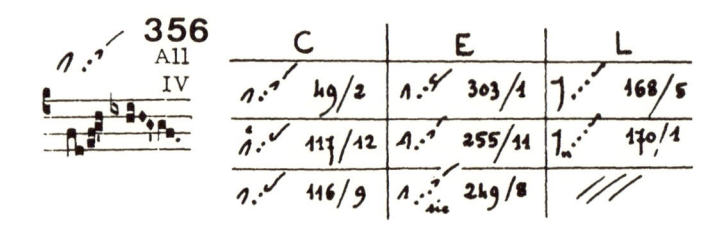

356 All IV

C	E	L
49/2	303/1	168/5
117/12	255/11	170/1
116/9	249/8	///

In this example L use the four-note scandicus twice; the third example is missing in this MS. C uses a salicus once and a scandicus twice. E uses the oriscus in all three of the examples; in the first case, this oriscus is tied to the virga, thus forming a pes quassus.)

These examples, chosen from the stereotyped melodic formulas for the alleluias from Modes VIII and IV, give some idea of the interchange that is sometimes found between the two symbols. If the difference between the salicus and the scandicus had been as great in former times as it has become today in current practice, the notators would not have been able to use the two signs so indiscriminately.

The following neume with a pes quassus in the center is found in a cadential formula from the Graduals of Mode III. As we will show in Chapter 17, this sign sometimes replaces the last two notes of the salicus when it is in combination.

357 Gr
III modo

Grad.	C	E	G
Tu es..tuam	✓ 61/8	///	✓ 32/2
Exs. n. pr..tuo	✓ 75/11	✓ 132/2	✓ 47/3
Exaltabo..me	✓ 87/15	✓ 172/11	///

C writes a light pes each time. Here, in combination, the choice of this sign underlines the second note which is followed by an expressive break at the ascending midpoint. The episema in the second case confirms this. E uses the pes quassus in order to express better the melodic tension towards the higher note. G uses both forms of the pes. (The episema in the rhythmic editions emphasizes a note of lesser importance and at the same time neglects LA, the only note which should in fact be underlined.)

Conclusion : the examples on the preceding pages clearly prove that the oriscus is far from being the most important note of the salicus. It conducts the melody onto the following note and indicates to the singer, by means of its special shape, the particular predominance of this note. The evidence in L makes this undeniable.

2. *salicus at the unison*

In this form of the salicus, the two first note are in unison. The interpretation remains the same ; the first two notes are light, there is a repercussion on the second and they both tend towards the third.

This neume is often found in the intonation of pieces in the deuterus (Mode II) :

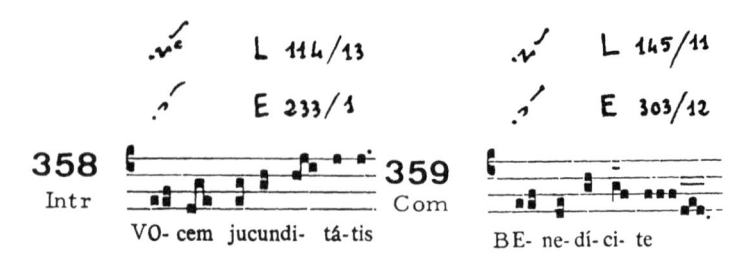

358 Intr — VO- cem jucundi- tá- tis — L 114/13, E 233/1

359 Com — BE- ne- di- ci- te — L 145/11, E 303/12

The correct execution of this salicus brings out the impulse of the two MI towards the principal note, FA, and gives a lively start to the piece. On the contrary, the current practice, which fuses these two MI into a single, static, two-beat note without any tension towards the FA, completely impedes the initial elan of the piece. L often adds a c to the oriscus of the unison salicus.

360 Off — Oravi De- um me- um e- go — tu- i : — L 156/7, E 327/9-11

361 Gr — Ego au- tem, — L 93/13, C 93/15, L 113/5, E 228/8

362 Com — E go sum * pa-stor bo- nus,

SALICUS

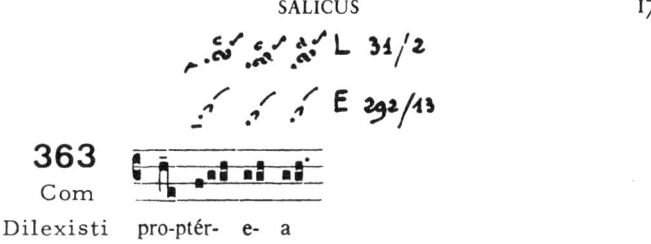

363
Com

Dilexisti pro-ptér- e- a

In ex. 363, L adds an ª to the last of the three oriscus in order to obtain a relaxation in the phrasing by enlarging the last two notes of this final salicus.

Furthermore, if this unison salicus did not tend towards the upper note, what difference would there be between the two following initial formulas?

364
Gr
CHri-stus * factus est

365
Intr
EX- áudi, * Dó- mi-ne,

The first example stresses the initial FA which is followed by a light ornamental pes starting with a repercussion on the same pitch. In this intonation formula, and in all similar ones, the melody is centered on FA. The other example begins with two light repercussed notes on MI, the weak semi-tone step, and these notes tend towards the FA. (In our example, as it is cited above, there has been, exceptionally, a transposition of the clef and so the half-step is written on LA and SI ♭.) The melody then descends to RE (that is, to SOL in our transposed example), and this serves as the point of departure for a new rise of the melody.

As a contrast to these intonation formulas, we ought to consider the formulas which are referred to as " inverted " cadences. Instead of coming down to rest on the cadential tone by means of a long clivis, the melody rises up one step. This gives a suspended character to the cadence and creates a close tie with the following melodic fragment.

366
Com

Acceptabis ju- sti- ti- ae, tu- um, Dómi- ne.

367
Resp

Ecce cor- de: et vi-ri iusti iu- stus, et ne- mo

The following examples are analogous to the inverted cadence:

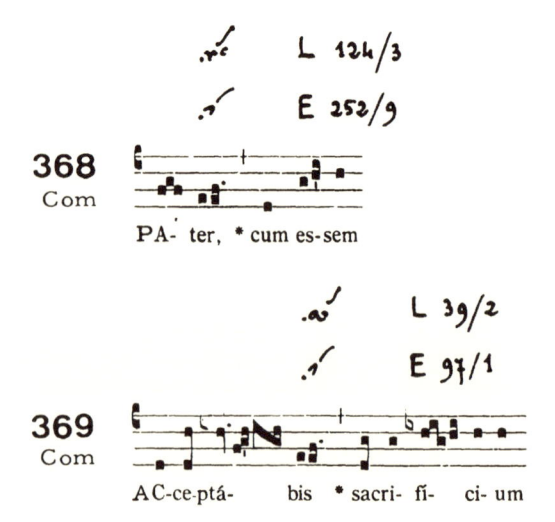

368
Com

PA- ter, *cum es-sem

369
Com

AC-ce-ptá- bis *sacri- fí- ci- um

SALICUS

3. special forms

In addition to the common light form of the salicus ⸝⸍ , other ways of writing the neume are occasionally found. We somewhat hesitate to simply call them " long forms " in the fear that this designation might give the impression that the special relation between the three ascending notes has been modified. Even though these symbols do underline the two initial notes, the third still remains the principle note of the group.

Nevertheless, it is difficult to explain why the copyists adopted one or the other of these forms. A special study has yet to be done on the subject.

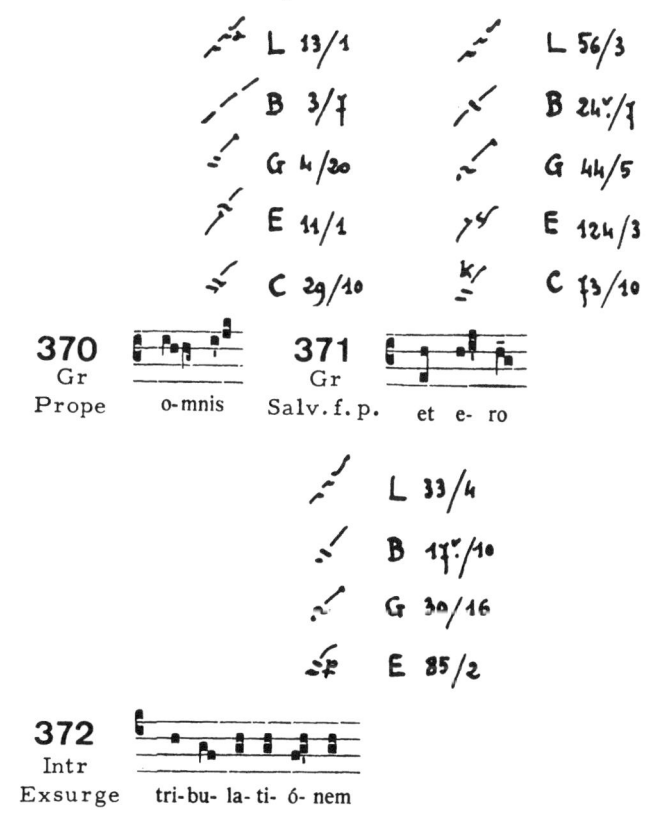

⸝⸍	L 13/1	⸍	L 56/3
⸍	B 3/7	⸍	B 24"/7
⸍	G 4/20	⸍	G 44/5
⸍	E 11/1	⸍	E 124/3
⸍	C 29/10	ᵏ⸍	C 13/10

370 Gr — Prope o-mnis

371 Gr — Salv. f. p. et e- ro

⸍	L 33/4
⸍	B 17"/10
⸍	G 30/16
⸍	E 85/2

372 Intr — Exsurge tri- bu- la- ti- ó- nem

In the first example nearly all the MSS write a long scandicus. E, which uses the oriscus to show the particular importance of the upper note, is the only exception. L adds an **a** between the two last notes and G countersigns the last note with an episema.

In the second example, only C and L notate a long scandicus. The others prefer a modified form of the salicus which expresses the fullness of the three notes. E alone gives additional importance to the first note by the use of an epismatic virga. It then ties the oriscus to the upper note, thus forming a pes quassus. G, on the other hand, modifies only the oriscus element of the ordinary sign : it has ᴧ́ in place of ᴧ́ , and this may signify an enlargement of the second note, a light crescendo from the first note to the third note of the group. The k (= klangor ?) added to the virga by C, probably underlines the importance of this note.

In the third example, whose melodic position is rather different, none of the MSS begin the salicus with a virga since the first note of this neume is lower than the preceding note. Both L and E write in this instance a long scandicus. The addition of ꝑ to the second note in E should be noticed. G and perhaps B use an oriscus to indicate the thrust of the group towards the culminating note.

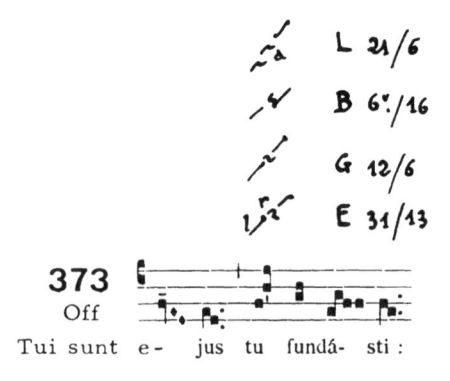

L 21/6
B 6ʳ/16
G 12/6
E 31/13

373 Off Tui sunt e- jus tu fundá- sti :

SALICUS 179

$\mathllap{m'}\ \ $ L 66/2
$\mathllap{\tau f}\ \ $ B 28/17
$\mathllap{/\!\!\prime}\ \ $ G 50/16
$\mathllap{e}\ \ $ E 143/1

374
Intr

Fac mecum ut ví-de- ant qui me odé- runt,

Here are two typical examples of the use of the salicus: in ex. 373 three notes are spread out over the interval of a fifth, with two successive thirds. In ex. 374 there is a unison salicus. In both cases, the culminating notes are followed by a large descending interval. This is why none of the St. Gall notators omit the oriscus which indicates the melodic tension towards the summit of the group. However, while some detach this oriscus from the virga, others unite the two notes into a pes quassus.

The letter f (= fragor), added by *B* in ex. 374 on the virga of the pes quassus, undoubtedly has the same meaning as the k from *C* in ex. 371.

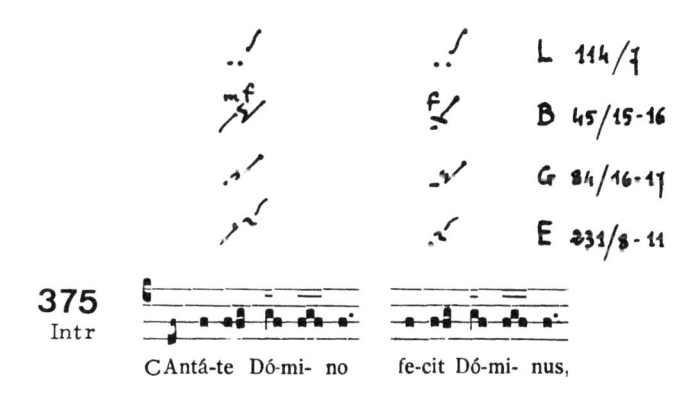

 L 114/7
 B 45/15-16
 G 84/16-17
 E 231/8-11

375
Intr

CAntá-te Dó-mi- no   fe-cit Dó-mi- nus,

180   SALICUS

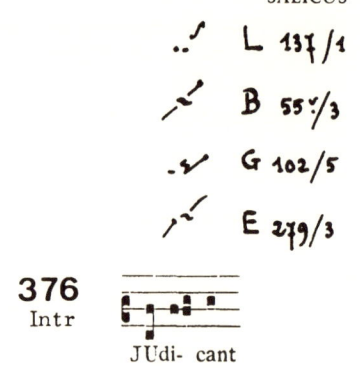

..∫   L 137/1

∕   B 55ᵛ/3

.∕   G 102/5

∕   E 279/3

376
Intr

JUdi- cant

Although L writes the same symbol in these three instances to indicate the lightness of the first two notes, the St. Gall copyists (with the exception of the first symbol in G) unanimously notate the salicus with signs different from the light form. (In ex. 375, we have restored the unison salicus, which was erroneously printed in the Vatican Edition as MI-FA-SOL.)

Another example of this special form of the salicus appears in the alleluia for Easter Day; the MSS notate it with a remarkable and rich variety of symbols and additions:

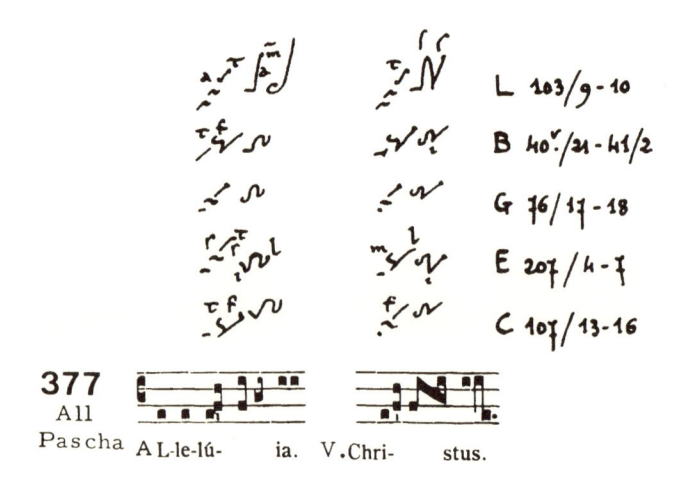

L 103/9-10

B 40ᵛ/21-41/2

G 76/17-18

E 207/4-7

C 107/13-16

377
All
Pascha   A L-le-lú-   ia.   V. Chri-   stus.

The melody leaps from SOL to DO with a special ardor. (C and B add an ♮).

There is no doubt that all of the copyists in the examples just cited wished to indicate a salicus which has a more than usual amplitude. But they evidently hesitated over the notation to use for the second note (and even the first). Nevertheless, they do clearly indicate that this note is not equal to either the first or the last note of the group. In various ways, each copyist experiments with the different possibilities of notation without ever being able to definitively choose any one symbol which could be systematically adopted.[39] As an element of the long salicus, the oriscus is a passing tone which must participate in the lengthening of the entire group without being equal to the other two notes. We will reexamine this problem after the study of the quilisma.

4. developed forms

The salicus of more than three notes is also found – often four notes form the group. In these instances the oriscus can be found as either the second or the third note. Here again, obviously, it is not the oriscus but the note following it that is the most important.

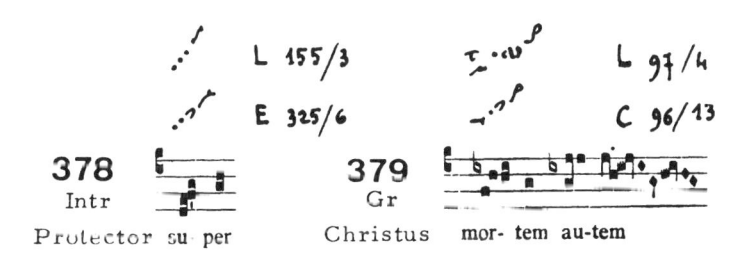

378 Intr — Protector su per

379 Gr — Christus mor- tem au-tem

When the oriscus is the second note, the fourth note shares the importance of the third and is also lengthened.

SALICUS

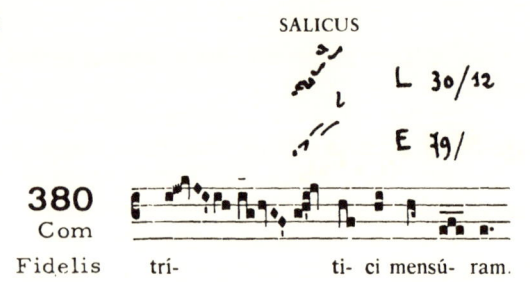

380 Com
Fidelis tri- ti- ci mensú- ram.

L 30/12
E 79/

Just like the scandicus, the salicus can be followed by one or more descending notes (salicus flexus, salicus subpunctis). It is then not rare for the copyists to use the salicus and the scandicus indiscriminately.

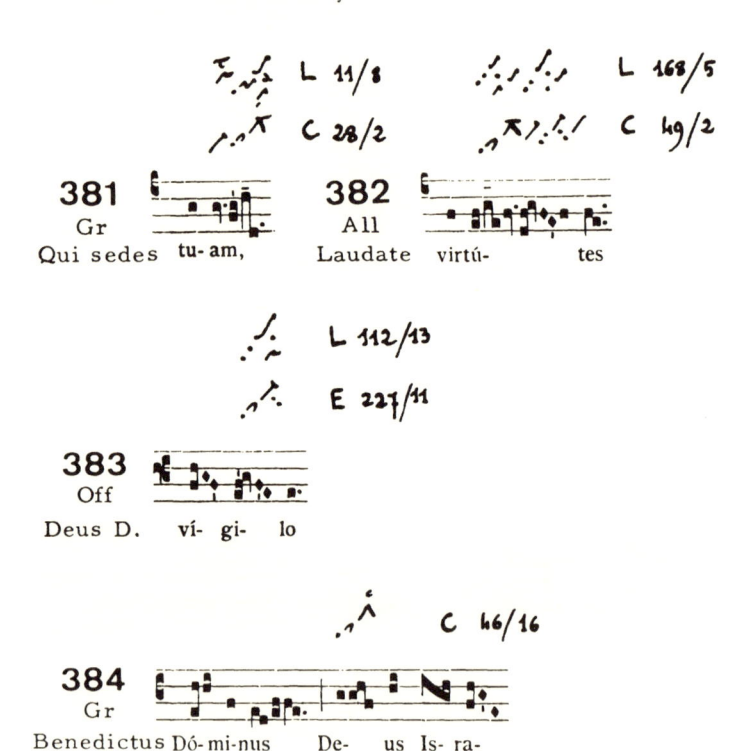

381 Gr
Qui sedes tu- am,

L 11/8
C 28/2

382 All
Laudate virtú- tes

L 168/5
C 49/2

383 Off
Deus D. ví- gi- lo

L 112/13
E 227/11

384 Gr
Benedictus Dó- mi- nus De- us Is- ra-

C 46/16

385 C 51/3
Gr

Gloriosus pro- dí- gi- a.

C writes ↗ in the first two examples, and in the last two ↗. This modification can be explained by musical analysis. By the addition of the c, the copyist wished to prevent the lengthening of the two notes in question, notes which are less important than those in the first two examples.[40]

PES QUASSUS

The pess quassus is a neume with two ascending notes, consisting in an oriscus and a virga.

I. SYMBOLS AND MELODIC SIGNIFICATION

Form 2 with the added episema is generally found in combination. As for form 3, it is perhaps the correction of an error. The copyist had written a pes quadratus. Wishing to correct it and to obtain greater precision he adds an oriscus above the grave accent.

II. INTERPRETATION OF THE SIGNS

In the St. Gall MSS the two notes of the pes quassus vary in value according to the use of the sign. To clarify the various significations of the neume the following subdivisions are made:

1. *isolated pes quassus*

a. as a neume for indicating the phrasing

The melody for the antiphons in Mode I generally revolves around FA and LA, the most important modal notes. In the following example, the word " fírmiter " carries three pes and the last, a pes quassus, underlines the predominance of LA :

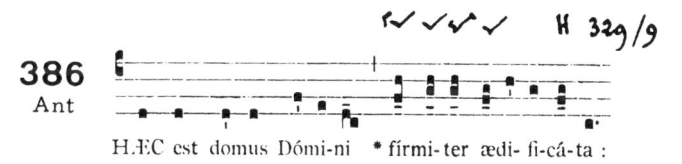

386
Ant

H.EC est domus Dómi-ni * fírmi- ter ædi- fi-cá-ta :

By indicating a stress on the first note of each of the three pes, the episemas of the rhythmic edition neglect the structural importance of the LA, which becomes a secondary note.

It is not surprising that the copyists almost always prefered to use the pes quassus in these first mode antiphon formulas, in order to emphasize the importance of the LA. Actually, the first two pes of "*fír-mi-ter*" already respect this importance since they both contain two broadened notes of equal value. But the notation of the third long pes as a pes quassus indicates that the second note is the more important one.

There are many similar instances :

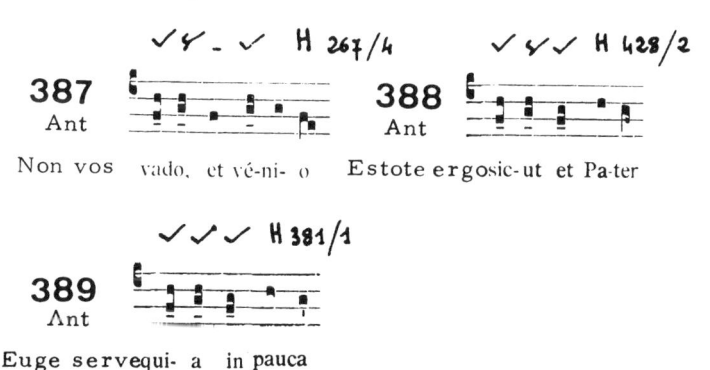

387 Ant
Non vos vado, et vé-ni- o

388 Ant
Estote ergosic-ut et Pa-ter

389 Ant
Euge servequi- a in pauca

In the last example, *H* notates the second pes as a mere pes quadratus ; he presumes that the singer is already familiar with the rhythm of this melodic motif and that he will automatically emphasize the second LA, even without the indication of the oriscus. Furthermore, this second pes quadratus carries an episema on its second note.

In the following formula from the Graduals of Mode V, the isolated pes quassus is equivalent to the pes quadratus in so far as the length of the two notes is concerned:

L 24/11
G 24/9
E 68/2
C 52/6

390
Gr
Timebunt in ma-jestá- te *su- a.

L 56/12
G 44/15
E 125/6
C 74/5

391
Gr
Propitius li- be-ra nos.

The melody of the last incise goes from FA to LA, and this note introduces the final formula which begins on the penultimate syllable. The situation is similar to the one in ex. 333. In ex. 390, E and C have done well in chosing a pes quassus for the third last syllable in order to bring out the strong thrust of the melody towards the pivotal note.[41] There is no doubt that the LA of the pes quassus keeps its structural importance even when some copyists write a pes quadratus in place of the more precise pes quassus. Besides, it is to be noted that C, which started with a pes quadratus in ex. 390, corrected it by the addition of an oriscus ℣.

b. pes quassus used as an intonation neume

The affinity of the pes quassus and the salicus from the point of view of the tension of the oriscus towards the important following note is clearly demonstrated in the following example :

392
Intr

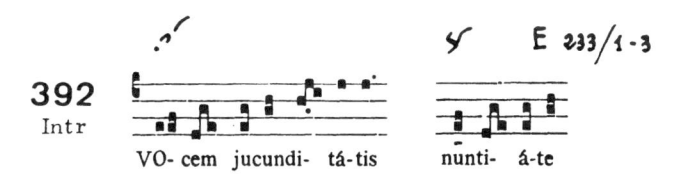

VO- cem jucundi- tá-tis   núnti- á-te

The melodic elan begins both times on MI. The first time the MI is repeated (with a light repercussion) because it is the beginning of the whole piece. The second time it is not repeated. But in both instances, FA is the principal note.

When an intonation formula starting on the lower degree of a semi-tone interval occurs in the middle of a piece, the MSS sometimes differ. Some place two light notes, *i.e.* a salicus at the unison, before the principal note ; others simply write a pes quassus :

393
Com
Pater   nunc au-tem   ad te vé- ni- o :

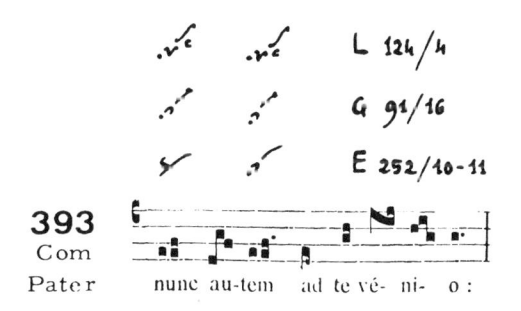

394 Gr
Exs.non   In convertén- do

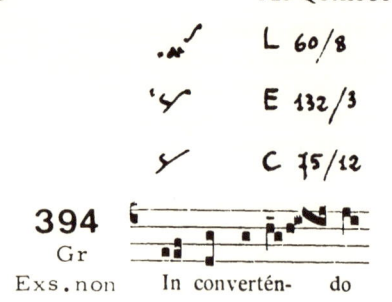

L 60/8
E 132/3
C 75/12

c. pes quassus used as a cadential neume

The pes quassus is found at the end of the psalmodic versicles in Mode III, after the Introit " Vocem jucunditátis " for example :

E 233/7

395 Jubilate deo... date glo-ri-am laudi e-jus

The importance of the upper note explains the frequent use of the pes quassus in inverted cadences :

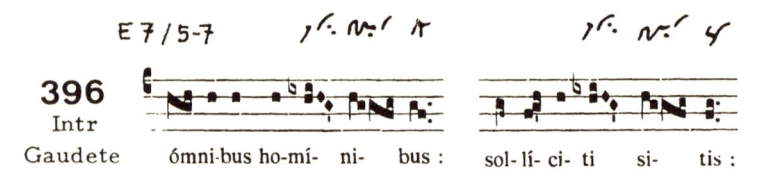

E 7/5-7

396 Intr
Gaudete   ómni-bus ho-mí- ni- bus :   sol- li- ci- ti si- tis :

On " homíni-bus ", there is a normal cadence. The melodic motive concludes on the FA of the final syllable. On " si-tis " however, there is an inverted cadence. The melody rises up from FA to the SOL with a rather accentuated tension indicated by the pes quassus. This gives this cadence a suspended character and introduces the following phrase.

Melodic incises are often treated in this way :[42]

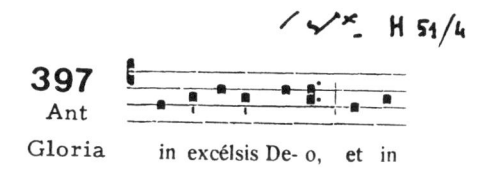

397 Ant
Gloria in excélsis De- o, et in
H 51/4

398 Ant
Isti s.s. et in sángui-ne Agni lavé-runt
H 366/13

399 Intr
Ad le lev. De- us me- us in te confí- do,
L 7/4
G 1/13

Conclusion :
All of the preceding examples and the analogous cases show that, although the two notes of the pes quassus have the same length as the corresponding notes in a pes quadratus, the pes quassus nevertheless gives an additional indication : the special importance of the second note.

2. *pes quassus in composition*

In composition, the pes quassus can be found : 1) at the beginning of a neume, 2) in the middle or at the end of a light neume, 3) at the same pitch as the preceding note.

a. pes quassus at the beginning of a neume

A typical case occurs in third-mode Graduals :

      L 35/1
      G 32/1
      E 88/10
      C 61/6

400
Gr
Tu es so- lus :

The melodic movement of the neume which begins on SOL, is immediately drawn towards the LA, and this is what the pes quassus clearly indicates (C : ✓ ; E : ✓ ; L : ✓). Note that the importance of the LA is again emphasized by the neumatic break which follows the quilisma-pes.

In eight pieces from the most ancient repertoire, this formula occurs 12 times, and in these cases the copyists used the pes quassus and the pes quadratus indiscriminantly. This is what the following diagram illustrates :

Grad.	C	E	G	L
1. Juravit				
2. Tu es				
3. Exsurge non				
4. Deus vitam				
5. Eripe me				
6. Deus exaudi				
7. Exaltabo te				
8. Benedicite				

Of the 36 St. Gall signs, 19 are pes quassus, 17 pes quadratus. It is however to be noticed that in the Gr. " Jurávit " where the formula occurs for the first time, the notators unanimously write a pes quassus. L, which unfortunately has a lacuna from the Feast of St. Stephen up until about the third Sunday after Epiphany, writes a pes quassus in the Gr. " Tu es ". In what follows, the three St. Gall agree only once, *i.e.* in the Gradual " Eripe " – in the use of the pes quassus. Elsewhere they use the pes quadratus and the pes quassus indifferently.

Since the oriscus is a sign which per se has a purely melodic signification, indicating the tension towards the following note, the use of a pes quadratus in its place simply clarifies, in a given instance, the rhythmic value of the oriscus. ✓ and ✓, far from contradicting one another, are complementary. ✓ indicates the melodic tension between the two notes and the predominance of the second and ✓ indicates the corresponding rhythmic value.

L 31/9
G 29/12
E 81/13
C 58/12

401
GR
Adjutor quó- ni- am non

In this additional example, the St. Gall MSS write a pes quassus ; L, has a unison salicus. Both signs emphasize the importance of the DO.

b. pes quassus in the middle or at the end of a neume

Light descending notes preceding a salicus sometimes create a notational problem for the St. Gall copyists. In such cases the principle of neumatic cutting does not permit them to write the usual sign ⸝. Instead, they use the pes quassus and join the first light note of the salicus to the descending group. For them the sign ⸝ represents an indivisible graphic unit. And thus, to give an example, the notation ⸝⸵⸝ would create the impression of a break at the descending mid-point and put the fourth note before the end into prominence. In order to avoid this, they prefer to write ⸝⸵⸝ (cf. ex. 406).

The following example is a good illustration of the problem :

402
A11

C 153/12

Beatus v.q.s. co- ró- nam

If the St. Gall copyists had used the same salicus sign on each of the two first syllables, the notation on the second syllable would have required the union of the first dot with the virga, which would have given ⸝⸝⸝. But this grouping would have given an undue importance to the third note (the fourth-last note). Consequently, St. Gall copyists continued the descending line of light notes up to the lowest point, and joined the oriscus to the virga ⸝⸵⸝. This was the only way to indicate the light movement of the melody from the MI at the beginning of the neume to the MI at the end of it.[43]

If, however, the fourth-last note is an important note, the normal salicus is used instead of the pes quassus :

L 46/3   L 39/4
C 68/15   E 97/7

403   **404**
Tr   Intr

De necess. é-ri- pe me,   Audivit   et mi-sér- tus

In these two examples the same notes are involved, FA-MI-FA-SOL. But in the first example, the light FA must be tied to the second note which gives a clivis followed by a pes quassus. In the second example, FA is the important note, and it is followed by an expressive neumatic break. The three last notes are therefore grouped together to form a salicus.

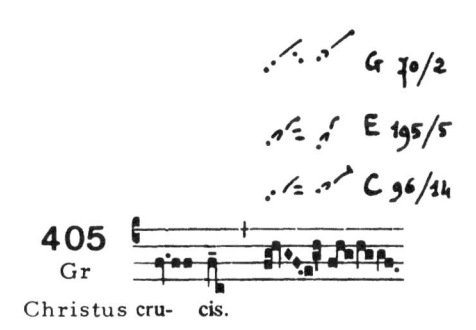

Although the first neumatic element of the second incise differs according to the copyists (G : an entirely light scandicus subbipunctis ; E : a salicus subbipunctis with the three last notes long ; C : a scandicus subbipunctis with the three last notes long), the three St. Gall MSS all emphasize the fifth note by the expressive break at the descending mid-point which follows this note and which then permits the use of a salicus.

Hence, in melodic designs of this type, the value of the fourth-last note is the determining factor. If this note is light, the pes quassus is used. If it is important, a salicus is used.[44]

The St. Gall notation is not always clear as to whether, in these cases, the first note of the pes quassus is light (i.e. equivalent to ✓) or long (i.e. equivalent to ✓). (In either case, the second note is invariably emphasized by the expressive nematic break which follows.) In order to decide which alternative is correct, we must refer to L :

406
Gr

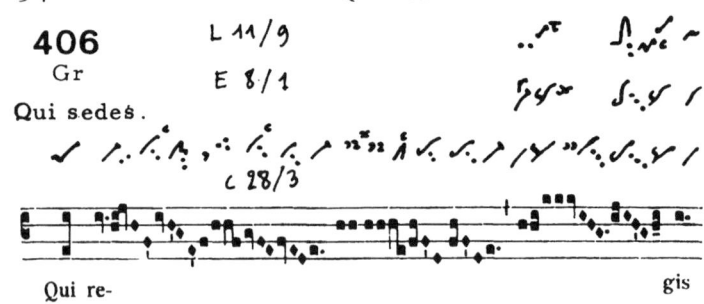

Qui sedes.

Qui re-   gis

The melody rises on " qui " with a wide jump from SOL to RE. A long melisma then follows, beginning on the RE, pivotal note of the whole period, and ending on this same note with a pes quassus. RE is also the base of the melodic peak which follows on " Israel ". The c which L places next to the oriscus indicates that the St. Gall pes quassus is equivalent to a light pes which is tending towards the upper note, the principal note of the group. (The episema which underlines the DO in the rhythmic editions is therefore erroneous.)

The function of the first pes quassus (the one immediately after the quarter bar) is to restate the importance of the RE after the first part of the melisma which was centered on DO. The second incise begins on DO followed immediately at the unison by a pes quassus which draws the melody to the note RE. Whatever value is given to this repetition of DO (L : ..♪; C : ♪; E : ♪), the RE undoubtedly remains the principal note (L : ᴛ ; E : ᴌ).

Here are two more examples in which the melodic structure clearly proves the predominance of the second note of the pes quassus, the first note being light.

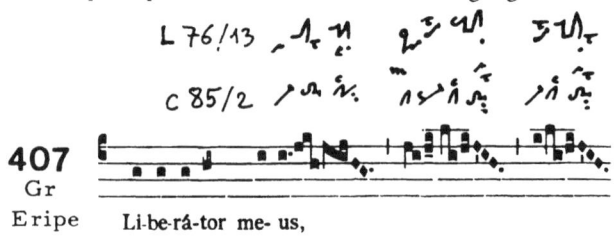

407
Gr

Eripe   Li-be-rá-tor me- us,

The last incise obviously repeats the melodic motive of the preceding incise but the initial ornament of three notes is omitted and only the RE remains. This is the principal note of the group and its importance is visibly underlined by the neumatic break which follows. In the first incise the RE is prepared by three light notes but it exercises the same function. The choice of the pes quassus clearly indicates that it is the pivotal note towards which the preceding ornamental notes tend and from which the following notes receive their force. The reprise of this melodic theme is similar to a rhetorical repetition — it is a form of insistance by repetition of the essence of what was already stated. The lengthening of the DO, which is suggested by the episema in the rhythmic editions, is therefore inappropriate here.

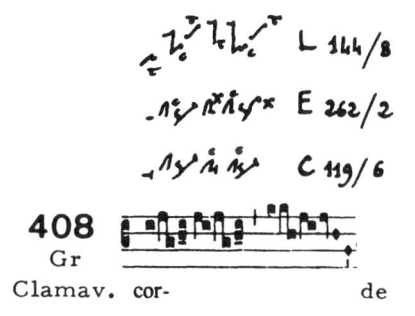

The melody rotates around RE and stresses this note each time it returns there. The initial RE, brought out by its neumatic separation from the following notes, gives these notes their impulse and then draws them back again by means of a pes quassus /\y. The same movement — from RE (E :/\x) to the following RE — is repeated after the light MI.

In spite of very clear indications in the MSS (episemas on the virga of the St. Gall pes quassus ; τ on the virga in L), the rhythmic edition does not underline a single RE, putting instead an episema on the two DO (oriscus) which L expressly modified by the addition of a c.[45]

c. pes quassus in unison with the preceding note

When a higher light note precedes a unison salicus, the salicus is replaced by a pes quassus, for the reasons already explained; the initial punctum becomes the last note of the preceding neumatic element.

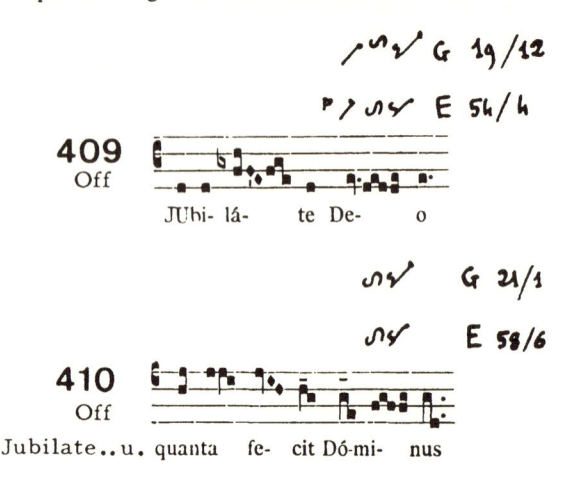

409 Off

JUbi- lá- te De- o

410 Off

Jubilate..u. quanta fe- cit Dó-mi- nus

Unfortunately the signs of L are missing for these pieces but there is a similar instance to which we can refer:

411 Off

Intonuit et Al-tís- si- mus

L clearly indicates a light neume which tends towards the last note, the only important one. In order for the St. Gall copyists to be able to write a unison salicus in this melodic context, the preceding note (the fourth from the last) would have had to be long; then they would have had ✓ɔ́. But this neume seems to be inexistent.

PES QUASSUS

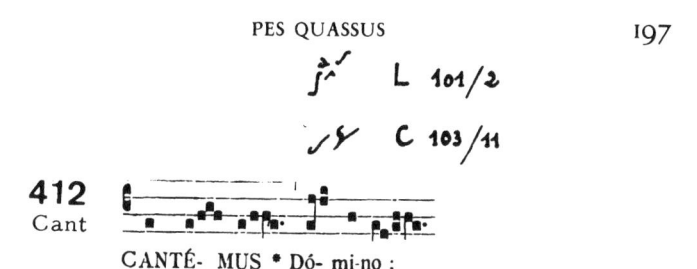

412
Cant

CANTÉ- MUS * Dó- mi-no :

Here we have one of the special symbols for the salicus, preceded by a light note. The second note of the pes, which brings the melody to DO, is long and marks a neumatic break near the melodic summit followed by an attack at the unison ; the pes quassus which follows carries the melody to the RE. The oriscus (second DO) takes part proportionally in the enlarging of the notes which surround it. (*L*'s notation makes this evident.) " Proportionally " because the following note remains the most important. An accurate performance should therefore involve the repercussion of the second DO which must be treated differently because of its special function.

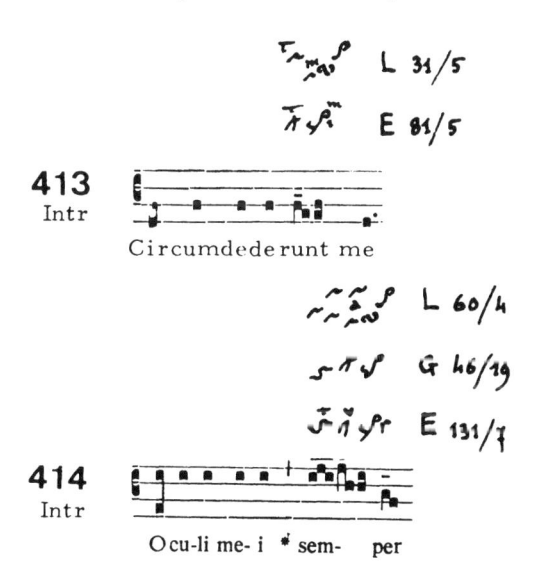

413
Intr

Circumdederunt me

414
Intr

Ocu-li me- i * sem- per

One or more long notes immediately precede the unison salicus. Practically speaking, it is this form ⌄, + the preceding higher note which is tied to the tractulus.

CONCLUSION

The oriscus of the salicus and of the pes quassus indicates the melodic tension towards a higher note. The note represented by the oriscus never stands out in the melody, either paleographically or melodically. In fact, while the oriscus may be accompanied by a c or even replaced by a simple punctum, the importance of the following note is very often brought to our attention by an episema or a τ.

When the salicus or the pes quassus are long, the note corresponding to the oriscus can also be lengthened, especially when the preceding note is also long, but this does not change the predominance of the last note.

To restore the true intention of the composers who emphasized in a refined way and with profond musical instinct the monodic expression, it would be necessary to rectify the signs in the rhythmic editions, bringing them up to date in light of modern paleographic research.

18

QUILISMA

I. THE SIGN AND MELODIC SIGNIFICATION

The quilisma is composed of two or three small semicircular loops ⌣ ⌣⌣. It is never found in isolation but is always tied to an ascending virga ⌣/⌣⌣/ forming a quilisma-pes.[46]

Normally this quilisma-pes is preceded by a note which is almost always at a lower pitch.[47] Most often this note is part of a quilismatic group (quilismatic scandicus) but sometimes it belongs to the preceding neume. In this case the quilisma is directly attached on a new syllable.

The symbol for the quilisma-pes undoubtedly has its origin in the question mark used by grammarians. The sign ⌣/, was used at the end of interrogative phrases at Corbie (a monastery near Amiens) in the second half of the eighth century. This is probably the first way in which this sign was employed since we cannot prove that any musical notation used ⌣/at the same era.

In addition, at the same period, the question mark used in the region around Tours ∕ suggests the quilisma-pes from L. The quilisma-pes from both the St. Gall and Messine schools may thus have a common source.

The copyist of the oldest of the St. Gall MSS (C) intentionally distinguishes the two forms of the quilisma-pes. The symbol with two semi-circles is reserved for those instances in which the notes are separated by a whole-tone whereas the sign with three semi-circles has no special melodic indication. The other St. Gall MSS distinguish the two forms but use them indiscriminately.

As to the melodic placement, the quilisma-pes usually terminates a minor third. Some of the Aquitaine MSS seem to have made a rigorous law of this. Sometimes, however, the quilisma-pes is written over an interval of a major third or even a fourth, and in such cases it can be difficult to determine with certainty which one of the intermediary tones really corresponds to the quilisma. Thus, in the intonation of the Antiphon " Veni sponsa Christi ", should perhaps be .

II. INTERPRETATION OF THE SIGNS

Before discovering the interpretation of the quilisma itself, it is necessary to examine the two notes which frame it.

1. *the note preceding the quilisma*

The notes which precede the quilisma are almost always written with long signs :

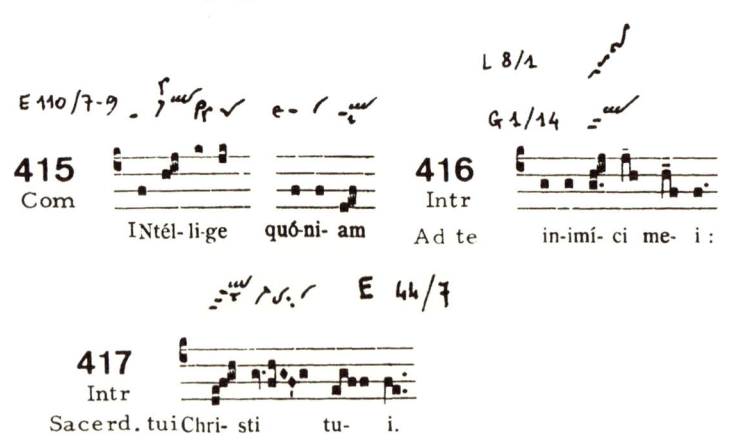

415 Com — INtél-li-ge quó-ni- am

416 Intr — Ad te in-imí- ci me- i :

417 Intr — Sacerd. tui Chri- sti tu- i.

QUILISMA 201

418 Cant
Cantemus ascen- só- rem

419 Intr
Laetare conso-la-ti- ó- nis ve- strae.

2. *the note following the quilisma*

Here it is necessary to examine the more developed forms:

420 Off
PRe-cá- tus est

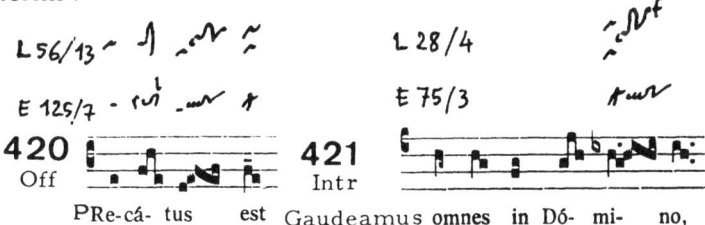

421 Intr
Gaudeamus omnes in Dó- mi- no,

The melody obviously tends towards the note which follows the quilisma. This note is brought into relief by the ornament which follows and by the fact that the same note is repeated as the first note of the next syllable.

422 Intr
Respice cau- sam tu- am

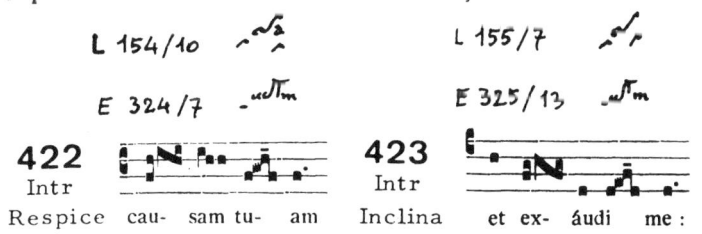

423 Intr
Inclina et ex- áudi me:

In these formulas, the St. Gall MSS underline the note which follows the quilisma by the addition of an episema to the clivis. Naturally, the second note of clivis is also lengthened. Let it be added, however, that in the formulas *with* the lengthening of the last two notes is so normal that copyists did not always think it necessary to point this out by the addition of an episema.

L indicates the length of the two notes by detaching them from one another and by the occasional addition of an a .

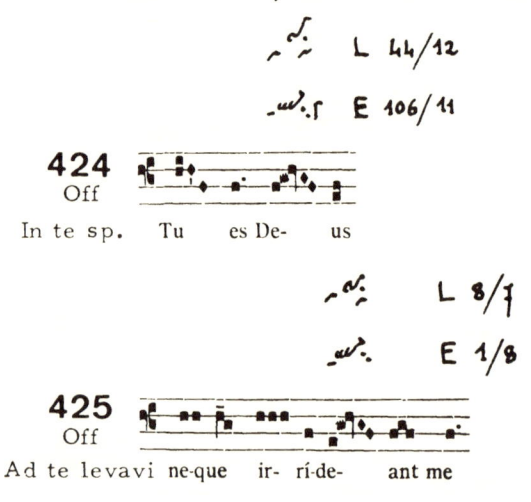

424
Off
In te sp. Tu es De- us

425
Off
Ad te levavi ne-que ir- rí-de- ant me

When the note which follows the quilisma is a " subpunctis ", the St. Gall copyists almost always underline its importance by the addition of an episema.

In the preceding examples, the note after the quilisma was the highest of the neume. There are also instances in which one or two higher notes follow the quilisma pes. These notes can be either light or long. But the virga after the quilisma still remains inportant. It is always followed by an intentional neumatic break and it often carries an episema.

First of all, here are two examples in which the quilisma-pes is followed by a light note. (Notice that in ex. 427 the virga of the quilisma-pes was underlined with an episema in E and with a c in L.)

L 96/7

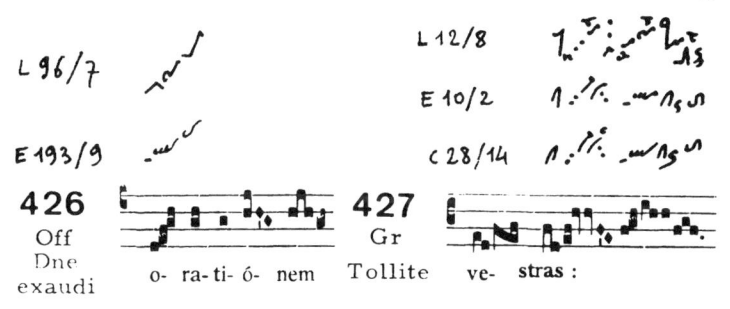

E 193/9

L 12/8

E 10/2

C 28/14

426 Off
Dne exaudi o- ra-ti- ó- nem

427 Gr
Tollite ve- stras:

In the following example, the quilisma-pes is followed by a higher oriscus, after which the melody returns to the recitation tone.

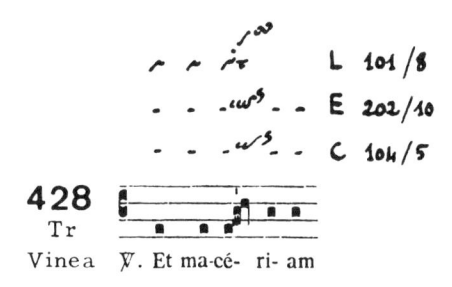

L 101/8

E 202/10

C 104/5

428 Tr
Vinea ℣. Et ma-cé- ri- am

The higher note which follows the virga of the quilisma-pes is sometimes the principal note, but this does not diminish the rhythmic value of the preceding note which is prepared by the quilisma.[48]

L 167/6

E 34/8

C 41/8

L 97/6

E 195/7

C 97/1

429 All
. Ví- de- o

430 Gr
Christus no- men,

3. the quilisma

The note represented by the quilisma is light. Here is the proof :

1º The melodic context : the quilisma is a light passing tone and as such has no special importance ;

2º The quilisma is sometimes added as an ornamental note between the two notes of a pes. Thus, it does not belong to the essential melodic structure ;

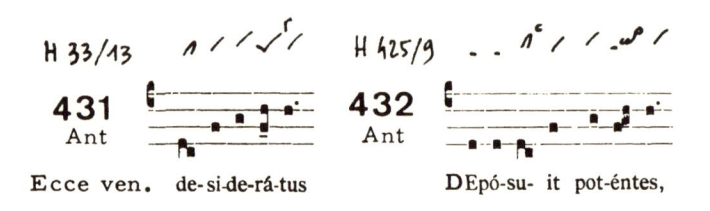

431 Ant — Ecce ven. de-si-de-rá-tus

432 Ant — DEpó-su- it pot-éntes,

433 Ant — Regnum tu- um, Dó- mi-ne, regnum

434 Ant — LOquebántur * vá- riis linguis

3º L habitually renders ⌇ by ⌇ . Sometimes however, the copyist entirely neglects the quilisma, using a simple punctum ⌇ instead. This has already been seen in ex. 428 ; here is another instance :

435 Intr

Resurrexi sci- én- ti- a

4° In the chapter dealing with the torculus, we saw that in the case of a short text lacking a syllable, the notes of the special passing torculus and the preceding note are united into one neumatic design. The weak note of the special torculus (the first one) is then written as a quilisma (cf. ex. 83, 84, 85).

5° The quilisma and the first note of the special torculus have a tendency to disappear in the MSS, precisely because of their weakness.

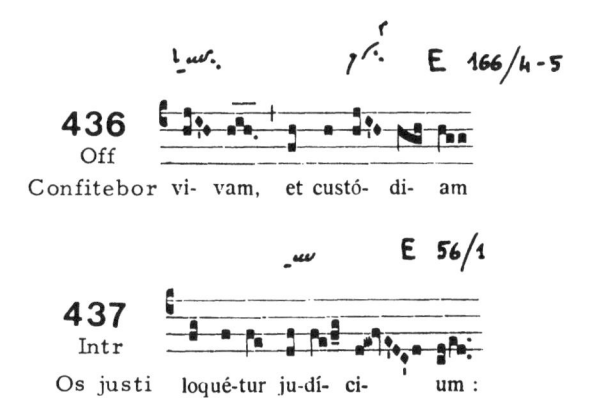

436 Off

Confitebor vi- vam, et custó- di- am

437 Intr

Os justi loqué-tur ju-dí- ci- um :

III. THE ISOLATED QUILISMA-PES

The quilisma-pes is generally preceded by a lower note on the same syllable. However, there are instances, mainly in the Antiphonary, in which it is found isolated on a new syllable.

QUILISMA

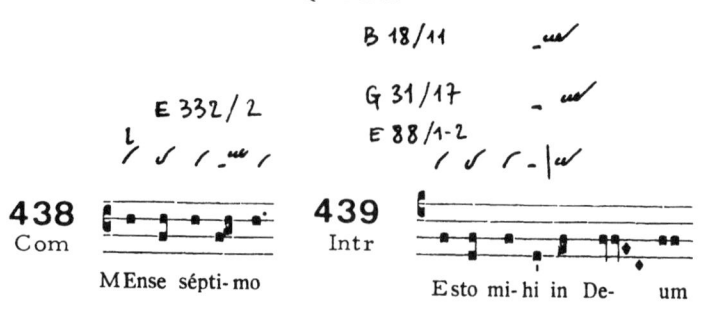

438 Com — MEnse sépti-mo

439 Intr — Esto mi-hi in De- um

This last example is simply the diaeresis of ⌐⌐, caused by the repetition of the two *i* vowels.

The following symbols are found in H at the final cadence of the Great " O " Antiphons :

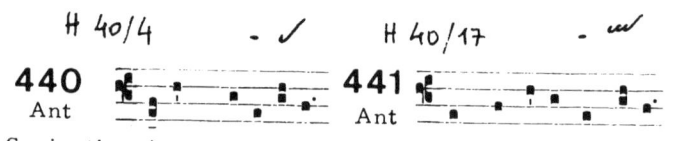

440 Ant — O Sapientia vi- am prudénti-æ.

441 Ant — O Rex quem de limo formásti.

The melody tends from DO to the FA (which is an important note in Mode II, serving as the recitation tone and situated a third above the final note), passing lightly across the weak note MI. The respective weight of the two notes MI-FA is expressed either by a light pes (twice ✓, and twice the liquescent form♪) or by a quilisma-pes (once ⌐⌐ and twice the liquescent form ⌐⌐). As has been seen, the quilisma is a weak passing note, which tends towards the more important note which follows. It keeps this character even when it is an isolated quilisma-pes. Consequently, it is not surprising that H uses the quilisma-pes in this formula instead of the light pes. This neume expresses in a clearer way the tension of the weak first note towards the important second note. This is also why H uses it readily on the half-step SI-DO and MI-FA, just as the other St. Gall copyists do in the following example (in

QUILISMA

which an office antiphon is used as a communion antiphon in the Missal) :

      B 61/6

      G 111/20

      E 305/7

      H 289/9-10

442 Ant
Vos qui sec. tri-bus Isra- el, di- cit Dóminus.

Unfortunately, with the exception of the " O " antiphons and a few other instances, the Monastic Antiphonary has almost always put the episema on the first note of the pes, and this contradicts the very nature of quilisma.

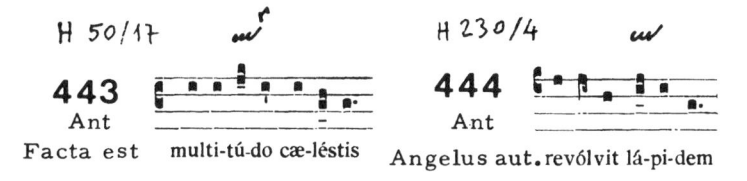

H 50/17   H 230/4

443 Ant   **444** Ant
Facta est multi-tú-do cæ-léstis Angelus aut. revólvit lá-pi-dem

In a few instances, the Monastic Antiphonary renders the quilisma-pes as a single note, DO or FA — the second note of the neume. This reading is based on MSS in which the first weak note is already disappareared.

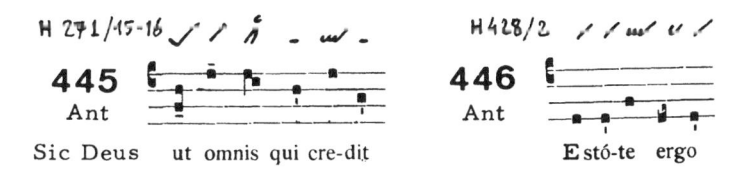

H 271/15-16   H 428/2

445 Ant   **446** Ant
Sic Deus ut omnis qui cre-dit   Estó-te ergo

In other cases, the Monastic Antiphonary, following more recent MSS, has only the first note – the weak, quilismatic element – whereas the important final virga, clearly stated in *H*, has been suppressed :

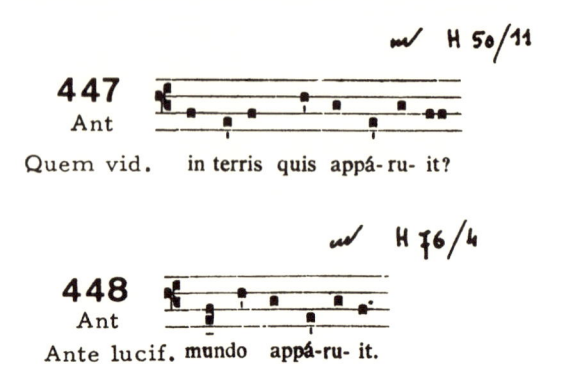

447
Ant
Quem vid. in terris quis appá-ru- it?

448
Ant
Ante lucif. mundo appá-ru- it.

The isolated quilisma-pes is also found at the end of versicles for Introits and Communions in mode VII :

449 Qui regis Isra-el intende,

qui deducis velut ovem Joseph.

IV. PARTICULAR CONTEXTS

In rare instances, the quilisma follows a note at the unison. This presents no difficulty for practical execution if the repercussion is regularly observed :

450 Off — Justitiae re- ctae,

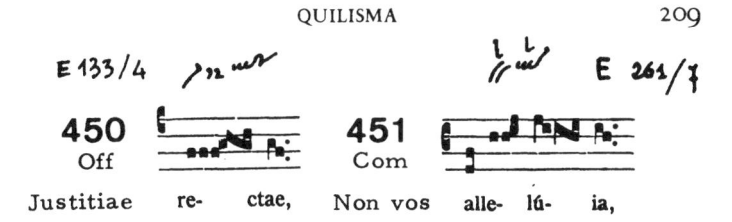

451 Com — Non vos alle- lú- ia,

The following instances are rather exceptional :

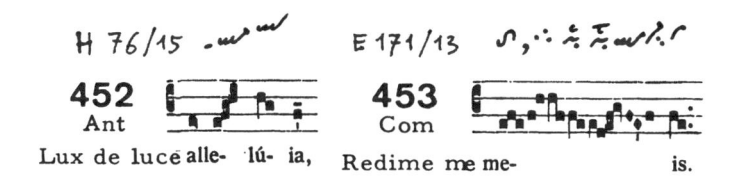

452 Ant — Lux de luce alle- lú- ia,

453 Com — Redime me me- is.

V. THE QUILISMATIC SCANDICUS AND SALICUS

There is a certain resemblance between the quilisma and the oriscus of the salicus since they are both passing tones in a group which ascends towards a principal note. But the degrees of the musical scale upon which they are found differ in quality :

− The quilisma, a passing tone preceded by one or several lengthened notes is normally placed on MI or SI − weak degrees of the scale.

The oriscus of the salicus a passing tone preceded by one or several light notes is usually found on the important degrees : FA or DO.

There are also cases in which one copyist used an oriscus and others a quilisma :

QUILISMA

L 24/12
G 24/11
E 68/7

454 Off
Dextera fe- cit vir- tú- tem,

L 70/11
G 54/1
E 152/7

455 Off
Exspectans exspectá- vi

L 35/2 L L 31/11
C 61/7 C C 58/16

456 Gr
Tu es vir- tú- tem

457 Gr
Adjutor páu- pe- rum

In these four examples, L writes an oriscus, using the design of the salicus in order to express more clearly the melodic tension towards the highest note of the group. E does the same in the first two instances, whereas G as well as C in the last two examples, uses a quilisma. The two notations indicate the same melodic and expressive idea concerning the note which follows the oriscus or quilisma. They differ only in respect to the preceding note – this note is always long before a quilisma but it is normally light before an oriscus.

In the last instance, the quilismatic scandicus and the salicus are followed by a higher note. This fact has caused some observers to express doubt as to whether the principle of neumatic cutting still holds true. They advance the following objection : Since it is graphically impossible to join the virga coming directly after an oriscus or quilisma to a higher note which follows, a neumatic break becomes inevitable. But perhaps the copyist did not intend to emphasize the penultimate note. He was simply incapable of realizing a graphic liaison. And thus the resulting neumatic break is not necessarily an expressive one, even though it is found at the ascending mid-point.

This objection is improperly formulated because it turns things upside down. It is the melody which came first chronologically, together with its rhythmic pecularities, and later the copyist had to notate these by the use of signs. Therefore, in these particular instances, he chose the sign most capable of indicating motion towards an important note which was followed by a higher note. The choice of the symbols was determined by the nature of the notes and not the reverse ! Therefore, when a lower, important note was followed by several ascending, light notes, the copyist did not use the quilisma. This can be demonstrated by opposing two quotes belonging to the same piece :

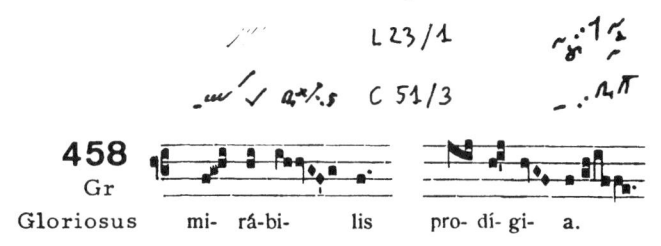

458
Gr

Gloriosus   mi- rá-bi-   lis   pro- dí- gi-   a.

In the first fragment, the FA, terminus ad quem of the quilismatic scandicus, is followed by a SOL which is also important. (The following pes quadratus reaffirms the importance of the two notes and the FA only regains its prominence in the neume which follows.) In the second fragment the melody reaches its peak on LA (pro-dí-gia);

then, by means of the FA on the next-to-last syllable, it reaches the cadential RE, an important note underlined by an initial neumatic break and by an ornamentation on three light ascending notes which lead to the second RE (note carrying an episema in *C*). Now it is clear that although the copyist uses a tractulus as the first note of the last neume, he avoids using a quilisma on the next note since the FA is light.

In recognizing the principle of neumatic breaking, we are merely rediscovering and respecting the true intention of the composer.

A complementary symbol :
THE PES STRATUS

In order to complete the Table of St. Gall Symbols, we included, on the last line (24) a sign whose use and signification is very different from those of the other symbols. The pes stratus is never found in C (at least in its first redaction), the best representative of the St. Gall school. Elsewhere, it denotes melodic and rhythmic pecularities which are foreign to the authentic Gregorian repertoire.

It is used in pieces " imported " from the west (Spain, Aquitaine, Gaul, England), in the Offertory " Elegérunt... plenum... lapidavérunt " for example.

The pes stratus is composed of a light pes to which an oriscus has been tied :

The Vatican Edition renders it with a light pes followed by a punctum in unison with the second note. The Monastic Antiphonary has correctly replaced the punctum by an oriscus (as in the final melisma of the Antiphon " O Crux benedícta... allelúia ".

The St. Gall MSS only use the pes stratus as a neumatic element – in composition. But the custom of using it at the end of an incise or of a melodic entity – at the end of the strophes in the sequences for example – prevents the establishment of any relation between the pes stratus and the other, authentic St. Gall symbols. Here the oriscus entirely lacks that quality of tension towards the following note which we recognized earlier as its principal characteristic.

Nevertheless, the last note of the pes stratus must be repercussed. The best proof of this is that the pes stratus of the sequences is regularly distributed in the prose text over three-syllable words. The fourth phrase of the sequence " Occidentana ", for example, was notated this way in St.Gall 484, p. 281/4 : (look out ! the pages of this sequentiary are written from the bottom of the page going upwards) and the corresponding text in the prosa " Sancti Spíritus adsit " is the following :

Spíritus alme illustrátor hóminum

" Hóminum " is capable of being notated by ♪ because the second note of this sign is the weakest of the three and because the rhythmic movement comes to a rest on the last repercussed note of the pes stratus.

N.B. – In some later MSS the pes stratus is found isolated. This gives the melodic formulas SOL-DO-DO and LA-DO-DO which are simply corruptions of the melodic designs SOL-DO-SI and LA-DO-SI which were previously notated by a special intonation torculus. The same holds true for all similar combinations on FA and SI ♭. (Some of the most recent MSS only retain the pes SOL-DO or LA-DO.) Needless to say, this practice deprives the symbol of all all resemblance to the pes stratus as it was employed by the St. Gall copyists of the authentic Gregorian era.

CONCLUSION

At the end of our analysis of St. Gall symbols, an all inclusive glance over the studied instances of unison notes manifests that in each case undeniable arguments in favor of the repercussion of each note has been presented. In Gregorian chant, at the time of the earliest notation, sounds were never " blocked " together, and long sounds were not made by uniting several notes. Nor were there ever any " trilled " notes as certain people have mistakenly pretended. There were only repercussed sounds : each note bearing its individual importance in the rhythmic order of the whole.

19

LIQUESCENCE

I. DEFINITION AND FUNCTION

Liquescence is a vocal phenomenon caused by the articulation of a complex combination of syllables. This requires the vocal organs to momentarily assume a position which diminishes or impedes the sound.

In the MSS this phenomenon is expressed in a more or less precise way. This is the object of our particular study in this chapter.

Because of its nature, liquescence is never found in the course of a melisma[49], neither is it found at the juxtaposition of two vowels or two simple syllables. In this latter case however, there are exceptions for the consonants m and g which can, each one by itself, cause a liquescence on the last note of the preceding syllable.

In *Paléographie Musicale* Dom Mocquereau has provided a classification of the different instances:

1. *Two or three consecutive consonants*

1st type : Two or three consonants the first of which is a " liquid " sound (l, m, n, r) : *e.g.*, salvi, òmnia, osténde, cordis.

2nd type : Two consonants the first of which is a dental plosive (d, t) : *e.g.*, ad lápidem, et sémitas.

3rd type : Two consonants, the first of which is a sibilant (s) : *e.g.*, Fílius Dei, Israel.

4th type : The consonant group *gn* : *e.g.*, magni.

5th type : Two consonants, the second of which is *j* (or *i*, according to the spelling followed in recent books), the first consonant varying (b, d, m, n, r, s, t, and even l) : *e.g.*, adjútor, ovem Joseph, injúste, et jam.

2. *Consonants* m *and* g *between two vowels*

Here, the liquescence is called " antecedant " because the consonants *m* and *g* have an effect on the vowel which terminates the preceding syllable : *e.g.* petra melle, altíssimus, regit.[50]

3. Diphthongs au, ei, eu : e.g. gaudéte, aures, eléison : " euge " belongs both to this category and to the preceding one.

4. J *or* I *between two vowels :* *e.g.* ejus, cujus, majéstas, allelúia.

The phenomenon of liquescence is relative in the sense that the coincidence of consonants and diphthongs enumerated above does not provoke the use of liquescent neumes in a uniform or consistant fashion. From this point of view there is great diversity between the various schools. Benevento is the richest in liquescent signs.

Furthermore, an identical complex articulation is not always treated in the same way in the same MS. For example, in the psalmody of Tone I, at the first accent of the median cadence, we find :

misericórdias Dómini with ⌐ (E 60/4) and with ✓ (E 308/8).

II. AMBIGUITY AND UNCERTAINTY OF VALUE

The liquescent sign is a modification of the normal neume and most often consists in a light loop at the end of the neume. (Cf. the Table of Neumatic Signs, columns *g* and *h*.)

Study of the melodic formulas clearly proves that, at least at St. Gall, one liquescent sign can correspond to two different normal neumatic signs. Thus, in the following examples, the sign ⸓ (cephalicus) corresponds respectively to a virga and to a clivis:

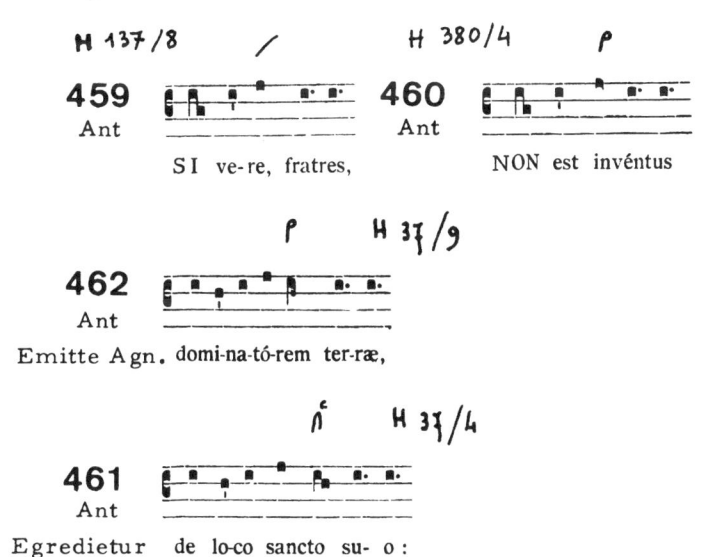

459 Ant — SI ve-re, fratres,

460 Ant — NON est invéntus

462 Ant — Emitte Agn. domi-na-tó-rem ter-ræ,

461 Ant — Egredietur de lo-co sancto su- o :

Therefore, in order to interpret a liquescent sign, it is necessary to refer to parallel formulas without liquescence (in cases involving stereotyped melodies) or to evidence from other MSS. Without such comparison it is difficult to accurately reconstruct the melody.

Here are some analogous instances of ambivalent liquescence:

- ᴗ = 1 note   or   2 notes
- ⸓ = 2 notes   or   3 notes
- ⸓ = 2 notes   or   3 notes.[51]

The sign ⌣ can actually have four meanings; it can indicate:
- the augmentation of ✓ and
- the diminution of ⌣✓ as well as
- the diminution of the salicus ✓ and of the scandicus with a terminal break ⌣✓. This is illustrated by the following examples in which the same formula is found with and without graphic liquescence:

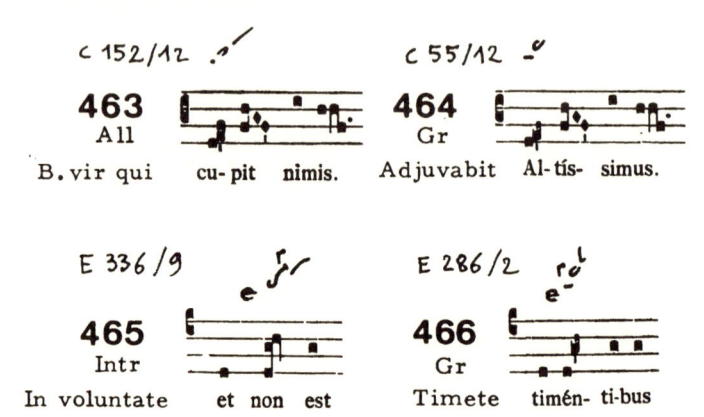

463 All — B. vir qui cu- pit nimis. (C 152/12)

464 Gr — Adjuvabit Al- tís- simus. (C 55/12)

465 Intr — In voluntate et non est (E 336/9)

466 Gr — Timete timén- ti-bus (E 286/2)

The type of liquescence that the neume receives is determined by the melodic importance of the last note:

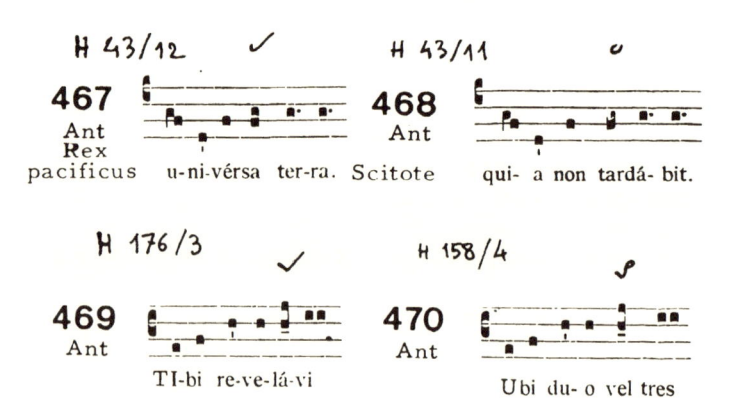

467 Ant Rex pacificus — u-ni-vérsa ter-ra. (H 43/12)

468 Ant — Scitote qui- a non tardá- bit. (H 43/11)

469 Ant — TI-bi re-ve-lá-vi (H 176/3)

470 Ant — Ubi du- o vel tres (H 158/4)

The liquescent sign ␣ corresponds to the light pes ␣ of the first example; the second note SOL is merely the anticipation of the following cadential SOL and it can therefore be somewhat reduced. In the other instance, on the contrary, the second note of the pes quadratus ✓ is important. Hence the sign ␣ is used. It indicates that the importance of MI must be completely respected before beginning the complex articulation.

III. AUGMENTATION AND DIMINUTION

The preceding examples show that, practically speaking, liquescence brings about an augmentation or a diminution of the normal neume. It augments an important note and diminishes a weak note.

The terms "augmentation" and "diminution" are, needless to say, relative; they do not concern directly the liquescent signs themselves, but refer to the normal sign which is augmented or diminished. Although this at first seems contradictory, since the objective rhythmic value in the second instance is longer than in the first, ␣ can be either an augmentation ␣ or a diminution ␣. ␣ is, in fact, an augmentation of a ␣, and is the diminution of ␣. The same thing holds true for the other signs. In a few cases, the diminution and the augmentation become "exaggerated":

1. The last note of the normal group completely disappears and the diminution affects the preceding note ·

471 Resp   H 218/14

Tenebrae excla- má- vit   Je-   sus vo- ce   ma- gna :

2. Other notes are added to the last note of a group and the last of these is diminished :

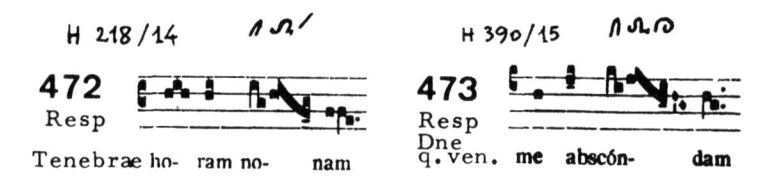

472 H 218/14
Resp
Tenebrae ho- ram no- nam

473 H 390/15
Resp
Dne
q. ven. me abscón- dam

These two phenomena are not fortuitous. The melodic formulas which our examples illustrate are modified in these two ways in every case of liquescence.

With regard to the diminutive liquescence, a remark must be made concerning the value of the liquescent note, the little note of the Vatican Edition. Although there actually is a reduction of sonority because of the momentary contraction of the vocal organs, the liquescent note conserves its normal rhythmic value. It has approximately the same value as the adjacent notes. The note itself is certainly not a long note ; on the contrary it is shortened somewhat since a weak sound tends to grow thinner. It is however best not to consciously attempt to obtain this shortening but to let it happen as a simple consequence of natural articulation. The liquescence can be assured by good pronounciation and clear articulation.

When, on the other hand, there is an augmentative liquescence the last note of the liquescent sign should be lengthened slightly. The articulation should follow the normal duration of the note but without giving rise to any other distinct sound, melodically or rhythmically, which would give the impression not of an augmentative liquescence but of the diminutive liquescence corresponding to the graphic element containing one additional note.

MELODY AND LIQUESCENCE

The following conclusions have been drawn from numerous analyses concerning the relation between liquescence and melody :

1. The liquescent sign is never found
   a. on a final syllable (of a piece or of an incise);
   b. on the accented syllable of a redundant cadence ;
   c. in the course of a recitation at the same pitch ;
   d. in an ascending melodic line when the next syllable is on a higher note.

2. The liquescent sign is almost never found on a syllable in the middle of a descending melodic line (below the preceding syllable but higher than the following one) unless the syllable which follows is cadential.

3. Liquescent signs are used with a certain amount of consistency on light, high ornamental notes. This liquescence is normally diminutive when the ornament is not important and augmentative when it has some importance in the melodic structure.

4. The augmentative liquescent sign is almost always found on culminating notes, isolated or at the end of a neume.

5. On the contrary, the diminutive liquescent sign is always found on the light clivis situated at the bottom of melodic curves, that is. when the following syllable is higher than the second note of the clivis.

Diminutive liquescence is normally found in three instances :
   a. at the lowest point of a melodic curve ;
   b. on anticipations ;
   c. on a simple light ornament of an accent.

MUSICAL EXPRESSION AND LIQUESCENCE

There remains the study of the liquescence as a special sign for musical expression. This function seems to justify the copyist's choice of the sign in cases such as the following :

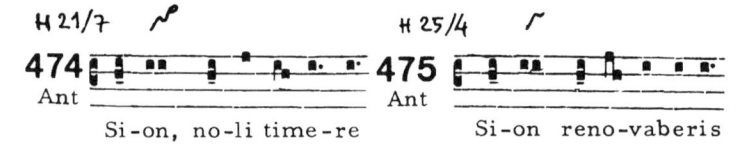

474 Ant — Si-on, no-li time-re   475 Ant — Si-on reno-vaberis

The different treatment given in these two, nearly identical syllabic articulations shows the function of the liquescence in the first example ; the concise and intense expression of the text is brought out well by the liquescent sign. In similar fashion, particular words like *magíster* and Johánnis (on this saint's feast-day) were underlined by liquescence in cases where the special importance of these words aroused the attention of the notator.

An excellent application of liquescence is also found in H in the Responsory versicles. Here, there is a contrast between the mediant cadence (lighter ; built on an accent with three preparatory syllables), in which the diminutive symbols predominate, and the final cadence (broader ; built on the cursus planus), where augmentative symbols are in the majority.

Finally, here is an example in which four versions of the same verbal incise confirm the expressive role of liquescence :

476 Intr — Ad te levavi non confun- dén-tur.

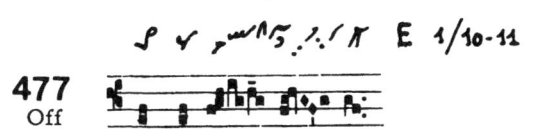

477 Off
Ad te levavi non confun- dén- tur.

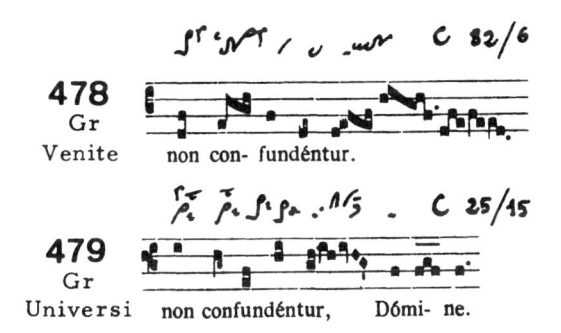

478 Gr
Venite non con- fundéntur.

479 Gr
Universi non confundéntur, Dómi- ne.

CONCLUSION

Diverse combinations of three elements – text, melody and expression – explain the more or less optional character of the written liquescence. Perhaps our modern, rationalistic mentality has some difficulty in understanding it. Yet, even if precise, firm rules cannot be established, certain tendencies which agree perfectly among themselves can be recognized. Only study conducted on a vaster scale can hope to provide more precise and categorical conclusions.

ALPHABETICAL SIGNS

Ekkehard IV, chronicler of St. Gall (c. 1036) attributes the introduction of the particular letters found in the Gregorian chant MSS, to the monk Romanus. Previously, Notker (c. 912) had explained their signification in a letter.[52]

They may have a :
- melodic signification indicating

    an elevation   : ſ (ursum), а (ltius), ʟ (evate)
    a unison   : ҽ (qualiter)
    a descent   : ι (inferius, iusum), ⅾ (eprimatur)

- or a rhythmic signification, indicating

    a slower movement : τ (enete), ж (expectare)
    an acceleration
    : c (eleriter).

Some adverbial letters specify the meaning of the preceding letters : ƀ (ene ; τƀ : tenete bene) ; m (ediocriter ; ſm : sursum mediocriter) ; v (alde ; ιv : inferius valde).

The following letters seem to concern vocal technique in the performance of the ornamental notes : ꜰ (remitus, frangor), g (uttur), k (lamor, klangor).

In addition, one finds different first letter abbreviations :
ᴄō (njunguntur, conjunctim) : often attributed to the pressus ;

ft (atim) : indicating a direct link between the notes where it is found ;

simul : for the unison ;

fid (eliter, fidenter), len (iter), moll (iter), par (atim), per (fecte).

Some letters are frequently used – ſ above all, ʟ and а, as well as c, τ, ҽ, and ж ; – others, especially ꜰ, g, k, and the last mentioned first letter abbreviations are vey rare.

The horizontal prolongation of certain letters, chiefly ⌒ ⌐, indicates that their effect extends over several neumatic signs.

The position of the letters, relative to each of the notes of the neume, must be taken into account :

As for the letters whose sionification is uncertain, it is best not to urge their interpretation.

Letters are sometimes used to correct a neumatic symbol :

They can also have a signification *contrary* to their usual one. Thus, in the symbols ⋀ɾ or ⋀ₐ (⋀ʟ is exceptional), the second note is undoubtedly lower than the first ; nevertheless, the letters ɾ or ₐ are used to indicate that the note descends by the smallest possible interval, generally a halfstep.

The inhabitual use of a letter is often explained by the context. The letter then has a relative signification determined by its relation to another letter which is used in the normal fashion. Thus, in the Tracts of Mode II :

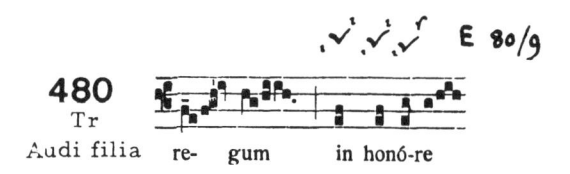

480
Tr
Audi filia   re-   gum   in honó-re

The letter ₄ has an absolute signification on the first note of each of the pes (which always begins lower than the preceding note). On the second note of the first two pes however, its signification is in relation to the " s " on the second note of the third pes. The interval of the first two pes (DO-RE) is smaller than the interval of the pes which carries the ɾ (DO-FA in the Vatican Edition and DO-MI in *Ben.*)

Notice also the two following fragments in which the letter ⲅ indicates a smaller descending interval than the letter ⲗ :

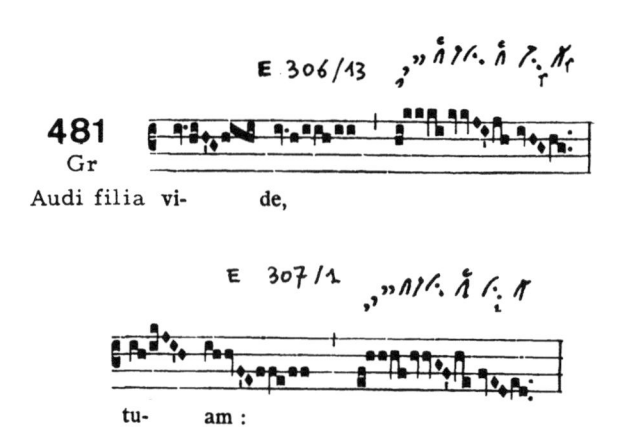

481
Gr
Audi filia vi- de,

tu- am :

In the case of the Introit "Miserére mihi quóniam... " the ⲅ added to the second note of the clivis DO-LA can be explained by reference to a parallel instance in which the melody is identical up until the clivis and then descends a fourth, justifying the use of an ⲗ :

482
Intr
Miserere m. quo-ni- am trí- bu- lor

483
Intr
Miserere m. quó-ni- am ad te clamávi

Last of all, here is a neume in which the relation between the diverse notes is indicated by two groups of letter :

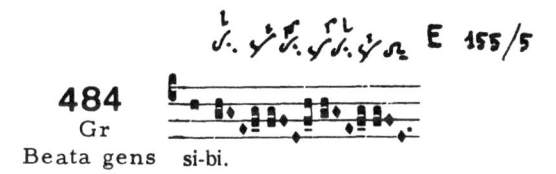

484
Gr
Beata gens si-bi.

There is opposition between L𝑝 and L𝑟. Since ⌣ indicates a note that is lower than 𝑟, 𝑝 must be lower than L . (This neume, which is a perfect example of a " clarifying context ", makes it possible to discover the meaning of a rare and unknown letter.

CONCLUSION

The letters of Romanus furnish nuances and precisions which are rather important both for the restoration of Gregorian melodies and for their interpretation. Their abundance in some MSS is, therefore, justified.

NOTES

1. J. Hourlier, *Paleografia musicale* in *Enciclopedia cattolica italiana*, IX, 580-585.

2. We will use the following abbreviations to designate the various MSS, nearly all published in Solesmes' collection. *Paleographie Musicale* (= P.M.) :

B = Bamberg, lit. 6
C = Cantatorium, St. Gall 359, *P.M.* 2nd series, II
E = Einsiedeln 121, *P.M.* IV
G = St. Gall 339, *P.M.* I
H = Hartker, St. Gall 390-391, *P.M.* 2nd series, I
L = Laon 239, *P.M.* X
M = Montpellier, Ec. Med. H. 159, *P.M.* VIII
Y = St. Yrieix, Paris, B.N. lat. 903, *P.M.* XIII
Ben = Benevent, VI 34, *P.M.* XV
Cha = Chartres 47. *P.M.* XI

Antiphons are always cited according to the Monastic Antiphonary.

3. In order to simplify things, we have restored the correct final note SI, even through the Vatican Edition, which relied on later MSS, used a DO.

4. There are, however, some instances in which the copyist uses a tractulus before the melodic curve reaches its lowest point. He sometimes does this on the final syllable of a word in order to respect the verbal unity when this last syllable is higher than that which follows but lower than that which precedes :

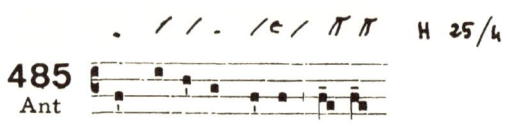

485 Ant Sion renov. et vi-dé-bis justum tu- um,

NOTES

5. There is a " redundant cadence " when the accented syllable of the last word is already situated on the cadential note, the final syllable concluding on that same degree. The last accent is thus integrated into the cadence.

6. A rigid conception of the rhythm (/ = one rhythmic beat ; ∧ = two rhythmic beats) would bring about the same incoherence in the following stereotyped formula :

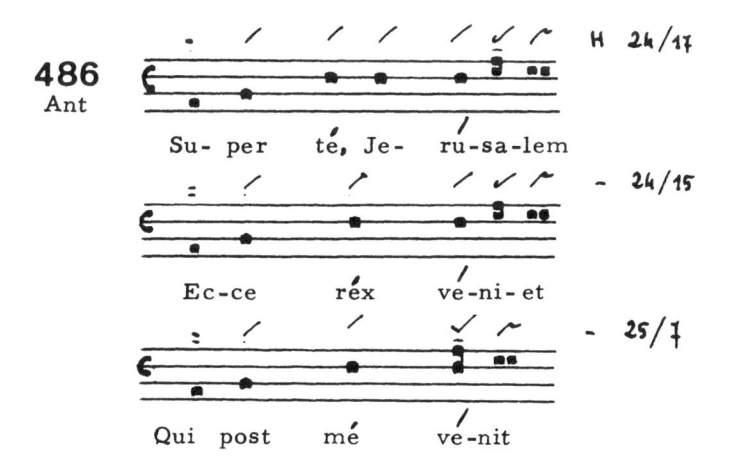

486
Ant

Su- per té, Je- ru-sa-lem   H 24/17

Ec-ce réx ve-ni- et   - 24/15

Qui post mé ve-nit   - 25/7

1st case :   4 beats (2 + 2) before the important accent towards which the text and melody verge.
2nd case :   4 beats (2 + 2) if one accepts – " dato, non concesso " – that ∧ is worth two beats.
3rd case :   3 beats (2 + 1) before the accent. The word " me " is less important than " rex ", and consequently it does not have an episema.

This stereotyped formula does not have a precise, measured rhythm, but rather, it is free, corresponding to the text in each instance.

7. We can also cite instances in which the accented syllable of a word is underlined with an episema :

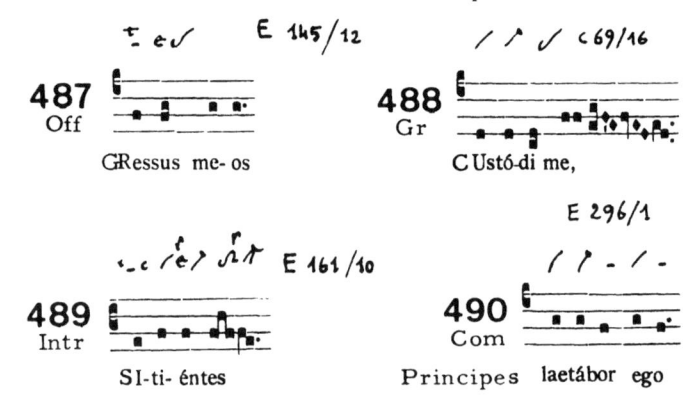

487 Off
GRessus me- os

488 Gr
CUstó-di me,

489 Intr
SI-ti- éntes

490 Com
Principes laetábor ego

The episema corresponds, in the musical domaine, to the rhetorical accent which does not have double the rhythmic value of a simple syllabic beat.

8. The Vatican Edition writes ⸺. But St. Gall did not write //-/ and we have consequently restored the unison indicated by the copyists.

9. The two following examples clarify the last two points. Ex. 491 clearly proves that the difference between the virga, the tractulus and the punctum is purely melodic.

491 Gr
Tu es Deus   ℣. Li- be- rásti

The pretonic syllables move towards the accent of the word which, for its part, causes the melody to rise from SOL to SI. In this example, as well as in ex. 28 and the following ones, L uses a punctum. E and C differ. E writes tractuli because of the SOL's relation to the notes of the melody which follow. C, however, writes two virgas, placing the SOL in relation to its antecedant context. But both copyists add a c to indicate the lightness of the sounds which were notated in different ways.

The second example demonstrates the complete liberty with which the copyists used differentiated rhythmic signs. It involves the intonation of five versicles from the Graduals of Mode V, + one instance in which the intonation is slightly altered but the first two notes are the same as the others :

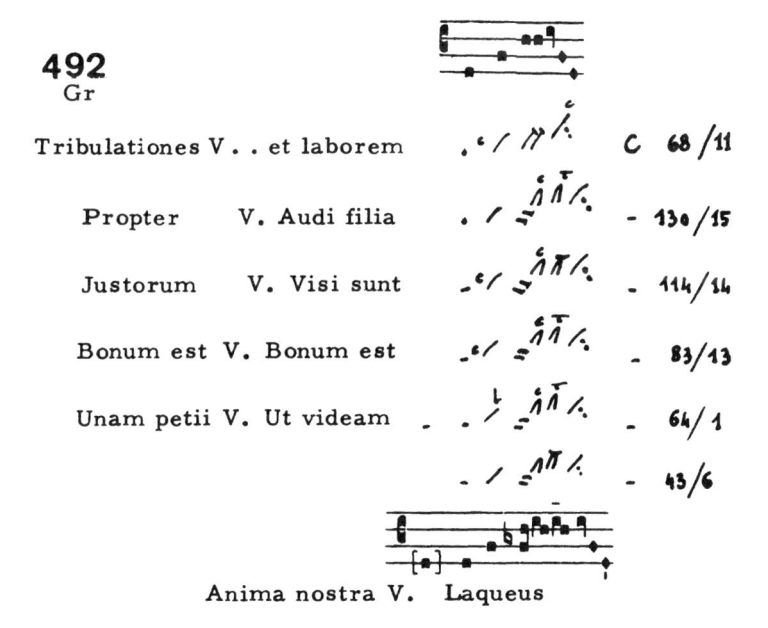

492
Gr

Tribulationes V . . et laborem		C	68/11
Propter V. Audi filia		-	130/15
Justorum V. Visi sunt		-	114/14
Bonum est V. Bonum est		-	83/13
Unam petii V. Ut videam		-	64/1
		-	43/6
Anima nostra V. Laqueus			

These six examples present four different ways of writing the same light notes FA-LA; twice a tractulus and a virga, twice the same signs with an added c, once a punctum and a virga, and once these same signs with a c.

In the face of such evidence, how can a metric conception of the value of the signs be justified ?

10. In E 147/10, over "in his" there is a light pes without an episema on the second note. This does not mean that E ignores or even disagrees with the particularity expressed in C by the sign. The copyist of E simply saw no point in indicating it, since singers could scarcely neglect this musical phenomenon. There are even some instances in which the upper note of the pes (the DO in the example below) has such an active force that the first note disappears completely in certain recent MSS. Vide :

493
Gr
Misit et sanávit   V. mi-se-ri- córdi- ae

11. A similar phenomenon was observed in a series of clivis in ex. 37. In cases of this type, however, the successive pes or clivis are not always stressed ; they can also be light :

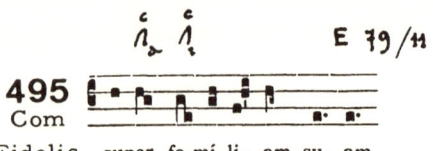

494
Intr
In excelso quem adó- rat

495
Com
Fidelis super fa-mí-li- am su- am

12. The syllabic beat, represented by ‑ and ∕ , remains essentially a point of reference for all the " long " neumes, for example :

⁓ = 3 syllabic beats (L :⁓⁀) ;
ഗ = 3 diminished syllabic beats (L :𝄐).
∕₌ = 3 syllabic beats (L : ⁀) ;
∕. = 3 diminished syllabic beats (L : ⁀.).
⸝ = 3 syllabic beats (L :⸝) ;
∕ = 3 diminished syllabic beats (L in composition :∙∕).

13. B. Pugliese : *La strofa di apposizione nel codice di San Gallo 359*, Rome, 1960 (typewritten).

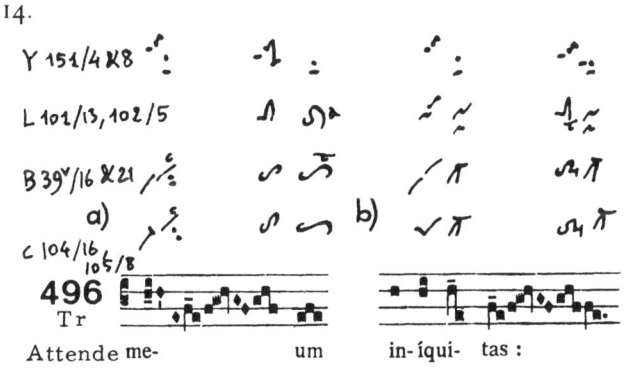

14.

Y 151/4 X8
L 101/13, 102/5
B 39ᵛ/16 X 21
   a)
C 104/16, 105/8
496
Tr
Attende me-   um   in- íqui- tas :

Formula a) is sometimes found in eighth-mode tracts ; b) is an adaptation and modification of this fixed formula for a proparoxytone word ; each of the first four notes are lengthened, whereas in a) only the first was long. The pes quadratus clearly underlines the verbal accent but this fact is not indicated in the rhythmic edition where an episema only appears on the clivis of the following weak syllable. It is, however, the end of the melodic motive which interests us principally here. In a), the last syllable carries a special torculus which is reduced to a long clivis in b), because of the lack of a syllable. This is a convincing example of the intimate connection which exists between text and melody, even in fixed melodic formulae.

234 NOTES

15. The following example corresponds exactly to what we have pointed out:

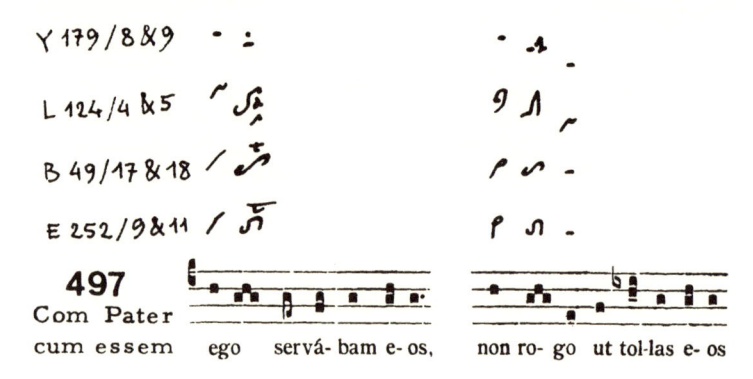

Y 179/8 &9

L 124/4 &5

B 49/17 &18

E 252/9 &11

497
Com Pater
cum essem ego servá- bam e- os,   non ro- go ut tol-las e- os

Here are two torculus on the same notes: SOL LA SOL. The first is a special torculus because it is found on the final syllable and is lower than the preceding note. The second, on the other hand, is a normal torculus because it coincides with the accented syllable. Consequently, it preserves its initial note, even in the Y's tradition.

16. When a new " Gregorian " mass has to be composed, it is necessary to look for a melody which is adaptable to the new text. In such a case, one must be careful not to forget this peculiarity of the passing torculus. This is why the adaptation done for the Communion of the Mass for the Holy Family is inexact:

498
Com
De scendit et e- rat

It should read:

et e- rat

17. Copyists from the various schools treat in the same way some other cases more or less akin to the categories here explained.

18. The only two instances in which an isolated ./ is found in C are probably errors of a distracted copyist. In numerous similar instances this same copyist writes a salicus, just as the other St. Gall notators did, even in these two cases :

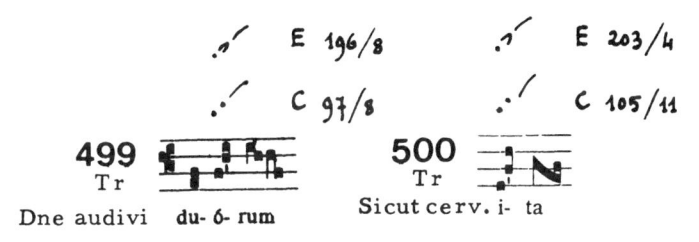

499 Tr — Dne audivi du- 6- rum

500 Tr — Sicut cerv. i- ta

19. The Vatican Edition only rarely writes this neume in a way that corresponds to the authentic tradition of the MSS :

501 All — Eripe me me- us : in me libera me.

20. Unfortunately the Vatican Edition does not distinguish ./ (entirely light) and ./ (with the second note emphasized). Both are printed as ♪. This habitual fragmentation of ascending notes into binary groups is the only truely serious defect of the Vatican Edition in regards to neumatic breaking.

21. Notice that the sign ♪ can also be a " special " torculus resupinus. As has been seen, there are some instances in which the special torculus is not expressly notated (ex. 80, 81, 82); similarly, for the torculus resupinus, we find this instance, among many others :

⋎	Cha 15/20
⁔	Y 39/5
⋏	E 62/8
⋏	C 50/5

502
Gr

Specia tua intén- de,

This is the same phenomenon as the passing torculus. Here, the torculus resupinus represents the crasis of the special torculus with the following virga. This crasis is caused by the fact that the accent here is preceded by a single syllable (In·tén·de) instead of two (cf. ex. 83 mise·ré·ris). Consequently Y and Cha also omit the first weak note here.

22. The following chart demonstrates the perfect unanimity in writing the three cited examples, not only of the St. Gall writers among themselves, but also between the St. Gall family of manuscripts and those of other quite different families and regions.

503			
S.Gall 339	15	29	98
Einsiedeln 121	41	81	270
S.Gall 359		58	122
Graz Un.807	20	40	134

NOTES

Laon 239		31	132
Roma Ang. 123	36	59	165
Chartres 47	10	20	75
Mont Renaud	6 (?)	12	29
Paris Maz 384	13	47	117
Paris B.N. lat 46.511	156	27	153 / 188
Paris B.N. lat 776	18	31	100
Benevent. VI 34	26	56	201
Sarum	17	24	214

23. The SI (fifth note of " Dó-*mi*-nus ") ought to be a DO, as is proven in *Ben* which makes use of two lines, FA and DO, and places the notes on very exact intervals. But this does not alter the problem.

24. The comparison of the examples from column A and B with those from column C proves beyond a doubt that both of the notes of the epismatic clivis or of the squared pes must be lengthened. Today it is common pratice to limit this lengthening to the first note, thus reducing the second note (the one immediately preceding the neumatic break) to a light rhythmic value. Such a procedure corresponds

correctly to signs indicating an initial neumatic break, but not to those in column C.

The examples from the chart are taken from the following pieces :
   A1 : Intr. Adoráte Deum ;
   A2 : All. Hic est discípulus ;
   A3 : Off. Eripe me ;
   B1 : Off. Exspéctans ;
   B2 : Intr. In excélso ;
   B3 : All. Quóniam Deus ;
   C1 : Intr. Ego clamávi ;
   C2 : Ant. Ab Oriénte ;
   C3 : Dicit Dóminus, impléte.

25. Three exceptional instances of an isolated distropha are found in the versicles for the two following Offertories :

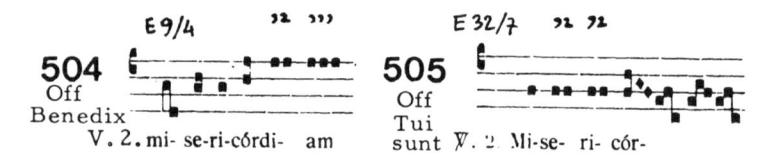

504 Off Benedix V. 2. mi- se-ri-córdi- am

505 Off Tui sunt V. 2. Mi-se- ri- cór-

26. Cf. E. Cardine, *Théoriciens et théoriciens,* in Etudes Grégoriennes, II, 1957, p. 29-35.

27. This last example with the final formula

is found also in various forms. One or more light notes can precede the important SOL, which is detached from the following distropha, without changing the rhythmic structure of the formula. Two neumatic separations remain, one at the descending mid-point after the SOL and the other after the distropha above the final torculus.

506 Intr — adó-ret

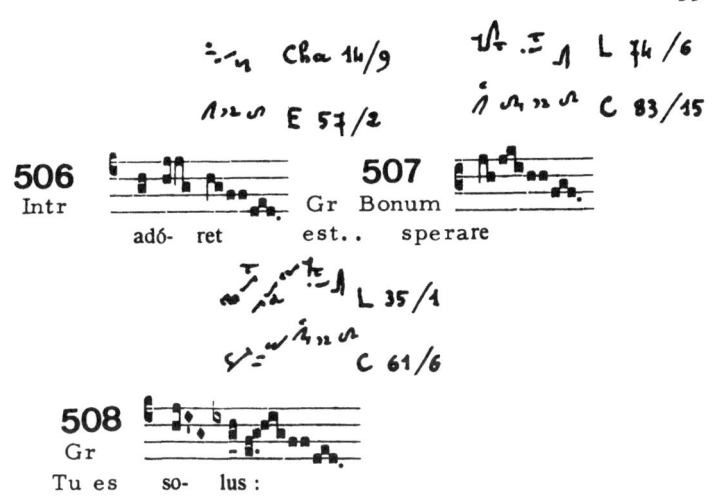

507 Gr Bonum est.. sperare

508 Gr — Tu es so-lus:

In spite of the clear paleographic indications and the evident analogy of the examples, the rhythmic edition fails to countersign the SOL with a lengthening dot.

28. If this stropha were light, the copyists would have had to join it to the following climicus by writing (cf. the erroneous transcription in the Vatican Edition given in ex. 209).

29. It is interesting to note that L, which does not have a sign for the stropha, writes the first time that this formula appears. The small horizontal mark added to the design of the light clivis visibly expresses the unison with the preceding note (Gr. Tollite... aeterná-*les*). It seems, however, that this sign was an obstacle to flowing script and so the copyist modified it in the subsequent case to, and eventually to the sign of the normal porrectus.

30. L has no special sign corresponding to the St. Gall trigon. It writes the tristropha with a lower first note, and quite logically it notates ∴ by .

31. Cf. E. Cardine, *Théoriciens et théoriciens* in *Etudes Grégoriennes*, II, 1957, p. 29-35.

32. The repercussion itself is not as difficult as it may seem at first sight. We often do repercussions without noticing them, *e.g.* when we say Aaron, meae, fílii, coopéruit, or tuum ; in the case of " Zébee et Sálmana " or of " fílii Israel " there is a tristropha.

It suffices to simply observe what takes place when we pronounce " tu·um " or " me·ae " and then repeat the process several times as in " tu·u·u·um " or " me·e·e·e·ae ".

33. Stropha, bivirga, and trivirga (and also the virga strata) in the present editions.

It is easy to identify ⁄⁄ and ⁄⁄⁄ , as well as ʺ ʺʺ and ⁄ in the old MSS. The modern editions, however, generally fail to establish distinctions between these symbols. Some progress was nevertheless made after the Vatican Edition. (Proof of this can be found in *Liber Usualis*, a collection of pieces drawn from various official books.)

In the Roman Gradual (1908), except in very rare cases (" in composition ", *e.g.* Off. " Emítte Spíritum... in saécula "), the bivirga and trivirga are printed as two or three ordinary punctums ■■■ . The rhythmic editions add nothing to these notes.

In the Antiphonary (1912), the official edition has kept this imprecise sign, but the rhythmic editions have printed horizontal episemas on these punctums : ▬▬▬ .

The books edited after 1922 (Office for Holy Week and the Octave of Easter) are much more faithful to tradition and print these neumes as tailed virgas ₉₉, which quite naturally carry episemas in the rhythmic editions : ₉₉.

The Monastic Antiphonary (1934) goes even further. In place of

⁄⁄ it prints ₉̄₉̄
⁄⁄⁄ it prints ₉̄₉̄₉̄
⁄ it prints ■■
ʺ it prints ✦✦

Even in the Gradual it is possible to recognize most of the bivirga. When two notes at the unison are found on the same syllable (without the addition of any other note) the neume is almost certainly a bivirga. In the authentic repertory only

four cases exist where the MSS use the virga strata in place of the bivirga :
Com. *Vox* in Rama
Com. *Servíte Dómino... pereátis*
Com. *Mense séptimo... tabernáculis*
Com. *Vos* qui secúti.
There are also some instances where ♦♦ = ✓ but, here, the performance of a bivirga is correct (as in the old MSS ✓ ‹› //).

When, on the other hand, there are three unison notes isolated on one syllable the neume is invariably a tristropha (except for the already cited instance in the Offertory " *Repléti... delectáti sumus* "). Even for those who are unaware of these exceptions there is practicaly no possibility of error.

As for the identification of the bivirga or the trivirga " in composition " in the Gradual, it is almost impossible without having recourse to the MSS.

34. Sometimes the letter c is drawn out over a long neume ⌒ , even though it is made up of rhythmically different elements. This c is not meant to equalize all the notes or to correct an erroneous symbol but it reminds the singer that, without leveling off the expression of each of the elements in any way, he must chant the entire melisma in a subtle and fluid manner. Here is another example :

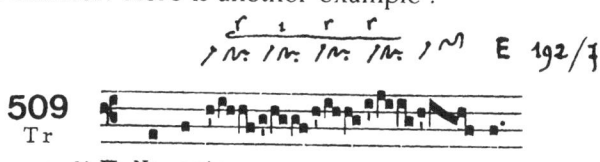

509
Tr
Dne exaudi ℣. Ne avér-   tas

35. Cf. A. Mocquereau, *N.M.I.* p. 304 (arguments in favor of the fusion of notes)

36. One of Dom Mocquereau's arguments in favor of the interpretation of the pressus by a single, two-beat sound is based on the fact that the same formula can be represented in the MSS by two different symbols. Here is an example :

510 Tr — C 65/16
Qui habitat mil- le,

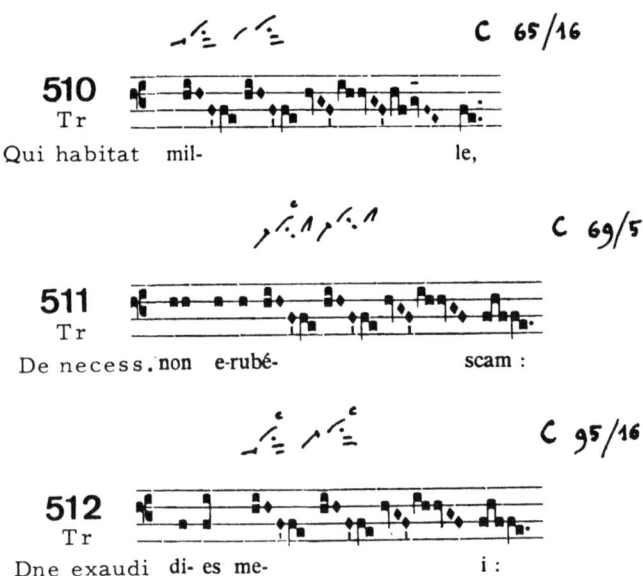

511 Tr — C 69/5
De necess. non e-rubé- scam :

512 Tr — C 95/16
Dne exaudi di- es me- i :

How can it be explained that the two, melodically identical groups have five notes in the first and third instances and six in the second ? (Notice from the page numbers that the examples appear in the chronological order in which they were written.) This is the case not only in all of the St. Gall MSS but also in L and throughout nearly the entire manuscript tradition.

We must admit that the copyist of the archetype has written these three examples of the same formula in different ways and that the majority of the later copyists reproduced the original notation. But this is not a real argument in favor of the fusion of the two notes at the unison. When a note was broad and solid, as in the case of RE (the penultimate note of the first two groups), the singers, habitually used to repercussions, repeated it without conscious effort, in order to express its importance. Experience clearly proves this.

37. It is very rare for a pressus to be followed by a neumatic break :

NOTES

513 All
Dne Deus sal. AL-le- lú- ia. * *ij*.

38. The letter ℯ (= aequaliter) which is found in E between the oriscus and the torculus, does not contradict our melodic restoration, since copyists sometimes used this letter to indicate the half-step.

39. The following chart of the symbols used by H for notating an identical formula clearly shows that there was indecision in the choices made :

514

Resp	Vidi Dominum ..plena erat		H	416/8
Resp	Gaude Maria ..erubescat		-	119/3
Ant	Ecce nunc ..in his		-	147/15
Resp	Deus meus ..eripe me		-	165/9
Resp	Super salutem ..caelorum		-	189/2
Resp	Sancti tui ..validis		-	367/15
Ant	Ab Oriente ..magi		-	11/12

40. The salicus in the Vatican Edition.

The salicus is unrecognizable in the Vatican Edition. It is normally transcribed by the sign ♪ . In order to make the neume recognizable, the rhythmic editions place a vertical episema *under* the second note, which is then considered to be the most important note : ♪ .

But the Vatican Edition does not always use this grouping, sometimes printing ♪ , which is also the sign used to transcribe the scandicus ✓ . The rhythmic editions were obliged here to place the vertical episema over the second note (*e.g.,* the Introit " Ecce advénit... *et* impérium ") as had been done for the scandicus of the " Státuit " type (ex. 103).

In addition, the rhythmic editions place a vertical episema under the second note ♪ for the ✓ form of the scandicus (cf. ex. 100). The A.M. has tried to improve this transcription. It does often underline the importance of the first note by a horizontal episema ▁✓ = ♪ but it omits the blank space between the punctum and the pes which it normally uses in the more extended forms. This blank space has, on the contrary, been reserved, just as in the Vatican Edition, for the salicus where it is in no way justified.

41. This formula from the Graduals of Mode III containts another example of the pes quassus as a neumatic element for phrasing :

515
Gr
Adjutor (non)

42. At the coincidence of two equivalent vowels, the pes quassus may be separated into two distinct signs, *e.g.* :

516 Com
Dne Dns n. quam admi-rá-bi-le est

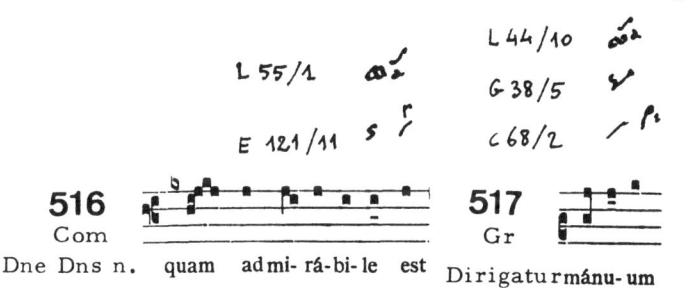

517 Gr
Dirigatur mánu-um

43. L is unacquainted with this problem. It retains the normal form of the salicus when the oriscus is preceded by a punctum (a succession of at least three descending notes) :

518 Off
Benedixisti ple-   bis

On the contrary, when the oriscus is preceded by a torculus or a clivis (a succession of two descending notes), L joins the oriscus to the preceding sign .

44. There are also some analoguous instances of the decisive role played by the fourth last note in certain formulae for final and median cadences :

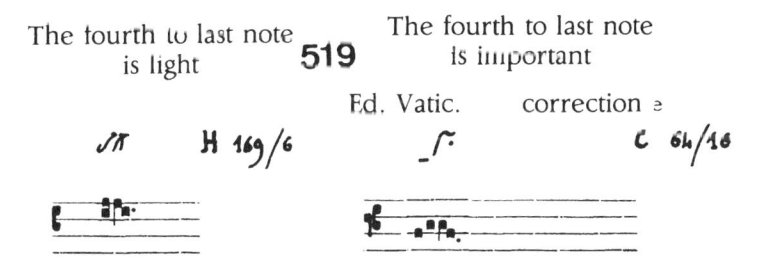

519

The fourth to last note is light

The fourth to last note is important

Ed. Vatic.   correction

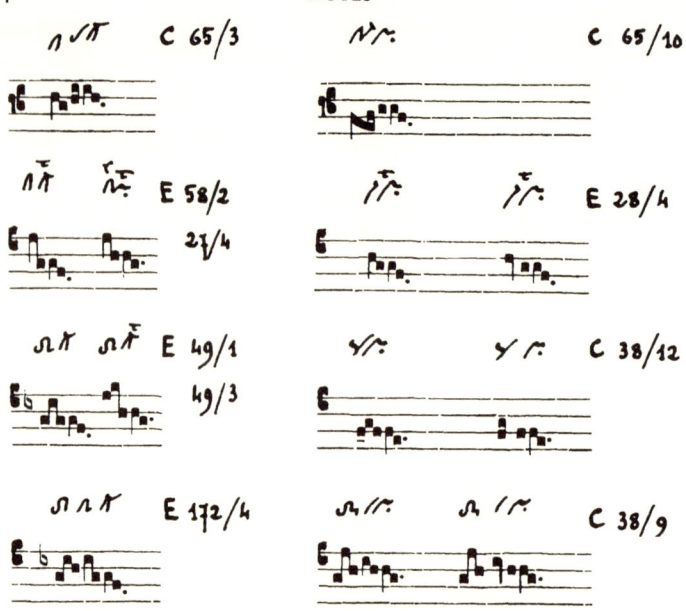

45. The following formulae are special cases; the signs and are equivalent here in the sense that both final notes are long. However the pes quassus expresses more clearly the melodic tension towards the higher note which is followed by a descent of the melody on the next syllable.

NOTES

46. E writes the quilisma-pes in this way: ⌇⌇⌇. These symbols always represent two notes even if the sign of the virga is scarcely visible.

47. It is very rare for the quilisma to be in unison with the preceding note:

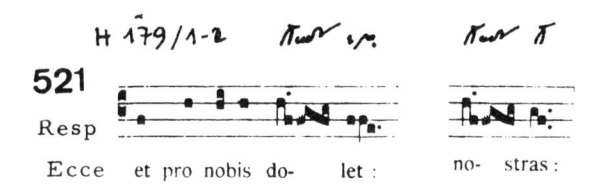

521
Resp
Ecce et pro nobis do- let : no- stras :

48. The following formula, which appears several times in the repertoire, shows one of the rare instances in which two long higher notes come after the quilisma-pes :

522
Com
In salutari De- us me- us.

The three important notes here are RE FA, and LA, and in between there is first a rather light passing note (MI) and then another note which tends strongly towards the accented summit (SOL→LA).

49. The error of the Vatican Edition which, in the Gradual " Sciant gentes... omnem ", anticipates the second syllable by three notes, is due to the fact that it recopied faithfully the Liber Gradualis of Dom Pothier (Solesmes, 1895), even though Dom Mocquereau had in the meantime restored the melody according to the MSS (Liber Usualis, 1903).

50. This shows that the contemporary Roman pronunciation is the one which corresponds best to the established facts (ge, gi), and even to the MSS from German regions.

51. Unfortunately, the Vatican Edition prints only the diminutive liquescence (by a " small note "). For the ancus (a diminutive form of the climacus), it prints the second and third notes as diamond shaped notes which are smaller than those used for the ordinary climacus (*e.g.* Off. " Tóllite... portae " ; Of. " Exaltábo te... super me "). It is clear, however, that only the last note is actually diminished ; the reduction of the size of the central note is due exclusively to visual aesthetics. In addition to the diminutive liquescences already indicated by the Vatican Edition, the Monastic Antiphonary uses ♩ to render both ♪ and ♫. This transcription is correct only in the first instance ; ♫ ought to be rendered by ♩. In an analoguous manner, it should have introduced other signs, *e.g.* ♩ ♩ ♩.

52. Cf. J. Froger, *L'épître de Notker sur les Lettres significatives. Edition critique*, in Etudes Grégoriennes V, 1962, p. 23-71.

INDEX OF EXAMPLES

Introitus

Accipite	88
Ad te levavi	66, 228, 399, 416, 476
Adorate	150
Audivit	404
Cantate Domino	375
Circumdederunt	413
De ventre	23
Deus in loco	167
Dominus dixit	157
Dominus fortitudo	92, 157, 236
Dum clamarem	22
Dum sanctificatus	174
Eduxit	111
Ego clamavi	150
Esto mihi	115, 231, 243, 439, 520
Etenim	58, 82, 173, 520
Ex ore	144, 145, 503
Exaudi	365
Exspecta	60
Exsurge	312, 372
Fac mecum	374
Factus est	346
Gaudeamus	73, 421
Gaudete	74, 285, 396
Hodie scietis	116
In excelso	150, 311, 494
In medio	2bis, 159, 208, 216
In voluntate	133, 465
Inclina Domine	77, 423
Invocabit	127
Judica me	245
Judicant	376
Lætare	135, 419
Loquebar	239
Lux fulgebit	124
Miserere... ad te	348, 483
Miserere... tribulor	482
Misereris	83
Multæ tribulationes	68
Ne timeas	179
Oculi mei	48, 309, 414
Omnes	233
Omnia	242
Omnis terra	182, 506
Os iusti	130, 437
Protector	244, 344, 378
Puer	47, 81, 110, 168, 325
Reminiscere	35, 304
Respice Domine	166, 422
Respice in me	177
Resurrexi	72, 435
Sacerdotes Dei	209
Sacerdotes tui	417
Salus	332
Sapientiam	207
Si iniquitates	259, 284
Sitientes	489
Spiritus	229
Statuit	103
Suscepimus	53ter, 131
Terribilis	192
Veni	310
Verba mea	11
Viri	114
Vocem	358, 392

Gradualia

A summo	219, 334
Ad Dominum	4, 176
Adiutor	134, 136, 147, 279, 401, 457, 503, 515
Adiuvabit	251, 464
Anima nostra	492
Audi, filia	29, 481
Beata gens	308, 484
Benedicam	146, 314
Benedicite	195, 400
Benedictus Dominus	384
Benedictus es	186
Bonum est confidere	492, 507
Bonum est confiteri	55
Christus	55, 94, 364, 379, 405, 430
Clamaverunt	32, 71, 212, 408
Constitues eos	123
Custodi me	201, 488
Deus exaudi	152, 193, 218, 400
Deus vitam	98, 211, 400
Diffusa est	274
Dilexisti	54
Dirigatur	517
Discerne	315
Dñe Deus virtutum	290, 336
Domine prævenisti	313
Domine refugium	267
Ecce quam bonum	148, 503
Ego autem	361
Eripe me	28, 162, 195, 307, 400, 407
Ex Sion	118, 260
Exaltabo	195
Excita	288, 335
Exiit	55, 143
Exsurge... et intende	106, 195
Exsurge... non præ.	175, 195, 357, 394, 400
Fuit homo	520
Gloriosus	70, 385, 458
Hæc dies	93
Hodie	57, 190
In Deo	55
In sole	289, 333
Inveni	183
Jacta	109
Juravit	195, 400
Justorum	492
Lætatus sum	42
Liberasti	213, 256
Locus	281
Miserere mei	200
Miserere mihi	255, 271
Misit	234, 493
Oculi	125, 306
Omnes	24
Pacifice	354
Posuisti	138
Probasti	43
Prope est	30, 370
Propitius	220, 391
Propter veritatem	492
Qui sedes	199, 381, 406
Respice	273
Salvum fac	203, 371
Sciant	165, 218
Si ambulem	214
Specie tua	502
Tecum	56, 191, 337
Tenuisti	62, 137, 215, 268, 269, 286
Timebunt	158, 188, 222, 240, 390
Timete	466
Tollite	235, 241, 287, 427
Tribulationes	492
Tu es	195, 357, 400, 456, 401, 508
Universi	479
Venite	478

TABLE OF EXAMPLES

Viderunt 278, 353
Vindica 189

Versus alleluiatici
Adducentur 340
Beatus vir qui suffert . . 402
Beatus vir qui timet . . 463
Dies sanctificatus 96, 181, 343
Domine Deus salutis . . 513
Emitte 84
Eripe me . . 143, 341, 501
Excita 85, 270
Hic est dicipulus . . . 150
In die 298
Lætatus sum 144
Laudate 382
Multifarie 275
Ostende 246
Paratum 339
Pascha 155, 377
Posuisti 347
Qui timent 108, 204
Quoniam Deus 150
Te martyrum 95
Veni Domine 338
Video 342, 429

Tractus et cantica
Ad te levavi 46, 69
Attende . . . 303, 330, 496
Audi filia 480
Cantemus . . 126, 226, 302, 412, 418
De necessitatibus 143, 319, 403, 511
De profundis 39, 76, 154, 194, 258, 272, 283
Deus, Deus . . 31, 44, 156
Domine audivi 61, 129, 499
Domine exaudi 262, 509, 512
Eripe me 9, 33, 238

Jubilate 320
Laudate 128
Qui confidunt 143
Qui habitat . 10, 40, 90, 97, 301, 510
Sæpe 36
Sicut cervus 500
Vinea 428

Offertoria
Ad te levavi . . . 425, 477
Anima nostra 52
Ave Maria . . . 144, 205
Benedicite 99
Benedictus es... in . . . 185
Benedictus qui venit . . 149
Benedixisti . . . 504, 518
Confirma 140
Confitebor . . . 53ter, 436
Confortamini 141
Desiderium 223
Deus Deus meus . . . 383
Deus enim 170
Dextera 89, 454
Diffusa est 210
Domine Deus 217
Domine exaudi . . . 426
Elegerunt 49
Eripe... Deus 248
Eripe... Domine . 150, 160
Exaltabo 351
Exspectans . . . 150, 455
Factus est . . . 257, 266
Gressus meos 487
Immittet 153
Improperium 265
In die 263
In te speravi 424
In virtute 34
Intonuit 261, 411
Jubilate Deo omnis . . 409

Jubilate Deo universa	180, 410
Justitiæ	450
Lætamini	227
Lætentur	196, 197, 350
Miserere mihi	328
Oravi	323, 360
Perfice	132, 184, 198
Portas cæli	113, 161
Precatus	75, 178, 420
Reges	202
Repleti	224
Si ambulavero	139
Sicut	230, 329, 331
Sperent	119
Tollite	299
Tui sunt	142, 373, 505

Communiones

Acceptabis	366, 369
Adversum me	305
Benedicite	359
Cantate	64
Cum invocarem	78
Data est	112
Descendit	498
Dicit Dominus: Implete	150
Dicite	327
Diffusa est	237, 280
Dilexisti	363
Domine Dominus	516
Dominus dabit	221
Dominus Jesus	91
Ego clamavi	50
Ego sum	362
Erubescamt	79
Exiit	169
Factus est Dominus	104
Factus est repente	105
Feci	187
Fidelis	380, 495
Hoc corpus	65, 206
Honora	63, 282
Illumina	45, 51
In salutari	522
In splendoribus	122
Inclina	117
Intellige	415
Introibo	67
Jerusalem	326
Manducaverunt	322
Mense septimo	292, 438
Non vos	451
Panem	349
Pascha	232
Pater cum essem	368, 393, 497
Posuerunt	254
Principes	490
Quis dabit	59
Redime me	453
Revelabitur	80, 86, 144
Servite	293
Surrexit	352
Tollite	37
Tu es Petrus	120
Video	100
Viderunt	87
Vovete	345

Antiphonæ

Ab Oriente	150, 514
Adoramus te	324
Angelus autem	444
Ante luciferum	448
Ascendens	38
Cantate Domino	6
Commendemus	14
Da mercedem	295
Deposuit	432
Domine non sum	18
Domine si tu vis	17
Dominus veniet	225, 250
Ecce nunc	514

TABLE OF EXAMPLES

Ecce Rex	5, 21, 486	Simile est	291
Ecce veniet	431	Sion, noli	13, 53, 474
Egredietur	461	Sion renovaberis	475, 485
Emitte	294, 462	Spiritus Domini replevit	8
Estote ergo	388, 446	Stans a dextris	249
Euge serve	249, 389	Stella ista	121
Exiit	321	Super muros	249
Exspectetur	53	Super te	486
Facta est	443	Tibi revelavi	469
Gloria in excelsis	397	Tradetur	1
Gratia Dei	26	Tu es qui venturus es an	276
Hæc est domus	386	Tu es qui venturus es Dñe	19
Homo quidam	16	Ubi duo	470
Isti sunt sancti	398	Urbs	247
Loquebantur	434	Vade mulier	53
Lux de luce	452	Videntibus	316
Magi	41, 102	Viri Galilæi	297
Maria et flumina	163	Vos qui secuti	442
Nativitas	2		
Non est	460	**Responsoria**	
Non vos	387	Deus meus	514
O mors	53	Domine quando veneris	473
O rex	441	Ecce quomodo moritur	367
O sapientia	264, 440	Ecce vidimus eum	252, 521
Quærite	12	Gaude Maria	514
Quando natus	318	Judas	101
Quem vidistis	20, 296, 447	Sancti tui	514
Qui post	486	Super salutem	514
Qui hic	25	Surgens	253
Regnum tuum	433	Tenebræ	471, 472
Rex pacificus	467	Vidi Dominum sedenetem	514
Sacerdos	277	Vidi speciosam	164
Sancti tui	317	Viri sancti	7
Satiavit	53		
Scitote	468	**Versiculi**	
Senex	107	in modo III	300, 395
Si vere	459	in modo V	11
Sic Deus	445	in modo VII	449
Sicut fuit	15	simplex	3

TABLE OF CONTENTS

Introduction 7
1. Isolated notes 17
2. Clivis 32
3. Pes 35
4. Porrectus 42
5. Torculus 47
6. Climacus 59
7. Scandicus 63
8. Complex symbols 68
   − Porrectus flexus 68
   − Pes subbipunctis 69
   − Scandicus flexus 72
   − Torculus resupinus 74
9. Neumatic break 79
10. Stropha 92
11. Trigon 108
12. Bivirga & trivirga 116
13. Pressus 124
14. Virga strata 145
15. Isolated oriscus 155
16. Salicus 163
17. Pes quassus 184
18. Quilisma 199
    Pes stratus 213
19. Liquescence 215
20. Alphabetical signs 224
Notes 228
Index of examples 249

Imprimé en France. - JOUVE, 18, rue Saint-Denis, 75001 PARIS
N° 296841J. - Dépôt légal : Juillet 2001.